British Cultural Memory and the Second World War

EDITED BY LUCY NOAKES AND JULIETTE PATTINSON

BLOOMSBURY

LONDON • NEW DELHI • NEW YORK • SYDNEY

Bloomsbury Academic

An imprint of Bloomsbury Publishing Plc

50 Bedford Square
London
WC1B 3DP
UK

1385 Broadway
New York
NY 10018
USA

www.bloomsbury.com

Bloomsbury is a registered trade mark of Bloomsbury Publishing Plc

First published 2014

British Library Cataloguing-in-Publication Data
A catalogue record for this book is available from the British Library.

ISBN: HB: 978-1-4411-6057-7
PB: 978-1-4411-4226-9
ePDF: 978-1-4411-0497-7
ePub: 978-1-4411-4927-5

Typeset by Fakenham Prepress Solutions, Fakenham, Norfolk NR21 8NN
Printed and bound in India

CONTENTS

LIST OF ILLUSTRATIONS

NOTES ON CONTRIBUTORS

Rebecca Bramall lectures in media and cultural studies at the University of Brighton. Her research interests lie in cultural theory, popular culture and twentieth-century British history. Bramall's current research examines discourses of austerity, drawing on debates about history, heritage and memory, and emergent work on ethical consumption and the environment. *The Cultural Politics of the New Austerity* is forthcoming from Palgrave Macmillan (2013).

Geoff Eley is Karl Pohrt Distinguished University Professor of Contemporary History at the University of Michigan, Ann Arbor. His most recent works include *Forging Democracy: The History of the Left in Europe, 1850–2000* (2002); *A Crooked Line: From Cultural History to the History of Society* (2005); (with Keith Nield) *The Future of Class in History: What's Left of the Social?* (2007); and *Nazism as Fascism: Violence, Ideology, and the Ground of Consent in Germany, 1930–1945* (2013).

Martin Francis is the Henry R. Winkler Professor of Modern History at the University of Cincinnati. His most recent monograph is *The Flyer: British Culture and the Royal Air Force, 1939-1945* (Oxford University Press, 2008). He is currently researching the cultural history of the Desert War, the novels of Robin Maugham and representations of King Faruq of Egypt in British and American culture.

Frances Houghton is currently completing a PhD at the University of Edinburgh. She is researching published post-war memoirs of British Second World War servicemen, focusing particularly on the experience and remembrance of frontline combat.

Lucy Noakes lectures in history at the University of Brighton. She researches in the fields of gender, war and memory, with a particular focus on the social and cultural history of Second World War Britain. Publications include *War and the British* (1998) and *Women and the British Army 1907-1948* (2006). She is currently researching death, grief and bereavement in Second World War Britain.

Juliette Pattinson, who is a Reader in History at the University of Kent, is a socio-cultural historian of the Second World War with particular interests in gender and personal testimonies. Publications include *Behind Enemy Lines* and an edited collection with Ben Shepherd entitled *War in a Twilight World*. She is currently writing a monograph on the First Aid Nursing Yeomanry and is embarking on a new project with Arthur McIvor on men who were in Reserved Occupations.

Corinna Peniston-Bird lectures in history at Lancaster University. She researches in the fields of gender, war and memory, with a particular focus on the social and cultural history of Second World War Britain. Publications include *Contesting Home Defence* (with Penny Summerfield, 2007) and *History Beyond the Text* (with Sarah Barber, 2008). She is currently researching gendered commemoration in Great Britain.

Penny Summerfield is Professor of Modern History at the University of Manchester. She has published widely on the social and cultural history of the Second World War including *Reconstructing Women's Wartime Lives: discourse and subjectivity in oral histories of the Second World War* (Manchester, 1998) and (with Corinna Peniston-Bird) *Contesting Home Defence: Men, Women and the Home Guard in the Second World War* (Manchester, 2007). Her current project is on the popular memory of the Second World War in Britain since 1945.

Wendy Ugolini lectures in British History at the University of Edinburgh. Her research interests lie in the field of war, identities and memory and she is currently researching constructions of Britishness within the army during the Second World War. Her book, *Experiencing War as the 'Enemy Other'. Italian Scottish Experience in World War II*, was awarded the Gladstone History Book Prize 2011.

Janet S. K. Watson is Associate Professor of History at the University of Connecticut. Her first book, *Fighting Different Wars: Experience, Memory, and the First World War in Britain* (Cambridge University Press, 2004) won the Tomlinson Prize for the Best Work of History on the First World War. She is currently completing a project, *Telling War Stories*, that uses Second World War commemoration to examine British politics and society.

ACKNOWLEDGEMENTS

This book developed out of an international, interdisciplinary conference held at the University of Brighton in 2011: 'The Second World War: Popular Culture and Cultural Memory'. As this volume would not have been possible without the conference, we would like to thank all of those who participated. In particular, we would like to thank our co-organizer, Dr Petra Rau, and the conference administrator, Dr Sam Carroll, for their academic and administrative support and collaboration, and student helpers from the University of Brighton for all their help. We would also like to thank the School of Humanities and the Centre for Research in Memory, Narrative and Histories at the University of Brighton, the Centre for European and International Studies Research at the University of Portsmouth and the School of Humanities at the University of Strathclyde for their generous support of the Conference. The Mass Observation Archive will be a familiar and valuable source for many people who work on the history of mid- and late-20th century Britain. Over the years, Mass-Observation has lost its original hyphen to become Mass Observation. In this volume, we have hyphenated Mass-Observation only when referring to earlier publications where this form is used. Material from the Mass Observation Archive is reproduced with the permission of the Trustees of the Mass Observation Archive.

Every effort has been made to trace relevant copyright holders for material cited in this volume. We would appreciate being contacted if there are any oversights.

FOREWORD

Memory and the historians: Ordinary life, eventfulness and the instinctual past

Geoff Eley

Invited some 15 years ago to write a foreword for a volume on *War and Memory in the Twentieth Century*, I took the chance to reflect on what seemed at the time to be a veritable 'boom in memory'.[1] After a few signature volumes of the 1970s, either with a mainly literary emphasis or else working creatively with oral histories – Paul Fussell's *The Great War and Modern Memory*[2] and Ronald Fraser's *The Blood of Spain*[3] each come to mind – the mid-1980s saw a cluster of interventions whose effects helped remake how we think about the 'history and memory' complex. In a time of ferment among historians at large, amid key political changes and challenges to well-tried assumptions of intellectual life, works by Carolyn Steedman, Ronald Fraser and Patrick Wright in Britain, by Alessandro Portelli and Luisa Passerini in Italy, by Lutz Niethammer and his collaborators in West Germany, and by Pierre Nora in France opened up exciting new avenues for study.[4] These drew much impetus from wider developments in the arts, education, public policy and popular culture – from the growth of new museum practices and pedagogies, from the commemorative excess of the Second World War anniversaries and the French Revolution's bicentennial, from prestigious historical exhibitions, from the growth of heritage industries and the proliferating of historical sites, from the making of memorials and monuments, and from varieties of nostalgia in entertainment and consumer culture. Long-smouldering controversies about the recent twentieth-century past would also intermittently burst into fire, country by country, most notably perhaps in Germany over *Vergangenheitsbewältigung* (coming to terms with the past), but also in Italy via the routines and rituals of anti-fascism, in France over the legacies of Vichy, and so forth around the map. Holocaust memory was also finding its powerful contemporary impact. As professional historians responded, the new journal *History and Memory*, launched in 1989, initiated and welcomed much of the resulting discussion.

Since the time of my earlier reflection in 1997, the shelves have become thick with discussion. Holocaust historiography, and more recently comparative genocide studies, provide an especially elaborate and intense set of examples, accelerating into the new century as events in former Yugoslavia and Rwanda laid down their effects. Traumatic memory, questions of restitution, crises of human rights, commissions for truth and reconciliation, cases before the International Criminal Court in the Hague – each offered spurs to historical research. Film, television, photography, artworks, exhibitions, architecture, landscape, the built environment – all kinds of visual representation afford rich materials for studying collective remembering and forgetting. Processing the Nazi past in Germany offers only the most salient of many other examples: debate over how exactly the Third Reich is to be remembered remains an ever-fertile source of contro- versy and scandal, each instance proving no less contentious than the last.

While often simplifying and sensational, media events also inspire an immense amount of inquiry, casting light back onto earlier twentieth- century problems while drawing growing attention in their own right. The memory work and memorializing of the past few decades have now themselves become an object of historical study. For some years now, whether in national historiographies or for Europe's history as a whole, this has been a primary means of addressing the impact and legacies of the Second World War. Tony Judt's highly regarded *Postwar* makes 'memory' into the organizing principle of its whole account, for example. Framing Europe's post-1945 history in such a way becomes entirely natural.[5] The first quarter of one recent volume of essays on reconstruction between 1945 and 1958 is devoted to 'collective memory' and the 'burdens of the past'; another anthology on the transnational dimensions of contemporary European history does the same, staging its treatments via an argument about 'contested memories'.[6]

Building the architecture of a postwar history around 'memory' has definite implications. In Judt's case it suggests the underlying continuity of a burdensome past that overshadows and disables, presenting a series of constraints and inhibitions, even as the resulting silences about the war and the earlier part of the century helped a certain common ground of societal reconstruction to be assembled. For Judt, postwar memory functioned mainly as a negativity, as the nightmare sent from 'the house of the dead' to weigh on the brains of the living. After the divisiveness and destruction of the earlier twentieth-century and the wartime, he argues, the selective memorializing of the period between the 1950s and 1970s then worked productively for the rebuilding of society's cohesion, just as the changes of the 1980s and 1990s (and the receding immediacy of 1945 per se) allowed aspects of the wartime experience to be faced more openly: 'The first postwar Europe was built upon deliberate *mis*-memory – upon forgetting as a way of life. Since 1989, Europe has been constructed instead upon a compensatory surplus of memory: institutionalised public remembering as the very foundation of collective identity.'[7] This affords one means of making the memory boom intelligible, historicizing its appearances to a particular period in the delayed, protracted and recursively uneven working through of the trauma of a long-lasting post-Nazi condition. Fredric Jameson's 'nostalgia for the present' is another, making 'memory' a source of bearings and locatedness during a time of severance and the precarious rapidity of change, where narrating and visualizing the present as history offers promiscuous consolation, in a surrogate claim to continuity.[8]

Where are we now with historical studies of memory? In contrast with the situation 15 years ago, the widely proliferating activity has become more explicitly theorized, made into a collective conversation, codified into a field. Earlier, the proposals of a few pioneers engendered excitement but remained idiosyncratic, their ideas and methods embedded in the brilliance of particular *oeuvres*. Characteristic in that respect was Raphael Samuel's remarkable *Theatres of Memory* published in 1994, an omnibus of unexpectedness and insight, an exhaustive array of possible ways of thinking about how societies remember and historians seek to capture the past.[9] A handful of generalizing works long held a place for theory as such, but since around 2000 the landscape has become markedly transformed.[10] Especially significant were three volumes edited by Susannah Radstone and Katherine Hodgkin, whose contents combined cases with theoretical treatments drawn from across the disciplines in latter-day cultural studies mode.[11] Alongside a profusion of publications on particular countries, including every possible aspect of the Holocaust, a variety of anthologies of European and sometimes global reach now appeared.[12] Above all, historians have acquired a systematic basis in theory, with one major anthology, *The Collective Memory Reader*, gathering together most of the major voices, both classical and contemporary, in 88 short extracts, and another, *Memory: Histories, Theories, Debates*, commissioning 30 original contributions organized into three parts: 'Histories' (with sub-sections on 'Epochs' and 'Imagining Modern Memory'); 'How Memory Works' (sub-sections on 'The Inner Self', 'Subjectivity and the Social' and 'Public Memory); and 'Controversies'. From multiple perspectives and a range of relevant disciplines, these volumes provide excellent access to the ground from which the questions of 'history' and 'memory' can now be engaged.[13]

This manifold activity has brought undoubted gains. Rather than talismanic invocations of Maurice Halbwachs and a few other classics, along with the contemporary salience of Nora's 'sites of memory', we now have an explicit and much broader theoretical basis for thinking about memory, one far more solidly grounded in appropriate interdisciplinary knowledges.[14] Of course, the great wave of current enthusiasm is rarely innocent, but on the contrary harbours a variety of ulterior purposes, angling in one way or another for the instatement of a new official version of the particular national past. Such renormalizing implications are nowhere more palpable than in the grand narrative ambitions of Nora's *Les lieux de mémoire*.[15] With popular memorializing also comes much complicating of access to the past: not only the events of history are now being recalled – in the present volume, the past of the Second World War and its legacies – but also the intervening welter of representations where those events may now be obscured. For example, in the proliferating anniversaries and commemorations of the past three decades not just the events themselves are being remembered, but all of the cultural sedimentation built up around them between the 1940s and now. As I argued on a previous occasion:

> History enters popular circulation at the beginning of the twenty-first century through such confusions of mass-mediated meanings. [These] construct the national past via a compulsive simultaneity of connotations, in a promiscuous mélange of imagery and citation, creating a dense palimpsest of referentiality. Symbolic capital accumulates thickly around national history's grand events in this manner, encumbering our access to their meanings. This is nowhere stronger than in popular culture's teeming archive of visual representations in film, television, advertising, magazines and the daily press.[16]

With respect to British historiography of the Second World War, I have three brief observations. One concerns the now well ensconced emphasis on ordinary popular experience as something distinct from the various versions of the longer-running official story. A strong set of assumptions foregrounding material life and its superior authenticities – the mundane continuance of everyday rhythms, the quotidian micro-political entailments of securing a wartime livelihood, the new social relations and cultural practices arising in a highly mobilized and unexpectedly shaken-up society, and the often messy pragmatics of finding ways of making it through – are set deliberately *against* the stalwartness of the older patriotic narrative, with its heroic mythologies, well-worn iconicities and Churchillian grandeur (the 'Dunkirk spirit,' the 'Valiant Years'). If, many years before, Angus Calder's classic account of *The People's War* had already debunked much of that earlier rhetoric of shared patriotic sacrifice, then the image of 'everyone pulling together' in the hour of the nation's need still kept remarkable staying-power.[17] But over the past two decades several distinct literatures have now been questioning this consensual claim in its relationship to '1945' and the postwar settlement. Left-wing versions emphasize popular radicalisms going far beyond what the Clement Attlee government was actually prepared to achieve, while more 'realist' approaches see rather the ineffectual, costly and generally misguided quality of the post-1945 reforms. Pushing into the gap between government and people is yet a third view, which queries the depth or extent of popular interest in reform *per se*, insisting that 'the majority of the public were ill-informed, lacked "social solidarity", and supported neither state intervention nor altruistic welfare policies' in the first place.[18] As Geoffrey Field puts it:

> In an effort to break through the impeding layers of nostalgia and demythologize the war years, historians have paid growing attention to aspects of life omitted from the 'orthodox' heroic version, such as looting, black market activities, absenteeism, strikes, cynicism, and low morale. Some imply that the average person often has few opinions worth the name – and caution that the idea of a popular wartime consensus for reform was largely a myth manufactured by intellectuals.[19]

These new histories look beyond and beneath the war's big events to explore those underlying dynamics of ordinary experience that social and cultural historians have always been so adept at addressing. But such studies easily run the risk of severing the 'people's war' from 'the people's peace' – that is, from the succeeding narrative of postwar reform and reconstruction that previously organized British collective memory and characterized the post-1945 consensus. Family, childhood and childraising, schooling, sexuality, courting, housing and neighbourhood sociality, domestic violence, crime and delinquency, dancing and cinema, workplace relations, hidden economies, black market – all these describe everyday settings where lives followed rhythms and patterns that remained relatively impervious to whatever government may have been trying to accomplish before or after 1945. These are indeed the uncharted territories gradually being mapped by some recent histories – ordinary childhoods, the dream worlds of teenagers, geographies away from London and other major cities, provincial landscapes away from the home counties, small and parochial lives of all kinds, especially those of women. These are what Carolyn Steedman has called 'lives lived out on the borderlands, lives for which the central interpretative devices of the culture don't quite work'.[20] Such lives contained, as Annette Kuhn remarks, 'ways of knowing and ways of seeing the world ... rarely acknowledged, let alone celebrated, in the expressions of a hegemonic culture.'[21]

Yet, there is no need for imaginative social and cultural histories of this kind to diminish or discard attention to the national narrative or the spectacular, eventful course of the war. This is the second point I want to make. In fact, the beauty of such studies is profoundly to complicate how we can think about the categories of politics, social policy and governance, enabling new fields of connection between the national and the local to be opened and viewed, where the 'local' describes all those quotidian spaces (family, household, neighbourhood, work, schooling, play, entertainment, sexuality) far away from the recognized and legitimate public frames we generally use for the assigning of political meaning. While the wartime may not have dislodged many continuities of cultural practice and social relations quite as radically as some older historiographies believed, its effects none the less included risk, fear, endangerment, death, loss, uncertainty, excitement and movement on the very largest of scales. We might see this as an existential disordering, a calling into question of the already available beliefs and assumptions through which people tended to think of their place in the continuum of the past and future social and political relations of their society. It was in such times that people could imagine how they might live differently in the future, particularly when the public rhetorics of citizenship, responsibility and governing actively urged them to do so, in the language of an unprecedented national emergency that placed not just the defence of the realm, but democratic freedoms and civilized values themselves at stake.

Of course, people might respond to this existential disordering in many differing ways. Large numbers were simply overwhelmed by the exigencies of an unmanageably difficult everydayness, with little practical room in their lives for thinking coherently or imaginatively about a future of any differing kind. *Politics*, as the professing of commitments and beliefs, as a practical domain of activism, or as an idiom of social being in the world, claims in any case only a limited and uneven resonance during ordinary times. For most people most of the time, politics in the conventional understanding of the term is an occasional presence, an encounter of the exceptional moment. But in the closing months of the war and its aftermath, as the killing stopped and the bombs ceased to fall, as a different kind of emotional, imaginative and practical space started to clear, political meanings might acquire unusual breadth of appeal. Those meanings embraced a variety of more optimistic or pessimistic ways through which the possible future might be thought.

Seeking to combine the new work on ordinary experience and popular memory with the classical frameworks of 'people's war' and 'people's peace', bringing more recent social and cultural histories into conversation with political histories of the war's spectacular eventfulness, will significantly shift the overall narrative, remaking our sense of what the category of the political might contain. A more complicated and nuanced *balance* between the national and the local, the dramatic and the everyday, the opening of new horizons and the persisting resilience of the old, will be the result. In this regard, a number of recent books can show us the way: Sonya Rose's account of the recasting of national citizenship, Geoffrey Field's study of the remaking of the working class, Martin Francis's treatment of class, gender and nation using the figure of the RAF flying hero, and James Hinton's use of the Mass Observation archive for examining nine exemplary lives.[22] Making these connections between the smallness of ordinary lives and the bigness of political history is exactly what attention to cultural memory, with its dialectics of the 'public' and the 'personal', can best enable us to do.

Finally, in moving from 'history' to 'memory' – from revisiting the dynamics of popular experience during the wartime itself to exploring how that experience became processed during the peace, including our contemporary moment of the present two decades – the aspects of visual remembrance become key. It is no accident that so much of the discussion in *British Cultural Memory and the Second World War* revolves around visual media and materials, including film and television, exhibitions and memorials, websites and material culture (though not, interestingly, photography), because such work requires a very different archive from the one conventional political historians have usually presumed. Imaginative writing – genre fiction, comics, children's literature, magazines, as well as poetry, novels and autobiography – together with private correspondence, personal diaries and the invaluable monthly journals collected by Mass Observation, provides a key form of written documentation.[23] But aside from the recognized visual media (film, photographs, television), the visual landscapes of the commercialized public sphere also become a rich resource – advertising and entertainment of all kinds, but also posters and postcards, multifarious collectors' cards (accompanying cigarettes, bubblegum, packets of tea), commercialized bric-a-brac, all the commodified images of an expanding economy of consumption. Given how densely and confusingly the imagery and citations composing this visual landscape can accumulate across any individual's lifetime, the prompting of memory may be not so much conscious and deliberate as *instinctive, visceral* and *sensory.*

In a complex and brilliant meditation on the workings of memory in their relation to the architecture of national identification and its spaces of ambivalence, Annette Kuhn begins with a famously diffused photograph of St Paul's during the Blitz in December 1940. 'A keystone in British popular memory of the "People's War"', this shows the cathedral rising unscathed above the smoke of fires and the ruins of burned-out buildings to become an icon of national belonging: '[It] comes to stand for the indomitability, under attack, of an entire nation. It offers uplifting testimony of survival through adversity. If it speaks of resistance, this is a resistance of endurance, of "taking it".' She ascribes an emotional immediacy to the meanings that continue to exceed whatever scepticism may now have developed around that mythology of national unity from the intervening historiographical judgements. As she writes, this photograph manages 'to speak to me – to interpellate me – in a very particular way', whether or not in her 'considered opinion' those older tropes of the 'people's war' have stood the test of time.[24] The ability of such images to elicit a spontaneous reaction, calling forth instinctual or intuitive knowledge from a kind of 'mute sensuality', expresses what Julia Adeney Thomas calls our *prediscursive* or *visceral* response to a photograph, which needs to be considered in addition to all of the careful contextualizing historians otherwise seek to apply.[25] Such a response gives access to the accumulated common-sense meanings that help organize our sense of history and belonging. In the unexpectedness of such an encounter between history's public appropriations and their personal resonance, the complex workings of memory and its archive – both collective and individual, explicit and unconscious – can create openings to knowledge where historians' more conventional practices might not.[26]

From this discussion, cultural memory emerges as an entire dimension of politics, one involving conscious and unconscious capacities, resources and interventions – that is, an apparatus of [mis]remembering (or forgetting), a complex of media and sites (film, television, radio, song, photographs, advertisements, museums, commemorations, tourist spots, fictions, ceremonial, buildings, popular histories, sermons, political speeches and more), a collective common sense, an entire repertoire of cultural scripts that are given to us, become memorized, are subject to all sorts of political influence and dispute, and by these complicated processes enable coherent understandings to be secured. In postwar popular memory, a particular rendition of the 1930s and 1940s became an especially persuasive story of how the present came to be, one that lasted well into the 1960s and 1970s. That powerful suturing of the Depression and the Second World War into a discourse of democracy and public good then passed into disarray. In many respects, the given story was brought forcefully and often brutally under attack, so that by the 1990s Thatcherism and other versions of a new right-wing politics seemed to have carried the day. The place of the war in cultural memory seemed to have been successfully re-narrated, leaving only a wasteland of ruined solidarities and dead metaphors behind. For thinking about that outcome – whether or not it proves perduring, and in what precise ways – this volume will prove an excellent guide.

Notes

1   Eley, G. (1997), 'Foreword', in M. Evans and K. Lunn (eds), *War and Memory in the Twentieth Century*. Oxford: Berg, vii–xiv. Here vii–xiii.

2   Fussell, P. (1975), *The Great War and Modern Memory*. Oxford: Oxford University Press.

3   Fraser, R. (1979), *The Blood of Spain*. London: Allen Lane.

4   Steedman, C. K. (1987), *Landscape for a Good Woman: A Story of Two Lives*. New Brunswick, NJ: Rutgers University Press; Fraser, R. (1984), *In Search of a Past: The Manor House, Amnersfield, 1933-1945*. London: Verso; Wright, P. (1985), *On Living in an Old Country: The National Past in Contemporary Britain*. London: Verso; Portelli, A. (1991), *The Death of Luigi Trastulli and Other Stories: Form and Meaning in Oral History*. Albany: State University of New York Press; Passerini, L. (1984), *Fascism in Popular Memory: The Cultural Experience of the Turin Working Class*. Cambridge: Cambridge University Press; Niethammer, L. (ed.), (1983), '*Die Jahre weiß man nicht, wo man die heute hinsetzen soll*': *Faschismuserfahrungen im Ruhrgebie* and '*Hinterher merkt man, daß es richtig war, daß es schiefgegangen ist*': *Nachkriegserfahrungen im Ruhrgebiet*.

Bonn: Dietz; Nora, P. (1984–92), *Les lieux de mémoire*, 7 vols. Paris: Gallimard, trans. (1996–8) as *The Realms of Memory: The Construction of the French Past*, 3 vols. New York: Columbia University Press, and (2001–10), *Rethinking France*, 4 vols. Chicago: University of Chicago Press.

5   Judt, T. (2003), *Postwar: A History of Europe since 1945*. New York: The Penguin Press.

6   The first of these volumes, Geppert, D. (ed.) (2003), *The Postwar Challenge: Cultural, Social, and Political Change in Western Europe, 1945-58*. Oxford: Oxford University Press, 25–97, titles its opening section 'Coming to Terms with the Past'; the second, Jarausch, K. H. and Lindenberger, T. (eds) (2007), *Conflicted Memories: Europeanizing Contemporary Histories*. New York: Berghahn Books, 23–77, has 'Contested Memories'.

7   Judt (2003), 829.

8   Jameson, F. (1991), 'Nostalgia for the present', in *Postmodernism, or The Cultural Logic of Late Capitalism*. Durham, NC: Duke University Press, 279–96. For my own thoughts, see Eley, G. (2005), *A Crooked Line: From Cultural History to the History of Society*. Ann Arbor: University of Michigan Press, 148–55; Eley, G, (2011), 'The past under erasure: history, memory and the contemporary'. *Journal of Contemporary History*, 46(3), 555–73.

9   Samuel, R. (1994), *Theatres of Memory, Vol. 1: Past and Present in Contemporary Culture*. London: Verso; Samuel, R. (1998), *Theatres of Memory, Vol. 2: Island Stories: Unravelling Britain*. London: Verso.

10 See, for example, Connerton, P. (1989), *How Societies Remember*. Cambridge: Cambridge University Press; Fentress, J. and Wickham, C. (1992), *Social Memory*. Oxford: Blackwell; Terdiman, R. (1993), *Present Past: Modernity and the Memory Crisis*. Ithaca: Cornell University Press; Hutton, P. (1993), *History as an Art of Memory*. Hanover, NH: University Press of New England; Connerton, P. (2009), *How Modernity Forgets*. Cambridge: Cambridge University Press.

11 Radstone, S. (ed.) (2000), *Memory and Methodology*. Oxford: Berg; Radstone, S. and Hodgkin, K. (eds) (2005), *Memory Cultures: Memory, Subjectivity, and Recognition*. New Brunswick, NJ: Transaction; Hodgkin, K. and Radstone, S. (eds) (2005), *Contested Pasts: The Politics of Memory*. New Brunswick, NJ: Transaction.

12 E.g. Peitsch, H., Burdett, C. and Gorrara, C. (eds) (1999), *European Memories of the Second World War*. New York: Berghahn Books; Müller, J.-W. (ed.), (2002) *Memory and Power in Post-War Europe: Studies in the Presence of the Past*. Cambridge: Cambridge University Press; Olick, J. K. (ed.) (2003), *States of Memory: Continuities, Conflicts, and Transformations in National Retrospection*. Durham: Duke University Press; Walkowitz, D. J. and Knauer, L. M. (eds) (2004), *Memory and the Impact of Political Transformation in Public Space*. Durham: Duke University Press; Geisler, M. E. (ed.) (2005), *National Symbols, Fractured Identities: Contesting the National Narrative*. Middlebury: Middlebury College Press; Friedman, M. P. and Kenney, P. (eds) (2005), *Partisan Histories: The Past in Contemporary Global Politics*. Houndmills: Palgrave Macmillan; Lebov, N., Kansteiner,

W. and Fogu, C. (eds) (2006), *The Politics of Memory in Postwar Europe*. Durham: Duke University Press; Kuhn, A. and McAllister, K. E. (eds) (2006), *Locating Memory: Photographic Acts*. New York: Berghahn Books; Paletschek, S. and Schraut, S. (eds) (2008), *The Gender of Memory: Cultures of Remembrance in Nineteenth and Twentieth-Century Europe*. Frankfurt am Main: Campus Verlag.

13 Olick, J. K., Vinitzky-Serousi, V. and Levy, D. (eds) (2011), *The Collective Memory Reader*. Oxford: Oxford University Press; Radstone, S. and Schwarz, B. (eds) (2010), *Memory: Histories, Theories, Debates*. New York: Fordham University Press. See also Perks, R. and Thomson, A. (eds) (2006), *The Oral History Reader*. London: Routledge.

14 The several anthologies mentioned in the preceding footnote provide the indispensable starting point.

15 See especially Schwarz, B. (2010), 'Memory, temporality, modernity: *Les lieux de mémoire*', in Radstone and Schwarz (eds), *Memory*, 41–58; Carrier, P. (2000), 'Places, politics, and the archiving of contemporary memory in Pierre Nora's *Les lieux de mémoire*', in Radstone (ed.), *Memory and Methodology*, 37–57; Wood, N. (1999), *Vectors of Memory: Legacies of Trauma in Postwar Europe*. New York: Berg, 15–37.

16 Eley, G. (2001), 'Framing the people's war: film, British collective memory, and World War II'. *American Historical Review*, 106 (3), 818–38. Here p. 819.

17 Calder, A. (1969), *The People's War: Britain, 1939-1945*. London: Cape; Calder, A. (1991), *The Myth of the Blitz*. London: Cape.

18 Lowe, R. (1990), 'The Second World War, consensus, and the foundation of the Welfare State'. *Twentieth-Century British History*, 1, 152–82. Here p. 175. For a summary statement of this view, see Fielding, S., Thompson, P. and Tiratsoo, N. (1995), *'England Arise!' The Labour Party and Popular Politics in 1940s Britain*. Manchester: Manchester University Press.

19 Field, G. (1992), 'Social patriotism and the British working class: appearance and disappearance of a tradition'. *International Labor and Working-Class History*, 42, 20–39. Here p. 27. Field himself does not share the view he describes. While questioning the degree of national unity grounded in social harmony, he shifts the emphasis onto the collectivism of working-class solidarity based in exactly the kinds of everyday wartime experience recent work has examined.

20 Steedman (1987), 5.

21 Kuhn, A. (2002), *Family Secrets: Acts of Memory and Imagination*. London: Verso, 9. For a brilliant allegory to this effect, see Briggs, R. (1999), *Ethel and Ernest: A True Story*. New York: Knopf.

22 See Rose, S. O. (2003), *Which People's War? National Identity and Citizenship in Wartime Britain 1939-1945*. Oxford: Oxford University Press; Field, G. (2011), *Blood, Sweat, and Toil: Remaking the British Working Class, 1939-1945*. Oxford: Oxford University Press; Francis, M. (2008), *The Flyer: British Culture and the Royal Air Force 1939–1945*. Oxford: Oxford University Press; Hinton, J. (2010), *Nine Wartime Lives: Mass Observation and the Making of the Modern Self*. Oxford: Oxford University Press.

23 For Mass Observation, see Hinton, J. (2013), *The Mass Observers: A History, 1937-1949*. Oxford: Oxford University Press; Hubble, N. (2006), *Mass Observation and Everyday Life: Culture, History, Theory*. Houndmills: Palgrave Macmillan.

24 Kuhn, A. 'Phantasmagoria of memory', in *Family Secrets*, 125–6.

25 Thomas distinguishes 'recognition' and 'excavation' as distinct strategies of understanding, each of which historians need to bring to their readings of photographs. On the one hand, historians need to 'interrogate photographs much like texts', treating them as the complicated effect or trace of past social and cultural relations whose character requires meticulous reconstruction, stressing 'the photograph's embeddedness in a whole network of social arrangements' or 'the historical matrix out of which it came'. We need to ask 'where, when, or even whether [a particular] photograph appeared in print, how it was made, what it was used for, who owns the copyright, or what its [original] title is.' But on the other hand, we need to acknowledge the inescapably 'precognitive' or 'prediscursive' and 'visceral' relations of historians to the photographs they seek to use. See Thomas, J. A. (2009), 'The evidence of sight'. *History and Theory. Theme Issue: Photography and Historical Interpretation*, 48(4), 151–68. Here pp. 151–3.

26 See also Kuhn, A. 'From home to nation', in *Family Secrets*, 147–69, with its six theses: '1. Memory shapes our inner worlds'; '2. Memory is an active production of meanings'; '3. Memory texts have their own formal conventions'; '4. Memory texts voice a collective imagination'; '5. Memory embodies both union and fragmentation'; '6. Memory is formative of communities of nationhood.' Also Radstone, S. (2010), 'Cinema and memory', in Radstone and Schwarz (eds), *Memory*, 325–42.

CHAPTER ONE

Introduction: 'Keep calm and carry on'

The cultural memory of the Second World War in Britain

Lucy Noakes and Juliette Pattinson

When the England football team played Germany in the European Championships in 1996, the *Daily Mirror*'s front cover superimposed tin hats on photographs of two England players, Stuart Pearce and Paul Gascoigne. This was accompanied by an article headed 'Pearce in our time' which reworked Chamberlain's declaration of war speech of September 1939:

> I am writing to you from the Editor's office at Canary Wharf, London. Last night the *Daily Mirror*'s ambassador in Berlin handed the German government a final note stating that, unless we heard from them by 11 o'clock that they were prepared at once to withdraw their football team from Wembley, a state of soccer war would exist between us. I have to tell you now that no such undertaking has been received, and that consequently we are at soccer war with Germany ...[1]

The adage 'Two world wars and one world cup' references England's previous victories. Indeed, the 1966 World Cup had featured in the 1969 film of the popular television series *Till Death Us Do Part* (1965–8, 1970, 1972–5). The main character, Alf Garnett, attends the England–West

Germany final and, following the opposition's first goal, taps a cheering German supporter on the shoulder, saying 'Same as in the war mate, same as in the war. Started it off well, started off well but got well clobbered in the end, didn't ya?'[2] The war is such a key aspect of British national identity that popular culture, in this case newspapers and film, frequently invokes it for comedic purposes.

Indeed, few historical events have resonated as fully in modern British culture as the Second World War. Despite it receding further into the distant past with that generation's passing, it continues to have a lingering and very vivid presence in British popular culture so that even those who were born in its aftermath have particular 'memories' of it. Later generations have acquired a learned historical memory informed by successive narratives conveyed in a range of media, thereby adopting the memories as their own. As Geoff Eley asserts, '"Remembering" World War II requires no immediate experience of those years.'[3] The memory of the war, which has remained potent and present throughout the past 70 years, has left a rich legacy in a range of media that continues to attract a wide audience: film, television and radio, photography and the visual arts, journalism and propaganda, architecture, museums, music and literature. The British memory of the war has also been maintained through cultural artefacts such as model aeroplanes and replica clothing, as well as mugs and bags adorned with punchy slogans such as 'Keep Calm and Carry On', and has lived on in advertising slogans such as those for Shepherd Neame's Spitfire beer: 'The Bottle of Britain'; 'Downed all over Kent, Just like the Luftwaffe'; 'No Fokker Comes Close'.

As Geoff Eley's foreword to this volume notes, the memory of the Second World War has become increasingly visible, and contested, in post-Cold War Europe. The numerous acts of memorialization and commemoration that have taken place since 1989 can be understood, at one level, as a means of attempting to assert a continuity between a rapidly changing present and a shared past. At the same time, because of the difficult and contested status of much of what is being 'remembered', these acts become sites of struggle.[4] In some instances, most visibly but not exclusively in Eastern and Central Europe, as Adam Krzeminski has argued, 'the Second World War is still being fought', albeit this time with museums and memorials, rather than armour and artillery.[5] The existence of national myths and memories of the Second World War is not, of course, anything new. Many nations have looked back to the war years, in different contexts, as a touchstone for their 'sense of self' in the post-war period. In France, for example, the cultural memory of the war focused for a long time on resistance: a memory increasingly challenged and undermined by questions around collaboration which began to open up after 1968.[6] In the Soviet satellite states of Eastern and Central Europe, and the former states of the USSR, memory of Nazi occupation was first framed by, and then overlaid with, the experience and memory of Soviet occupation. Entry tickets for the Museum of the

Occupation of Latvia, 1940–1991, for example, stated that 'the Museum shows what happened to Latvia, its lands and people under two occupying totalitarian regimes from 1940 to 1991'.[7] Over all of this lies the cultural memory of the Holocaust, increasingly positioned not only as the defining event of the Second World War, but as the defining event of the European twentieth century. In Tony Judt's striking phrase, the Holocaust has become the 'entry ticket' to contemporary Europe.[8] Despite its geographical isolation from mainland Europe, which protected it from the worst of the suffering that came with invasion, occupation, bombardment and internment during the war, Britain has not been immune to the impact of these 'memory wars', as the battle over the cultural memory of the war is restaged across a range of cultural texts, including academic and popular histories, museums and memorials. In recent years, for example, the isolated position of Britain in Europe in 1940 has been mobilized in support of opposition to British membership of the European Union,[9] while historians have fought over the historical memory of the 'people's war' and the meanings of consensus in the post-war period.[10]

The enduring presence of the war in all aspects of the public world is mirrored in its ongoing centrality in many personal and family memories, with stories of the Second World War being recounted through the generations. Many of the stories entered on the BBC's 'People's War' website, for example, were not written by those with personal experience of the war years, but by their families, using the space of the website to recount the stories that had circulated in their family and to open these up to a wider audience. One of the BBC's recommended entries on the website, entitled 'Coventry wartime memories: The night of the 14th', begins with the statement 'This is the story of my parents', and, after vividly recounting their experiences of the bombing of Coventry in November 1940, concludes that the entry was written 'as a tribute to my mother' who 'used to reminisce about the days in Coventry and say that she should have written about it.'[11] Marianne Hirsch, in her work on the ongoing impact of the Holocaust on survivors and their descendents, developed the term 'postmemory' to describe the multifarious means by which past events continue to shape the lives of survivors' families.[12] While Hirsch is writing specifically about the long afterlife of particularly traumatic memories, the continuing presence of the Second World War in twenty-first-century Britain suggests that the legacy of other events, not necessarily always experienced or remembered as traumatic, continues to frame family relationships and identities. Family stories, alongside medals, photographs and the other material artefacts of war, are often preserved within families, forming intergenerational links and shared points of reference.

Thus, the cultural memory of the war, which is present in family stories, in popular and material culture and in acts of commemoration in Britain between 1945 and the present, includes both *personal* memories and narratives of war as well as *publicly* produced war memories. These 'texts of memory'[13] are produced in the present, and are not a direct representation of events of the past; they have to be understood within the historical context of their creation and articulation.

Conceptualizing memory

Memory itself is a notoriously slippery term, one which can act to disguise the production of particular representations of the past as much as it enables analysis of this production. While memory may be understood in an everyday sense as the processes through which individuals store and recount past events, simply remembering what happened, memory itself, on both an individual and a cultural level, is anything but straightforward. On an individual level, and with the exception of a small number of memory savants, we select and interpret events from our lives, ordering them and drawing on them in order to create a narrative of who we are. Memory thus involves forgetting, as much as it does remembering. As the Popular Memory Group argued in 1982, we structure our memories to make sense of our past and present lives.[14] These individual memories, however, do not exist in a vacuum; they are shaped by time and place, by the forces of history, politics, culture, the economy and more that form the worlds in which we live. As Annette Kuhn asserts: 'If the memories are one individual's, their associations extend far beyond the personal. They spread into an extended network of meanings that bring together the personal with the familial, the cultural, the economic, the social and the historical.'[15] These forces provide not only the conditions for remembering and forgetting, but, arguably, the very language with which memories can be articulated. For example, in Alistair Thomson's oral history of the experience of Australian First World War soldiers, he found that many of the men that he interviewed made sense of their experiences by drawing on what he termed 'the myth' of the Anzac experience, with some relating scenes from the popular 1981 film *Gallipoli* as if they were their own personal experience.[16] Similarly, Penny Summerfield explored the ways that many of the women that she interviewed for *Reconstructing Women's Wartime Lives* made use of existing ideas about the Second World War, emphasizing stoicism, adventure and the forces of modernization and tradition to compose memories of their wartime selves which made sense in the present.[17] Formulations of memory may be, on one essential level, psychological, but they are also social and cultural.

Some individual memories, of course, deny composure, the two-fold process described by Graham Dawson as both the process of 'composing' memories so that they may be spoken or shared, and the achievement of personal composure through this process.[18] Experiences may not have been fully processed by the individual, and thus composure has yet to be

attained. Most dramatically, the experience of events that we might understand as traumatic and as outside of everyday understanding are recalled
differently than more mundane episodes. Some might recall vividly every
harrowing detail, others report without emotion and with matter-of-fact
detachment, while some repress memory. In some extreme cases, speech is
denied altogether, as with soldiers suffering from 'shell shock' during the
First World War who were unable to give voice not only to their experiences
but to anything at all, and to Second World War veterans suffering from
Post-Traumatic Stress Disorder, such as the New Zealanders interviewed
by Alison Parr who noted that 'silent coping strategies' were often adopted
upon their return to civilian life.[19] Traumatic memory is not the same as
amnesia, as forgetting.[20] As Cathy Carruth writes, 'to be traumatised is
precisely to be possessed by an image or event'.[21] Holocaust memories,
and the difficulties that survivors have often had in finding a means of
describing such extreme events, provide possibly the most apposite example
of traumatic memory.[22] As Craig R. Barclay states, 'There are no known
narrative structures that can be used as referents from which to reconstruct
traumatic experiences like those associated with the daily experience of
seeing others selected and exterminated.'[23] The absence of a framework
can impede the telling of traumatic memories; indeed, memories of painful
experiences often rely upon existing narratives for their articulation. This is
seen in some of the combatants' memories, entered on the BBC's 'People's
War' website, which made use of images and narratives in the film *Saving
Private Ryan* (1998) and the television series *Band of Brothers* (2001) to
describe the experience of the D-Day landings of 1944. Similarly, anniversaries and commemorative events can act as 'prompts', bringing difficult
memories to the surface and perhaps providing an audience for the telling
of these memories. Nigel Hunt and Ian Robbins found that the range of
public commemorations of the 50th anniversary of the D-Day landings in
1994 'acted as a reminder for many veterans', and the unveiling of a plaque
in 1993 commemorating the 1943 disaster at Bethnal Green Underground
Station, in which 173 people were crushed to death, enabled some survivors
to speak of their memories for the first time.[24] Psychological, social
and cultural factors can combine to make some memories difficult and
sometimes impossible to articulate, but they can also provide the historical
conditions in which such memories precisely can become visible.

Individual personal memories of an event or period are shaped by
public representations of the same, while public representations, equally,
draw on individual memories for recognition and validation. Thus, a
cultural circuit is in operation in which the public and the personal are
bound in a mutual and active cycle. Both individual memories and public
representations are shaped by the form in which they are expressed
and mediated: diaries, conversations, autobiographies, photographs, films,
novels, museum displays, websites and memorials, to name but a few, are
all sites through which memory is not only made visible but also formed.

Chapters in this book examine the production of memories of the Second World War across a range of different sites, including memoirs, memorials, interviews, ephemera, films, websites and Mass Observation, all of which impact upon and shape the formation of memory.

This complex relationship between the public and the private has led to the development of a range of sometimes competing, sometimes complementary, sometimes confusing, theoretical approaches and linguistic terms through which to analyse the production and articulation of memory. In addition to 'cultural memory', historians invoke various other concepts, often interchangeably, such as 'public memory', 'collective memory', 'social memory', 'popular memory', 'mass memory', 'vectors of memory', 'transactive memory', 'prosthetic memory' and 'multidirectional memory'. While it is difficult to give a precise definition, each has its own distinguishing peculiarities.[25] In what follows, each of these conceptualizations is briefly discussed with reference, where appropriate, to chapters from this collection.

'Public memory' is understood as being shaped by influential 'official' forces, such as the state. In 'closed' totalitarian societies this has far-reaching consequences, in that a particular approved version of the past suppresses memories that challenge the official view.[26] In 'open' societies, a more reciprocal and fluid relationship between official and personal memory can exist. Yet, even in liberal democracies, a static and selective version of the past, as presented in government-approved commemorative acts, memorials, museum exhibitions, archives and school curricula and textbooks, can muffle alternative memories, as Pierre Nora notes in his analysis of 'sites of memory'.[27] Thus, the exclusion of representatives of the Bevin Boys and the Women's Land Army on the Remembrance Sunday marches until 1998 and 2000 respectively constructs a public image of which groups merit commemoration. As Corinna Peniston-Bird discusses in her chapter in this volume, the creation of the Women's War Memorial, dedicated in Whitehall in 2005, brought to the fore a particular set of battles over women's participation in the war effort, as representatives and veterans of the women's auxiliary services fought unsuccessfully for a memorial which emphasized women's 'active' military role in wartime. This echoes debates over the creation of the Imperial War Graves Cemeteries, the Cenotaph and the associated two-minute silence that marked Armistice Day (and still marks Remembrance Sunday), in the immediate aftermath of the First World War.[28] Officially created, high-status sites of public memory can disguise the often fraught and contested nature of the creation of such sites.

If 'public memory' foregrounds the impact of *official* constructions of the past on personal memory, 'collective' and 'social' memory, terms coined by sociologist Maurice Halbwachs in 1925, signify that an individual's memories are inseparable from *group* memory: 'We can understand each memory as it occurs in individual thought only if we can locate each within the thought of the corresponding group.'[29] Personal memory is thus always configured, situated and preserved within the social group, and this serves to unite individuals communally. Memories that are at variance with those that are commonly agreed upon at the familial, local or national level receive bare acknowledgment and consequently fade. Halbwachs's notion of 'social memory' was developed in 1992 by Fentress and Wickham,[30] who assert that the act of articulating individual or personal memories is a process in which they become social. The BBC's 'People's War' website is one example of this.

Perhaps a less rigid interpretation of memory is that of 'popular memory', which allows for the relational interplay between individual and public memories. This was first conceived by Michel Foucault in the mid-1970s[31] and developed by the Popular Memory Group at the University of Birmingham in the early 1980s.[32] They assert: 'Private memories cannot, in concrete studies, be readily unscrambled from the effects of dominant historical discourses. It is often these that supply the very terms by which a private history is thought through.'[33] This notion focuses on popular culture such as cartoons and comics and asserts that, in any given culture, there is always conflict over the interpretation of the past that gains hegemonic status. There is never unanimity and nothing can be 'monolithically installed or everywhere believed in.'[34] Nevertheless, as with the conceptualizations above, popular memory theorists note that memories which are at variance to the dominant or hegemonic narrative are muffled. One example of this, discussed in Lucy Noakes's chapter on the BBC's 'People's War' website in this collection, is the difficulty many of those recounting their experiences of the aerial bombardment of civilians in wartime had in articulating any sense of fear that they may have felt. Fear, a universal emotion in wartime, and a 'common sense' reaction to the assaults on the self that war entails, has been marginal to most public accounts of British civilians under bombardment, making it harder, but not impossible, for those who experienced this emotion to express their memories of being scared.

Another way of understanding memory is not to foreground the 'popular' (sometimes regarded as 'of the people', an uncontaminated, truthful version of the past, free from political influence) at the expense of the 'public' (perceived as dominant, constructed, 'official' versions), but rather to focus on 'mass memory'.[35] Sue Harper, in her analysis of films of the 1940s and 1950s, uses the concept to emphasize the social diversity of the audience in terms of class, age and gender.[36] While working with the concept of popular memory discussed above, rather than 'mass memory' as defined by Harper, Penny Summerfield's chapter in this volume engages directly with the diversity of those who, in popular memory terms, are both the audience for, and producers of, memory. Focusing on the ways in which gendered and generational identities informed the responses of Mass Observation Project (MOP) panellists to a directive inviting them to reflect on 'What the Second World War Means to You', Summerfield demonstrates the mutability of memory.[37] She examines the panellists' diverse responses to illustrate the ways that life course and gender mould our response and relationship to cultural memory. Generation and gender, Summerfield argues, shape both our sense of self and our relationship to the past, but while gender appears to consistently shape the ways that we engage (or don't engage) with particular representations of the past, generational memory is shaped far more by the ageing process, and the individual's subsequent relationship to family and society, than by direct, personal experience of the events being recalled. The continued primacy of the cultural memory of the Second World War in British public and family life is illustrated here by the ability of those who were born long after the war none the less to 'remember' it.

Other influential concepts drawn upon by contributors to this volume include Henry Rousso's 'vectors of memory', in which he asserts that interpretations of the national past are conveyed to the public through a wide range of representations and sites. Rousso's aim in *The Vichy Syndrome* was to 'capture the full diversity of "collective memory" by recording all its visible signs.' Analysing key sites of representation of Vichy France in the post-war period, Rousso demonstrated how cultural and political representations of the period 1940–4 appeared and disappeared, driven by and intimately related to the contemporary political context and to what Nancy Wood has termed 'the affective dimensions that the evolving memories of Vichy had assumed in French public life.'[38] Drawing on Rousso's work, Juliette Pattinson in her chapter in this volume charts the myriad ways that the clandestine war in occupied France was revealed to the British public. While the Second World War is frequently configured as a man's war in memoir and film, female secret agents from the outset took centre stage in biographies, newspaper articles, films, memorials, television series, documentaries, museum exhibitions and computer games, all of them vectors of memory shaping the public's perceptions of the secret war.

Terms such as 'multidirectional memory',[39] 'transactive memory'[40] and 'prosthetic memory'[41] have also been coined recently. Multidirectional memory, used in this volume by Rebecca Bramall, is a concept developed by the critical and cultural scholar Michael Rothberg. Rothberg's work is an ambitious attempt to reconsider 'collective memory' in a post-colonial and globalized world, where competing memories meet and sometimes clash in multi-cultural societies. Arguing that memory should not be understood as a 'zero sum struggle over scarce resources', Rothberg instead develops a more positive view of memory battles in multi-cultural societies, insisting on them as dynamic processes which are 'productive and not privative'.[42] Rebecca Bramall's chapter in this volume draws on Rothberg's approach to offer an account of the cultural memory of austerity in twenty-first-century Britain. Bramall suggests that, in order to avoid what Susannah Radstone has termed the 'epistemological sleight of hand from representation to memory', by which certain cultural texts have been read by scholars *as* cultural memory, a productive examination of the cultural memory of austerity would be polysemic.[43] She argues that Rothberg's concept of multidirectional memory provides a useful concept through which the fluid and polysemic nature of the cultural memory of austerity in post-war Britain can be understood.

Building on Fentress and Wickham's argument that 'what makes memory social is talk', Graham Smith has drawn on cognitive psychology to develop the concept of transactive memory, defined as 'the combination of individual minds and the communication among them', to describe the ways that memories are shared.[44] Transactive memory provides a means to investigate the ways that we remember as members of a group that acknowledges the complex social processes involved in remembering, including the influence of cultural discourses within which people fit their personal stories, whilst avoiding the crude understanding of personal memory as externally constructed by allowing space for alternative recollections. Prosthetic memory, meanwhile, like Rothberg's work discussed above, is an optimistic account of the dynamic possibilities of cultural memory, in this case understood as mediated representations of the past experienced by the mass audiences of modernity, to produce new and empathetic identities. For Alison Landsberg, drawing on Pierre Nora's insistence on the importance of 'sites of memory' as anchors in the dislocations of modernity, the mass media, far from being a site where individuals are further alienated and objectified, becomes a transformational site where 'prosthetic memory emerges at the interface between a person and a historical narrative about the past, at an experiential site such as a movie theatre or museum.'[45] Prosthetic memory, as developed by Landsberg, suggests that audiences can 'take on' the memory of an event they did not experience, attaching it to their sense of self in the same way that one might attach a prosthetic limb, creating 'the conditions for ethical thinking precisely by encouraging people to feel connected to, while recognising the alterity of, the "other"'.[46]

These sometimes vague and often competing concepts have all been heavily criticized.[47] The collective, the social, the popular and the public do not possess their own memories but rather provide the context and the space for the expression of a cultural memory, sometimes widely agreed and sometimes contested, but always reliant on the agreement and recognition of individuals and social groups. After all, as Joanna Bourke reminds us, 'individuals "remember", "repress", "forget", and "are traumatized", not societies.'[48] The more recent conceptualizations of memory such as multi directional memory, transactive memory and prosthetic memory risk ignoring the power relations that shape the social world in which memories circulate and identities are formed. Taken together, however, the large body of work which attempts to theorize the production of memory is a useful, indeed necessary, endeavour.

The chapters collected in this volume draw upon a range of theoretical approaches in their analysis of the formation of the memory of the Second World War in Britain, but they are drawn together by a shared belief that cultural memory relies upon the interrelationship between the public and the private, the individual alongside the institutional, for successful adoption and circulation. Put simply, representations of the past that are created in the public sphere, on the public stage, that do not accord with the memories of enough of that public, will find it difficult to reach a wide audience. They need to have resonance with people's recollections, to fit, to 'ring true', in order to be considered authentic.

The Second World War in cultural memory

The cultural memory of the Second World War in Britain is notable for both its durability and its flexibility. Its resilience is evidenced both by its repeated articulation by individuals with no lived memory of the event, as discussed by Summerfield in this volume, and by the fact that post-1945 events are frequently seen through the lens of the war, with continual references to the spirit of Dunkirk or the Blitz, which are often used interchangeably. For example, in the aftermath of the bombing of the London Transport network in July 2005, references to the Blitz, and 'the Blitz spirit', were both immediate and omnipresent. Sir Ian Blair, then Metropolitan Police Commander, commented that 'if London can survive the Blitz, then it can survive four miserable events like this', whilst the *Daily Mirror* called on its readers to 'adopt the famous Blitz spirit', quoting Minister for Veterans Doug Touhig's call to 'keep up the spirit' which was shown in the 'grim days between 1939 and 1945'.[49] When research published in 2009 found a correlation between falling suicide rates and the attacks on New York and Washington DC in 2001, and on London in 2005, this was attributed by the researchers to a 'greater social cohesion, the Blitz spirit' found in the aftermath of these attacks.[50] As David Hoogland Noon's analysis of political rhetoric has demonstrated, the Second World War has frequently been invoked on both sides of the Atlantic in support of the far more nebulous 'war on terror' since 2001, the cultural memory of the 'good war' against European fascism and Japanese imperialism being mobilized in support of a simplifying rhetoric that places the West as 'good' and its enemies as 'bad'.[51] The cultural memory of the war, however, is also drawn upon to describe both non-conflict events and responses to them, often imbuing these responses with the image of the British public's 'stoical' response to the conditions of the Second World War. Media reportage of the clearing up operations following freak weather occurrences such as hurricanes and floods often refer to the Blitz in order to convey a sense of community spirit, tenacity and stoicism in trying circumstances. For example, in an article entitled 'Sheffield Floods Brought Out Blitz Spirit', local MP David Blunkett described residents' reactions to the 2007 flooding in the city as embodying a 'spirit' that 'was very much like that seen in the Blitz', and when Richard Branson's home in the British Virgin Islands was destroyed by fire in 2011 following a tropical storm, he was reported as saying, 'It's very much the Dunkirk Spirit here'.[52] The banking crisis also resulted in a glut of references to the spirit of the Blitz. In an article headlined 'Patience, good humour and a touch of the Blitz spirit', a 77-year-old man who was queuing up outside a branch of Northern Rock to withdraw his money was quoted as saying 'Out of tragedy comes togetherness – that's something you don't get very often these days. It's the same sort of experience as in the air-raid shelters. It has brought people together.'[53] As global stock markets were pitched into turmoil in the wake of Northern Rock, and a recession loomed, Gordon Brown in his 2009 New Year speech drew on the Blitz spirit, noting that the same qualities were needed to come through the current crisis.[54] These varied examples, which each draw upon a 'collective pool of knowledge'[55] about the war, illustrate the ways in which certain memories have become so ingrained in the public psyche that they are invoked continually, even when the events being described bear little relation to the memories being mobilized.

As well as being durable, memory is also elastic; it is not totally fixed and stable but instead is open to renegotiation, reinterpretation and sometimes contestation. Interpretations of the war alter over time as marginalized memories are recovered and incorporated and as present-day events prompt reconsideration. For example, the 1980s and early 1990s saw a struggle over the concept of the 'people's war', as a right-wing government engaged in wars in the Falkland/Malvinas Islands, Northern Ireland and Iraq gave voice to a memory of the period which emphasized bellicose Churchillian rhetoric over the memory of the creation of the Welfare State and a more egalitarian society. The historian E. P. Thompson, writing in 1980, expressed his frustration at the increasing hegemony of this right-wing memory of the war years, recalling the 'resolute and ingenious civilian army' and the 'anti-fascist and consciously anti-imperialist army' of his war, concluding that 'one is not permitted to speak of one's wartime reminiscences today'.[56] This reconceptualization of the war years provides the background to Janet Watson's chapter in this volume. Watson considers the foregrounding of the Second World War in popular culture and cultural memory through an examination of the growing importance of wartime anniversaries, and the concomitant marketing opportunities which accompanied them, during the 1980s and 1990s. Arguing that the Second World War has become a touchstone for a widely shared (yet still exclusive) concept of national identity, Watson's chapter demonstrates the ways that commemoration and commodification came together in the late twentieth century to produce a cultural memory of the war in which those who fought under flags of Empire were hidden from view, marginalized in the 1980s by the emphasis on white British veterans and in the 1990s by the expansion of veterans to include 'everyone' on the Home Front.

A similar attempt at politically mobilizing the memories of war is being undertaken by the Conservative–Liberal Democratic coalition government of the early twenty-first century, whose use of the term 'austerity' and frequent reminders that 'we are all in this together', discussed in this volume by Rebecca Bramall, invoke a cultural memory of the war years that foregrounds collectivity and stoicism in the service of a radical restructuring of the Welfare State that emerged out of the war.[57] In response, the grassroots opposition group 'UK Uncut' suggested that supporters hold 1940s-style 'street parties', arguing that post-war Britain was 'emerging from a World War and had a huge national debt' yet the country 'really was "all in this together"' as people 'partied in the streets and dreamt of what we could achieve as a people and a country'. Urging supporters to hold street parties in opposition to welfare cuts and National Health Service reform, UK Uncut attempted to mobilize a left-of-centre memory of the legacy of the 'people's war' and the progressive politics of the post-war years, claiming that 'the future's not what it used to be – let's get it back'.[58]

Some struggles over the memory of the war years, however, are more specific, focusing instead on the foregrounding or marginalization of particular groups or experiences. One example of a struggle over a specific war memory is the ongoing debate about the role of Bomber Command in the war, seen, as Frances Houghton demonstrates in her chapter in this volume, by some as heroes whose sacrifice has been unfairly excluded from a widely shared memory and culture of memorialization of the British war effort, and by others as representative of the barbarism of that war. As Houghton shows, some veterans of Bomber Command have made active attempts at carving out a space for their memories of the war years, and what they see as their unfair exclusion from both official acts of commemoration and popular narratives of the war. The actions of Bomber Command, who carried out large and devastating raids on German cities between 1943 and 1945, with heavy losses amongst both the civilians who were the targets of these raids and the British aircrews, have been notoriously difficult to fit within the British narrative of 'the good war', which opposes Nazi and fascist atrocities to an Allied commitment to 'decency' and humanitarianism.[59] Using Rousso's concept of 'vectors of memory', Houghton analyses the memoirs of Bomber Command veterans as 'carriers' of a particular memory of the war years which attempts 'a deliberate reconstruction of an event for a social purpose' – in this case, the incorporation into the wider cultural memory of the war of the actions of Bomber Command.[60] As a central London memorial to Bomber Command was dedicated in 2012, it could perhaps be argued that the veterans and their supporters have been successful, and that a memory of Bomber Command, albeit one that emphasizes sacrifice and bravery over the suffering of civilians, is becoming a part of the cultural memory of the war years.

While some aspects of the war years struggle for recognition, others, particularly what Sonya Rose has termed the 'signal events' of the war, Dunkirk, the Battle of Britain, the Blitz and the D-Day landings, continue to dominate the cultural memory of the period. These hegemonically dominant memories too need to be understood as having achieved their current iconic status through a process of struggle and negotiation.[61] They are by no means a permanent aspect of the cultural memory of the war but should be seen as having been produced in the present, under particular historical circumstances in which they make a particular kind of sense. None of Rose's 'signal events' have arrived at their current position at the heart of the cultural memory of the war years simply by chance or by some sort of 'natural' process. Indeed, while they are widely understood in the present as standing for Britain's 'finest hour' – as events in which Britain and the wartime British people 'pulled together' to overcome overwhelming odds before eventually emerging triumphant in 1945 – they are all also potentially unstable memories, memories which could, in other historical circumstances, invite very different readings. Dunkirk could as well be remembered as a military disaster as a victory, a disaster in which a routed army abandoned its weaponry in the retreat to the beaches, where they were left vulnerable to repeated attacks by the Luftwaffe.[62] Books such as Nicholas Harman's *Dunkirk: The Necessary Myth*, Clive Ponting's *1940: Myth and Reality* and Stuart Hylton's *Their Darkest Hour* attempt to rewrite 1940, the year of Dunkirk, the Battle of Britain and the Blitz, as a triumph of rhetoric over reality, while Angus Calder's *The Myth of the Blitz* offered a more sophisticated analysis of the creation of the cultural memory of the Blitz, and indeed the war itself, during the war years, whilst a re-thinking of the D-Day invasions of 1944 cast them as a sideshow to the *real* war that was being fought on the Eastern Front.[63] All of these events could be remembered differently; their role as 'signal' events embodying the British experience of the Second World War is in part due to myth-making during the war itself but is equally due to the demands of the present. While some historians problematically oppose 'myth' with 'truth'[64] and seek to debunk notions such as the Blitz spirit by focusing for example on the prevalence of looting, others have noted that truth and myth are not mutually exclusive; rather they are two sides of the same 1940 story. Mark Connelly asserts that historians should view these memories of the war as 'a particular explanation and interpretation of events rather than a cleverly designed falsification of reality'.[65]

While cultural memories of Dunkirk, the Battle of Britain and the Blitz have played a key role in defining Britishness, emphasizing *communal* stoicism in withstanding the onslaught of Nazi aerial bombing in a period when Britain stood alone, another aspect of war memory, one which illustrates *individual* activism in the struggle to liberate Continental Europe, erases 'other' nationalities and thereby collapses differences into a common Britishness. The 'British' secret agents who worked with the French Resistance, for example, and who are discussed in Juliette Pattinson's chapter in this volume, came from varied national backgrounds yet they have been remembered (or claimed) as British. In the immediate post-war period, there was an unwillingness to acknowledge the other nationalities and races involved. Noor Inayat Khan's name, for example, was frequently anglicized in newspaper coverage of her posthumous George Cross.[66] While her Indian identity is no longer obscured, with the unveiling of a bronze bust in 2012[67] and the announcement the same year that the film rights to a recent biography have been secured,[68] for other groups the dominant memory of the war has continued to marginalize their wartime contributions. This is made evident in Wendy Ugolini's chapter, which focuses upon post-war 'New Commonwealth' migrants to Britain and Polish refugees who settled here during and following the war. Drawing on rich oral history collections to trace the continuity between the marginalization of these groups in the wartime national community and, Ugolini argues, the marginalization of their wartime contributions in the cultural memory of the war, this chapter shows how the memory of the wartime Home Front has been constructed in a racialized manner that privileges and foregrounds both whiteness and a cultural Britishness. This construction serves not only to emphasize the 'finest hour' discourse of the war but also to exclude migrant groups from the national community that has so enthusiastically embraced this memory. Again and again, the interviews discussed by Ugolini contrast the relative acceptance and even welcome accorded to colonial and Polish troops during the war with a widespread rejection of their presence in Britain in the post-war period. The marginality of the wartime presence of these communities to the cultural memory of Home-Front Britain has acted to bolster their exclusion from the post-war, post-colonial, national community. Whilst privileged 'sites of memory' such as the Imperial War Museum in London and the Scottish United Services Museum at Edinburgh Castle have organized exhibitions which focus, respectively, on the contributions of West Indian and Polish servicemen to the war effort, black and non-British white communities continue to be marginal to the Home-Front-focused memory of the 'people's war' that circulates in late twentieth century and early twenty-first century Britain.

One of the key functions of the cultural memory of the Second World War in post-war Britain is to mask the decline of Empire and the economic and political decline of Britain as a world power. Britain's 'finest hour' has cast a long shadow over the post-war nation. Processes of decolonization and the 'end of Empire' have been both incorporated in, and at times obscured by, continued references to the war, a process which has ongoing consequences for post-colonial Britain as a multi-cultural nation.[69] Martin Francis provides us with a new reading of the war films of the 1950s, a period when, as Geoff Eley has argued, 'official and popular cultures were pervaded by the war's presence'.[70] In contrast to the predominant focus on a widely known corpus of films usually taken to represent the war film genre of this period, Francis discusses two lesser known war films of the period, *The Black Tent* (1956) and *Foxhole in Cairo* (1960), both of which examine the desert war. Focusing on the films' representation of racialized and sexualized 'otherness', Francis demonstrates the linkage between the cultural memory of the war and the end of Empire, arguing that it is not enough, as Paul Gilroy has argued, to understand this cultural memory as a means by which Britain failed to come to terms with its declining geo-political power.[71] Instead, as Francis demonstrates, remembering war in a time of decolonization does not have to mean forgetting empire; indeed, as these films show, 'race' and empire were deeply entangled in the cultural memory of the war years.

Another function of cultural memory has been to almost completely erase some aspects of the war. While some scripts are so central to British cultural memory, others are practically forgotten. This amnesia can be seen especially clearly in the case of the Far Eastern campaign. The humiliating fall of Singapore in February 1942 and Japanese successes in Burma were too painful to contemplate and were overshadowed by the war in Europe. Asked to name the date that the Second World War ended, many British people might say 8 May 1945, the day victory in Europe was attained; far fewer know the date of VJ Day and the actual end of the war. Defeat of the Germans was considered by many the primary goal, not least because the war against Japan was far away and did not impact so visibly upon the Home Front. Later victory in the Far Eastern theatre of war did not propel the conflict into the limelight. Burma's liberation, mainly by troops from the Commonwealth and Empire including Indians, India's independence in 1947 and then Burma's in 1948 gave the British, according to Mark Connelly, 'even less reason to celebrate this great imperial effort'.[72] They truly were the 'Forgotten Army'. The only aspects of the Far Eastern war that have a place in cultural memory are the prisoners of war, as a result of the popularity of films such as David Lean's *The Bridge on the River Kwai* (1958) and *A Town Like Alice* (1956) and the later television series *Tenko* (1981–4), and to a lesser extent the members of ENSA (Entertainments National Service Association) which featured in *It Ain't Half Hot Mum* (1974–81). Less palatable episodes have also been erased from cultural memory, such as the internment of 'enemy aliens' in Britain during the war,[73] the British sinking of the French fleet at the port of Mers-el-Kebir near Oran in Algeria on 3 July 1940 which resulted in 1297 Frenchmen losing their lives, and the incarceration, interrogation and alleged torture of German prisoners at the MI9-run London Cage, some of the files of which were only opened at the National Archives in December 2002.[74]

Conclusion

As the chapters gathered together here demonstrate, there is no singular, dominant and uncontested cultural memory of the British experience of the Second World War. At different points in time since 1945 different memories have dominated and different experiences have been empha-sized or marginalized. The cultural memory of the war is contingent, in that it is shaped as much by the period in which the war is being 'remembered' and represented, as it is by the multifarious experiences of the war themselves. One final example demonstrates the ways that the memory of wartime events shifts, shaped both by external cultural, social, political and economic factors and by the life course of individuals.

On Wednesday 3 March 1943, tragedy struck at Bethnal Green Underground Station in East London. The station had been used as a makeshift shelter by hundreds of residents since the Blitz of 1940–1 and, when air raid sirens sounded shortly after 8 p.m. that evening, many people hurried to take refuge in the station. At 8.27 an Anti-Aircraft Artillery battery in nearby Victoria Park opened up. Events immediately following this are unclear, but it appears that in the subsequent rush to take shelter a woman carrying a baby slipped on the stairs and within minutes hundreds of people trying to make their way down the stairs were crushed against one another. This 'quickly grew into a tangled mass of people who could not release themselves or be extricated for some time.'[75] A total of 173 people, including 62 children, died and a further 61 were injured, many seriously. Coverage of the disaster in the press was muted and the subsequent Home Office Inquiry was stamped 'Most Secret. To be kept under lock and key', as the government were anxious that details of the event should not reach Germany.[76] The event was reported in the national press, however, *The Times* describing how 'about 178 people were killed and 60 were injured when the crowd entering a London tube shelter after the alert on Wednesday evening tripped and fell on top of one another, blocking a stairway', and the Home Secretary, Herbert Morrison, made a public statement summarizing the disaster and announcing the inquiry.[77] Over subsequent decades, however, the tragedy was, if not forgotten, certainly marginalized within the dominant cultural memory of the bombardment of London. In the story of the British people during the Blitz that took shape in subsequent decades, there was little space for representations of fear, panic and death.

Gradually, however, the disaster at Bethnal Green began to enter the cultural memory of the war. The East End playwright Bernard Kops's dramatization of the event, *It's a Lovely Day Tomorrow*, was broadcast on ITV in 1975. Copies of the drama are unavailable, but *The Times* review the following day suggested that 'nostalgia had laid a soft and numbing hand over the whole enterprise'.[78] None the less, the existence of the drama demonstrates that the circulating cultural memory of the Blitz did have space for discordant and disquieting memories, even though the *TV Times* article that accompanied the drama invoked memories of the underground shelters where people 'lived out the night of the war underground as cheerfully and usefully as they could'. *TV Times* also noted the often squalid conditions, and that gangs of pickpockets operated in the shelters.[79] While descriptions of the more unpleasant and negative aspects of sheltering such as these may have been marginal to dominant and widely shared representations of the Blitz, in which the civilian response to bombardment had become a rhetorical device, shorthand for wartime unity and stoicism, they none the less existed and, at times, worked their way to the surface of cultural memory.

In 1993 a small plaque was unveiled at Bethnal Green Underground Station to mark the site of the disaster. This was the first time that the tragedy was officially commemorated, and the coverage and commemoration of the event appear to have enabled some of those with private, experiential memories to speak about them in public for the first time. One woman recounted how she had never been able to use the station since; another how she ritually counted the steps down to the platform every time she used them.[80] Following the erection of this first, small plaque, a campaign grew for a larger memorial to be placed outside the station. The 'Stairway to Heaven Memorial Trust' was formed to campaign and fundraise for a memorial, and an inverted stairway, with a memorial plinth beneath listing the names of the victims, began to be put in place outside the station entrance in 2012. MPs and public figures gave their support to the memorial campaign, and in 2011 Prime Minister David Cameron wrote to the Trust stating that 'a fitting memorial would be appropriate, as a tribute to those who died or were injured, and to ensure that younger people and future generations are aware of the tragedy that occurred there.'[81] By the early twenty-first century the tragedy at Bethnal Green had moved from being marginal to, and almost invisible within, the dominant cultural memory of the Blitz to a central position within representations of London at war, depicted in novels, discussed in parliament and the topic of numerous newspaper articles.[82]

Why, then, has this one event moved from the margins to the centre of the cultural memory of the war? There are a range of factors that can help to account for this. First, as identified by Jay Winter, a 'memory boom' developed in the late twentieth century.[83] This 'boom' or widely shared fascination with particular aspects of the past was driven by several factors: a desire to 'look back' and reflect on key events of the century and indeed, the millennium; the realization that veterans of the two 'total wars' of the century, widely understood to be the defining events of the period, were dying and reaching old age; the end of the Cold War and a re-evaluation of its impact; and the life course of individuals who had lived through these key events, and were often driven to record their experiences towards the end of their lives. These factors, though, account for the wider presence of the Second World War in popular culture and cultural memory, not for the increased visibility of the Bethnal Green disaster within this. There is, of course, some overlap. Older residents with personal memories of the tragedy were understandably anxious to have their experiences recognized and given a space upon the wider public stage of representation. Particular events of the late twentieth century may also have made memories of aerial bombardment, and its impact upon civilians, more visible and 'usable'. The bombing of Baghdad by a United States-led coalition in the Iraq War of 1991 was notable both for the deployment of 'smart' bombs, used to target specific buildings, and for the concomitant use of heavy area bombardment, which, on 13 February 1991, led to the deaths of hundreds of civilians using the Amariyah shelter. Media coverage of the bombardment led to the articulation of personal memories of sheltering during the Blitz by individuals writing for the Mass Observation Project in 1991, one woman writing:

> I suppose there are many who did not see the results of the blitz ... I saw a mentally and physically handicapped boy left in his wheelchair with his mother dying on the ground beside him.[84]

The end of the Cold War may also have enabled a wider range of more critical memories of aerial bombardment in the Second World War to appear on the public stage, as a newly united Germany began to explore the impact of the destructive Allied raids on German cities.[85] Memories of the Allied bombing of Dresden in February 1945 were mobilized by both the Left and the Right in Germany: by the Left as a symbol of the impact of war on civilians that could be used to protest against contemporary military actions, most notably the invasion of Iraq in 2003, and by the Right to argue for a moral equivalence between Allied and Nazi actions in the war.[86] Thus, a growing awareness of the impact of bombing on civilians, together with the wider aspects of the 'memory boom', created the conditions for an increased visibility of the Bethnal Green Underground disaster within the cultural memory of the Second World War in Britain.[87]

This, however, is not the end of the story. Representations of the tragedy remain partial and contingent. There is, for example, very little space within the dominant cultural memory of the war years for the entrenched anti-Semitism of that period that saw Jewish residents of Bethnal Green widely blamed for the disaster.[88] Other aspects of the event are exaggerated and distorted, with the government's wartime decision not to name the site of the accident being transformed into the disaster being 'censored from history', apparently on the express orders of Churchill himself.[89] The cultural memory of the disaster is mutable, dependent on a wide range of factors, some personal and some public, and the interactions between these, for the form that it takes at particular times and in particular places. Like the wider cultural memory of the Second World War in Britain to which it belongs, it is not fixed but fluid, not a direct and accurate representation of events of the time but subject to and filtered through the dominant beliefs and values of contemporary society.

The multiple 'sites of memory' examined in this collection are testament to the enduring presence of the war in post-war British society. Mass Observation directives, websites, family stories, oral history collections, films, television programmes, newspaper articles, memoirs, memorials, commemorative activities and consumer items all contribute to the continued pre-eminence of the Second World War in British culture since 1945. Whilst the cultural memory of the war may have been omnipresent since its end, the forms that this memory has taken, however, and the aspects of the war that have been foregrounded and marginalized, have varied, dependent as much on the moment of 'remembering' as on the war itself. Shifting and contested, constantly interrogated and regenerated, the cultural memory of the Second World War none the less remains a key aspect of post-war British life.

Notes

1   The *Daily Mirror*, 24 June 1996.

2   See Connelly, M. (2004), *We Can Take It!, Britain and the Memory of the Second World War*. Harlow: Pearson, 290–4.

3   Eley, G. (2001), 'Finding the people's war: film, British collective memories and World War II'. *The American Historical Review*. 106(3), 818–38. Here p. 818.

4   For an excellent overview, see Stone, D. (2012), 'Memory wars in the 'new Europe'', in D. Stone (ed.), *The Oxford Handbook of Postwar European History*. Oxford: Oxford University Press, 714–32.

5   Krzeminski, A. (2005), 'As many wars as nations: the myths and truths of World War II', *Sign and Sight*, 6 April 2005. Available online at http://www.signandsight.com/features/96.html/

6   Rousso, H. (1991), *The Vichy Syndrome: History and Memory in France since 1944*. Trans. by A. Goldhammer. Cambridge, MA: Harvard University Press.

7   Evans, M. (2006), 'Memories, monuments, histories: The rethinking of the Second World War Since 1989'. *National Identities*, 8(4), 317–48. Here p. 317.

8   Judt, T. (2005), *Postwar: A History of Europe Since 1945*. London: Heinemann, 803.

9   Reynolds, D. (2001), 'World War II and modern meanings', *Diplomatic History*, 25(3), 457–72. Here p. 470.

10 For key contributions to this debate see Fielding, S. (1992), 'What did "the People" want? The meaning of the 1945 election'. *The Historical Journal*, 35(3), 623–39; Lowe, R. (1990), 'The Second World War, consensus, and the foundation of the Welfare State'. *Twentieth-Century British History*, 1, 152–82; Fielding, S., Thompson, P. and Tiratsoo, N. (1995), *'England Arise!' The Labour Party and Popular Politics in 1940s Britain*. Manchester: Manchester University Press; Field, G. (2011), *Blood, Sweat and Toil. Remaking the British Working Class*. Oxford: Oxford University Press.

11 BBC 'People's War' website, at http://www.bbc.co.uk/history/ww2peopleswar/stories/97/a2038097.shtml/

12 Hirsch, M. (1997), *Family Frames: Photography, Narrative and Postmemory*. Cambridge, MA: Harvard University Press.

13 Harper, S. (1997), 'Popular film, popular memory: the case of the Second World War', in M. Evans and K. Lunn (eds), *War and Memory in the Twentieth Century*. Oxford: Berg, 163–76.

14 The Popular Memory Group (1982). 'Popular Memory: Theory, Politics, Method' in R. Johnson, G. McLennan, B. Schwarz & D. Sutton (eds), *Making Histories: Studies in History Writing and Politics*. London: Hutchinson, 205–52.

15 Kuhn, A. (1995), *Family Secrets: Acts of Memory and Imagination*. London: Verso, 4.

16 Thomson, A. (1990), 'Anzac memories: Putting popular memory theory into practice in Australia', *Oral History*, 18(2), 25–31. Here p. 26.

17 Summerfield, P. (1998) *Reconstructing Women's Wartime Lives: Discourse and Subjectivity in Oral Histories of the First World War*. Manchester: Manchester University Press.

18 Dawson, G. (1994), *Soldier Heroes: British Adventure, Empire and the Imagining of Masculinities*. London: Routledge, 22.

19 Shephard, B. (2000), *A War of Nerves*. London: Jonathan Cape; Roper, M. (2010), *The Secret Battle: Emotional Survival in the Great War*. Manchester: Manchester University Press; Parr, A. (2007), 'Breaking the silence: traumatised war veterans and oral history'. *Oral History*, 35(1), 61–70. Here p. 62.

20 For recent work addressing traumatic memory and conflict, see Dawson, G. (2005), 'Trauma, place and the politics of memory: Bloody Sunday, Derry, 1972–2004'. *History Workshop Journal*, 59, 221–50; Dawson, G. (2007), *Making Peace with the Past: Memory, Trauma and the Irish Troubles*. Manchester, Manchester University Press; Field, S. (2006), '"Beyond healing": trauma, oral history and regeneration'. *Oral History*, 34(1), 31–42.

21 Caruth, C. (1995), 'Trauma and experience: Introduction', in C. Caruth (ed.), *Trauma: Explorations in Memory*. Baltimore: Johns Hopkins University Press, 3–12. Here pp. 4–5.

22 Greenspan, H. (1998), *On Listening to Holocaust Survivors: Recounting and Life History*. Westport, CT: Praeger; Langer, L. L. (1991), *Holocaust Testimonies: The Ruins of Memory*. New Haven, CT: Yale University Press.

23 Barclay, C. R. (1995), 'Autobiographical remembering: narrative constraints on objectified selves', in D. C. Rubin (ed.), *Remembering Our Past: Studies in Autobiographical Memory*. Cambridge: Cambridge University Press, 94–128. Here p. 96.

24 Hunt, N. and Robbins, I. (1998), 'Telling stories of the war: ageing veterans coping with their memory through narrative'. *Oral History*, 26(2), 57–64. Here p. 59; Noakes, L. (1998), *War and the British: Gender and National Identity 1939–1991*. London: I.B. Tauris, 42–3.

25 Summerfield, P. (2008), 'War, film, memory: some reflections on war films and the social configuration of memory in Britain in the 1940s and 1950s'. *Journal of War and Culture Studies*, 1(1), 15–23.

26 See, for example, Ferro, M. (2003), *The Use and Abuse of History*. London: Routledge; Smith, K. E. (1996), *Remembering Stalin's Victims: Popular Memory and the End of the USSR*. New York: Cornell University Press.

27 Nora, P. (1984), *Les Lieux de Mémoire*. Paris: Gallimard.

28 Gregory, A. (1996), *The Silence of Memory: Armistice Day 1919–1946*. Oxford: Berg.

29 Halbwachs, M. (1992), *On Collective Memory*. London: University of Chicago Press, 53.

30 Fentress, J. and Wickham, C. (1992), *Social Memory*. Oxford: Blackwell.

31 Foucault, M. (1975), 'Film and popular memory: an interview with Michel Foucault'. *Radical Philosophy*, Summer 1975, 24–9.

32 The Popular Memory Group, (1982).

33 Ibid., 211.

34 Ibid., 207.

35 For a study that takes this somewhat uncritical approach to 'history from below', contrasting testimony with official narratives, but which is none the less illuminating about the construction of cultural memory, see Collier, R. (1961), *The Sands of Dunkirk*. London: Fontana. The publishers describe the book on its cover as 'the storm raising controversial best seller that lays bare the truth about Dunkirk'.

36 Harper, 'Popular film, popular memory'.

37 Mass Observation Project, Directive, 'World War Two', Spring 2009.

38 Rousso, *The Vichy Syndrome*, 219; Wood, N. (1999), *Vectors of Memory. Legacies of Trauma in Postwar Europe*. Oxford: Berg, 6.

39 Rothberg, M. (2009), *Multidirectional memory. Remembering the Holocaust in the Age of Decolonization*. Stanford: Stanford University Press.

40 Smith, G. (2007), 'Beyond individual collective memory: women's transactive memories of food, family and conflict', *Oral History*, 35(2), 77–90.

41 Landsberg, A. (2004), *Prosthetic Memory. The Transformation of American Remembrance in the Age of Mass Culture*. New York: Columbia University Press.

42 Rothberg (2009), 3.

43 Radstone, S. (2005), 'Reconceiving binaries: The limits of memory', *History Workshop Journal*, 59, 136.

44 Smith (2007), 79.

45 Landsberg (2004), 2.

46 Ibid., 9.

47 Critics of the term 'collective memory' include Marwick, A. (2001), *The New Nature of History*. Basingstoke: Palgrave; Portelli, A. (1997), *The Battle of Valle Giulia: Oral History and the Art of Dialogue*. Madison: University of Wisconsin Press.

48 Bourke, J. (2004), 'Introduction: remembering war'. *Journal of Contemporary History*, 39(4), 473–85. Here p. 483.

49 *Daily Express*, 9 July 2005; *Daily Mirror*, 9 July 2005.

50 *Daily Telegraph*, 5 January 2009.

51 Hoogland Noon, D. (2004), 'Operation enduring analogy: World War II, the war on terror and the uses of historical memory'. *Rhetoric and Public Affairs,* 32(3), 339–66.

52 *Sheffield Star,* 25 June 2012; *Guardian,* 22 August 2011.

53 *The Independent,* 18 September 2007.

54 *Daily Mail,* 1 January 2009.

55 Connelly (2004), 268.

56 Thompson, E. P. (1980), *Writing by Candlelight.* London: Merlin, 130.

57 See, for example, 'George Osborne tells Tory Conference "We're all in this together"', *Guardian,* 8 October 2012.

58 'UK Uncut's Great British Street Party – Because the Future's Not What it Used to Be', 11 April 2012. Available online at http://www.ukuncut.org.uk/blog/uk-uncuts-great-british-street-party/
    For analyses of the Second World War that emphasize its transformative nature, see Addison, P. (1975), *The Road to 1945. British Politics and the Second World War.* London: Jonathan Cape; Calder, A. (1965), *The People's War.* London: Jonathan Cape; Morgan, K. O. (1990), *The People's Peace. British History 1945–1990.* Oxford: Oxford University Press.

59 See Grayling, A. C. (2006), *Among the Dead Cities: Is the Targeting of Civilians in War Ever Justified?* London: Bloomsbury.

60 Rousso (1991), 219.

61 Rose, S. O. (2003), *Which People's War? National Identity and Citizenship in Wartime Britain, 1939–1945.* Oxford: Oxford University Press.

62 See Summerfield, P. (2010), 'Dunkirk and the popular memory of Britain at war, 1940–58'. *Journal of Contemporary History,* 45(4), 788–811. For an attempt to 'debunk' the myth, see Collier, (1963).

63 Harman, N. (1981), *Dunkirk: The Necessary Myth.* London: Coronet; Ponting, C. (1990), *1940: Myth and Reality.* London: Hamish Hamilton; Hylton, S. (2001), *Their Darkest Hour: The Hidden History of the Home Front 1939–1945.* Stroud: Sutton; Calder, A. (1991), *The Myth of the Blitz.* London: Pimlico.

64 See, for example, Ponting (1990).

65 Connelly (2004), 1.

66 *Sunday Express,* 5 June 1949.

67 Sculpted by Karen Newman and located at Gordon Square, Bloomsbury, London.

68 *Indian Express,* 26 September 2012.

69 Gilroy, P. (2004), *Postcolonial Melancholia.* London: Routledge.

70 Eley (2001), 819.

71 Gilroy (2004).

72 Connelly (2004), 251.

73 Ugolini, W. (2011), *Experiencing War as the 'Enemy Other': Italian Scottish Experience in World War II.* Manchester: Manchester University Press.

74 The National Archives, War Office (WO) 208/5381, Scotland, A. (undated), *The London Cage*. See also WO208/4294, Papers recovered from Lt. Col. A. P. Scotland: notes on operation of War Crimes Interrogation Unit, which were accessioned in May 1984.

75 Hansard, House of Commons Debates, 10 March 1943, Volume 387, Herbert Morrison, Col 668.

76 The National Archives, Home Office (HO) 205/233, Dunne, L. (1943), *Tube Shelter Inquiry*, 23 March 1943.

77 *The Times*, 5 March 1943.

78 Ibid., 9 October 1975.

79 *TV Times*, 1975, n.d. Available online at http://www.britmovie.co.uk/forums/looking-video-dvd-tv/102425-its-lovely-day-tomorrow-tv-play-1975-a.html/

80 *The Times*, 1 March 1993. *The Independent*, 4 March 1993.

81 Letter from the Prime Minister, David Cameron, to the Stairway to Heaven Memorial Trust, 13 May 2011. Available online at http://www.stairwaytoheavenmemorial.org/dcletter.html/

82 For a fictionalized account of the tragedy, see Kane, J. K. (2011), *The Report*. London: Portobello.

83 Winter, J. (2006), *Remembering War. The Great War Between Memory and History in the Twentieth Century*. New Haven, CT: Yale University Press.

84 Mass Observation Project, Gulf War Directive, 1990/1991, Panellist No. D666.

85 See, for example, Friedrich, J. (2006), *The Fire: The Bombing of German Cities* (trans. A. Brown). New York: Columbia University Press; Sebald, W. G., (2004), *On the Natural History of Destruction* (trans. A. Bell). New York: The Modern Library.

86 Huyssen, A. (2003), 'Air war legacies: From Dresden to Baghdad'. *New German Critique*, 90. 163–76.

87 The Hillsborough disaster, in which 96 football fans were crushed to death at Hillsborough football ground, and the subsequent campaign for an inquiry and findings regarding the South Yorkshire Police Force's culpability in their deaths, may also have enabled wider recognition of the Bethnal Green deaths.

88 See Bourke, J. (2005), *Fear: A Cultural History*. London: Virago, 236–8.

89 *Daily Mail*, 27 February 2008; *Daily Express*, 26 March 2011.

Key texts

Connelly, M. (2004), *We Can Take It! Britain and the Memory of the Second World War*. Harlow: Pearson.

Dawson, G. (1994), *Soldier Heroes, British Adventure, Empire and the Imagining of Masculinities*. London: Routledge.

Eley, G. (2001), 'Finding the people's war: film, British collective memories and World War II'. *The American Historical Review*, 106(3), 818–38.

Fentress, J. and Wickham, C. (1992), *Social Memory*. Oxford: Blackwell.

Halbwachs, M. (1992), *On Collective Memory*. London: University of Chicago Press.

Harper, S. (1997), 'Popular film, popular memory: the case of the Second World War', in M. Evans and K. Lunn (eds), *War and Memory in the Twentieth Century*. Oxford: Berg, 163–76.

Hirsch, M. (1997), *Family Frames: Photography, Narrative and Postmemory*. Cambridge, MA: Harvard University Press.

Kuhn, A. (1995), *Family Secrets: Acts of Memory and Imagination*. London: Verso.

Landsberg, A. (2004), *Prosthetic Memory. The Transformation of American Remembrance in the Age of Mass Culture*. New York: Columbia University Press.

Nora, P. (1984), *Les Lieux de Mémoire*. Paris: Gallimard.

The Popular Memory Group (1982), 'Popular Memory: Theory, Politics, Method', in R. Johnson, G. McLennan, B. Schwarz and D. Sutton (eds), *Making Histories: Studies in History Writing and Politics*. London: Hutchinson, 205–52.

Radstone, S. (2005), 'Reconceiving binaries: The limits of memory', *History Workshop Journal*, 59, 134–50.

Rousso, H. (1991), *The Vichy Syndrome: History and Memory in France since 1944* (trans. A. Goldhammer). Cambridge, MA: Harvard University Press.

Rothberg, M. (2009), *Multidirectional Memory. Remembering the Holocaust in the Age of Decolonization*. Stanford: Stanford University Press.

Smith, G. (2007), 'Beyond individual collective memory: women's transactive memories of food, family and conflict', *Oral History*, 35(23), 77–90.

Summerfield, P. (1998), *Reconstructing Women's Wartime Lives: Discourse and Subjectivity in Oral Histories of the Second World War*. Manchester: Manchester University Press.

—(2008), 'War, film, memory: Some reflections on war films and the social configuration of memory in Britain in the 1940s and 1950s', *Journal of War and Culture Studies*, 1(1), 15–23.

Thomson, A. (1990), 'Anzac memories: Putting popular memory theory into practice in Australia', *Oral History*, 18(2), 25–31.

Wood, N. (1999), *Vectors of Memory. Legacies of Trauma in Postwar Europe*. Oxford: Berg.

CHAPTER TWO

The generation of memory

Gender and the popular memory of the Second World War in Britain

Penny Summerfield

The impact of the Second World War on British society has, since the 1960s, been a favourite topic among historians.[1] More recently the perpetuation of its memory across the decades has commanded attention. In a much-cited article, Geoff Eley states that, for those living in Britain since 1945, '"Remembering" World War II requires no immediate experience of those years.' He continues, 'This is especially true of the immediate postwar generation (born between 1943–1945 and the mid-1950s), who grew up suffused in the effects of the war years but whose "memory" of them came entirely after the fact. During that generation's formative years (say, until the mid-1960s), official and popular cultures were pervaded by the war's presence ...'[2] Eley's article thereafter focuses on this cultural pervasiveness and its relationship to collective memory and changing ideas of British national identity, rather than on the history of the indirect memory of the Second World War which he so strikingly evokes. He was writing in the context of a rising tide of scholarship on the representation of the Second World War in British popular culture,[3] some of which explores the connections between cultural constructions and personal memories of that past.[4] Such work has not, however, investigated the phenomenon of remembering historical events that one has not experienced, nor has it interrogated Eley's generational claim concerning the indirect memory of the Second World War in Britain.

Scholars who address such problems work mainly in the field of Holocaust studies. Marianne Hirsch, for example, uses the term 'postmemory' to refer to 'the relationship that the generation after those who witnessed cultural or collective trauma bears to the experiences of those who came before, experiences that they "remember" only by means of the stories, images, and behaviors among which they grew up.'[5] Sources for such studies, whether focused on the Holocaust or other historical events, are difficult to find beyond individual memoirs. However, the project that Mass Observation (MO) initiated in 1981 provides a larger pool of testimony through which to address this type of 'remembering'.

Mass Observation, established in 1937 as a social research organization critical of 'the establishment' and committed to the creation of a democratic 'science of ourselves', amassed a huge amount of material about everyday life in Britain from 1937 to 1948.[6] A significant part of this came from volunteer observers and included responses to questions sent to them regularly, known as 'directives', as well as personal diaries that they submitted monthly. Historians and other scholars have drawn extensively on MO's archive, and some of the diaries have been published.[7] In 1981 MO's trustees revived one element of the original project by recruiting a 'panel' of 500 volunteers prepared to answer its questions several times a year. Directives sent out since 1981 have addressed matters as diverse as sex, pet food and the world financial crisis. They are not structured questionnaires that render standardized, comparable answers but prompts that elicit self-reflexive personal narratives. Critics have expressed concern that the panel does not constitute a representative sample of the population.[8] However, historians who have used the MO Project (MOP), such as Alistair Thomson, Lucy Noakes and Tony Kushner, have argued that whom 'the sample' represents in occupational or class terms is less important than what the panellists have in common.[9] Although the post-1981 panellists do not share the same politics or general outlook as their predecessors, argues Kushner, they are united by an 'impulse to write and a desire to express their independent views as against an increasingly powerful media and state which are perceived as manipulative and failing to represent public opinion fairly'.[10] The value of the material collected needs to be understood in the light of the meaning of writing for Mass Observation: the MO panellists are a self-selected and diverse group of literate individuals who believe that their contributions, however indirectly, enhance social knowledge.

In the spring of 2009 MO sent out a directive asking about the impact of the Second World War in the years since 1945 on panellists' lives from childhood to the present day. It invited panellists who were old enough to have lived through the Second World War to clarify their involvement in it, but emphasized an interest in the impact of the memory of the war on 'all of you, whenever you were born and wherever you were living'.[11]

Panellists were urged to consider what the Second World War 'means to you', an invitation to respond personally and reflectively. The enquiry encouraged retrospective accounts, but was different from an oral history project because of both the written form of the testimony and its focus on engagement with and responses to popular memory, rather than direct experience of events. Respondents do not appear to have had difficulties with the relatively abstract invitation to recall and relate their experiences of the shared memory of the Second World War. They had much to say about, for example, family stories, films and television programmes, books, the school curriculum, and traces in the landscape. Between March 2009 and June 2010 about 200 replies were received, of which 120 were from women, a response rate and a gender balance that is characteristic of the MOP.[12] Even if they did not mirror population distribution statistically, respondents were socially diverse: they came from all parts of the United Kingdom, and included factory workers and cleaners as well as retired professionals and university lecturers.[13] The oldest respondent was born in 1913 and the youngest in 1992.

The analysis that follows focuses on respondents born just before, during and after the war. It examines in particular the role of the family as a space of transmission, and the function of gender in relation to memory. It uses the concept of 'composure' favoured by oral historians, to illuminate both how the personal narratives that the MOP collects are composed or shaped, and what they contribute to the narrator's 'composure' or psychic equilibrium. It deploys the term 'discomposure' to indicate processes of narration that do not achieve the two goals of 'composure'.[14] The chapter addresses three broad questions: what is the importance of 'generation' for 'remembering' the Second World War; how do we understand the circulation and also the silencing of memories of the war within families; and what are the effects on 'remembering' the Second World War of the changing position of individuals in the life course and the shifts in public discourses that accompanied them?

Generation

Karl Mannheim suggested in the 1920s that 'generation' based on birth date could be used to explain social and political behaviours.[15] Since the 1920s scholars have wrestled with the definition of 'generation' and with Mannheim's argument that age cohort was crucial for the analysis of major crises in modern history. The problem exposed by the work of Mannheim and of later social scientists, such as Philip Abrams, concerns the identification of the generation in question and its social identity.[16] In the late 1970s Robert Wohl suggested an alternative way of thinking about 'generation', not as an objectively existing and quantifiable phenomenon, but as a literary and imaginative invention.[17] Historians in the last two decades, such as Mark Roseman and Anna von der Goltz, have taken up Wohl's insight that historical events are used in this process as 'signposts with which people impose order on their past and link their individual fates with those of the communities in which they live'.[18]

The subjective process of generation-building is visible in the personal testimony of the MO respondents. They make claims to membership of all sorts of 'age cohorts' whose titles are redolent of their constructedness: 'the wartime generation'; 'the make-do-and-mend generation'; 'the victory generation'; 'the baby boomers'.[19] They also differentiate themselves from other imagined cohorts: 'the lost generation'; 'the finest generation'.[20] Respondents use family generations to position themselves in relation to the Second World War: 'I grew up being told about the Second World War often – it was the backdrop to my childhood, though I was born in [19]64, and my parents in [19]42 and [19]43.'[21] There is much in the testimonies to support Eley's contention that those born in the 1940s and early 1950s were 'suffused in the effects of the war years', and there is also evidence that these effects extend well beyond those born in this period.

A common theme in these accounts is the importance of intergenerational relationships. It embraces both a sense of obligation to older generations and doubt about the understanding and appreciation of younger generations. Eric, for example, born in 1940, summarizes the 'huge' and 'lasting' effect of the war on his family: '… loss of family members. Disabled sons, family cohesion tested to the limit', and writes that the Second World War 'has formed a backdrop to much of my life, but paradoxically has given my generation a peace and a time to enjoy life I am always quietly conscious of. So I suppose [I feel] a massive sense of gratitude for all that WW2 gave my generation, and hope we justify their sacrifice.'[22] Doreen, born in 1943, describes listening to stories of family members 'as I was growing up after the war'. They impressed upon her 'how very brave and daring so many were [and] how they had been willing to "fight" for our nation', and she records her 'gratitude' to them for what they did, so 'that my generation could live in freedom'.[23] Her feelings were reinforced by post-war films such as The Dam Busters, Dunkirk and Carve Her Name with Pride. These films are among the 30 top box office hits of the 1950s and have been re-screened and shown on television many times since. Filmed in black and white, they have in common a focus on the struggles of small groups of British military personnel led by distinctive individuals against a formidable Nazi enemy within the wider collective endeavour of the Second World War, which they represent as an unquestionably just war, if one that was difficult for the Allies to win.[24] In reflecting on her appreciation of these films, Doreen draws attention to the specificity of her generational position: 'I always feel a sense of pride when I watch them, but remember I was born during the war, I doubt younger generations would feel the same.'[25]

The testimony of men and women born in the 1950s, however, suggests that it was not necessary to have been a war baby to feel as Eric and Doreen did. Susan, who still treasures the ration book issued to her as wartime rationing was phased out in 1952–4, writes: 'I was born in 1952 so although not actually alive in the war I'm one of the baby boomers: the generation born immediately afterwards when men and women discharged from the forces settled down and started families.'[26] 'The war' is of immense and continuing significance in her family: 'I admire the courage my parents and so many people displayed in those terrible times.'[27] Margaret (born 1956) writes: 'The Second World War played a huge part in the lives of my family – and I always felt that "the War" was like an extra live-in Great Aunt' who imposed values of stoicism and thrift.[28] In spite of the disciplinary function of this metaphorical persona, Margaret expresses a strong sense of indebtedness to participants in the war, which she couples with an anxious comparison with younger members of society: 'I feel proud, sad and grateful to them all. Often I wonder if this generation would behave so well in a similar situation.'[29] Angus (1959) writes of the war as 'an epic morality tale' given 'massive direct power' by 'stories from relatives'. Compared with the First World War, the Second was, for Angus, a 'Crusade': 'At school in the 1960s "Nazi" was a real term of abuse arising out of relatives' stories and the black and white war films shown on television.' He concludes, 'there is still a massive cause for pride in the Second World War'.[30] Angus feels that the lapse of time would make a difference to people's responses to the memory of the war. 'Each generation will become removed from that direct input from relatives that made the war so "real" and important to someone like me that didn't live through it.'[31]

Common sense, as well as some contributions to the scholarly literature on memory and generation, suggest that successive age cohorts would be attached, as Geoffrey Cubitt puts it, to 'different historical conceptions, articulating the experience … of different generations'.[32] There are indeed testimonies that support the view that the impact of the memory of the war slackened over time, but there are also those that contradict it.

Jill (born 1965) expressed a detachment from the war that she attributes to her familial generational structure: 'The generations in my family are spaced such that few of my relations were directly involved in the Second World War.' Her grandfathers were 'too old to fight on the front line' and her 'parents were children' aged 3 and 5 at the start of the war, 'so while they have memories of the war they are vague and are really more about their first bananas so not until the 1950s and the end of rationing'.[33] Likewise for Samantha (1978), 'stories of World War II don't really feature that much in our family', and she finds it difficult to connect with the popular memory of the war.[34] This is intensified by the war films shown on television: 'I can't really distinguish one from the other – just a lot of grainy black and white images of brave men and women. The films always seem very distant to me – I can't relate to them at all', with the result that the Second World War 'felt like something that happened a long time ago to people who were nothing like me.'[35] One might suppose that such detachment is the common pattern for most of those born in the 1960s and 1970s, but other accounts contradict such an assumption. Hannah, born in 1969 of parents whose ages in 1939 (2 and 5) were similar to those of Jill's parents, writes: 'Memories of the Second World War feature strongly in my family', and reports stories of a grandmother who worked in munitions and as a fire warden, a grandfather in army stores, of the black market and air raid shelters. In any case generational spacing is not the same for all those born at a particular time. Christopher, born in 1964, just a year before Jill, describes his parents, a soldier and a nurse, meeting during the war and states: 'I feel so much respect for the majority of this generation. I do think we will not see the calibre or fearlessness they portrayed [again]'.[36] Brian (1971) writes that his grandfather's stories of eating rats during the Siege of Malta 'made you aware of how lucky we are to live in freedom for their sacrifice and how much the youth of today takes that gift of freedom for granted.'[37] Wendy (1972) writes: 'I have had a great interest in the Second World War for as long as I can remember', nurtured by her grandfather's stories of army service and her grandmother's life in the Sheffield steel-works, and stemming from 'the fact this was a world so different to the one I inhabit yet it is so tangible'. Black and white films enable her to get 'lost in that other world', and she finds 'much to admire about that period compared to our own'.[38] Whereas Wendy's participation in the shared memory of the war is a source of comfort and pride, for Samantha the war contributes to neither composure nor discomposure; she simply cannot engage with the public discourses in circulation. Yet Samantha's testimony suggests that the reflexive process of writing for MO in 2009 was itself causing her to identify more closely with the memory of the war than previously, and to think of it in 'generational' terms. She concludes: 'Now when I think back to something that happened 20 years ago, I realize just how recent the reality of war is, and how people of my parents' generation grew up under its shadow with rationing and a failing economy.'[39]

The sense of respect and obligation communicated by respondents has been strong in British culture since at least the First World War, and, as Adrian Gregory argues, is institutionalized in the activities of the British Legion and the rituals of Remembrance Sunday.[40] The intergenerational pessimism is harder to explain but perhaps stems from representations in books, films and television of those who fought as heroic and hence, as a woman born in 1950 put it, 'so very different to us'.[41] It may also arise from the bad press given to the young after the ending of National Service in 1960, particularly in the context of the counter-cultural challenges of the 1960s and 1970s. Anxiety about the capacities of 'the youth of today', on the other hand, is possibly also endemic in personal understandings of a self differentiated by age. What is striking here is that the memory of the Second World War gives it a special reference point in the testimony of those born not only in the 1940s but as late as the 1970s.

Silences and censorship

Many testimonies refer to silences in family stories about the war. 'I don't think its memories featured much in my family's life', writes Victor, born in 1938.[42] 'I have little remembrance about any talk about the war in our house', said Barry (1945).[43] 'My grandparents never really talked to any of us about their experiences', writes Andrew (1968).[44] These respondents imputed this absence of war talk not to anything shameful or traumatic, but to the war's banality: 'it was something they just got on with', and to their parents' desire to 'put it behind them – like most people'.[45] The explanatory power of such common-sense understandings seems irresistible. However, oral historians urge the application of critical analysis to silences, sensitive to the effects of, for example, public discourses and gender.[46]

As scholars who work with personal testimony have pointed out, narratives are dialogic; they are produced for audiences.[47] These male respondents were remembering not only family members who did not tell stories but also, by implication, themselves as listeners whose boyhood expectations infused the relationship. Born in 1931, Bernard writes of three uncles whose war experiences involved, variously, salvaging planes in the RAF, surviving as a prisoner-of-war of the Japanese, and following the Allied troops into Europe after D-Day. He states: 'I don't remember these people talking about their war experiences all that much. As a bloodthirsty schoolboy I was perhaps disappointed that those Uncles I had were not exactly engaged in hand-to-hand combat with our enemies.'[48] Michael, born in 1958, 27 years after Bernard, writes in similar terms: 'When I was a child I was, if I'm honest, rather disappointed by the mundane nature of [family] recollections. No one in my family had flown a Spitfire or a Lancaster, or even been a paratrooper. Being on a train that briefly got shot up by a German aircraft didn't really count.'[49] Such relatives may have preferred not to face the crestfallen faces of young male audiences, conditioned by the comics they read and the films they watched to expect tales of masculine heroism: hence their silence.

The gendered discourse of war affected respondents' narratives in other ways too. Men who, due to their birth date, could not participate in military activity in the Second World War vividly describe their vicarious involvement. Such testimonies are legion among men born in the period from the 1930s to the 1960s. To give one example, Colin, born in 1944, vividly evokes what Michael Paris calls the 'pleasure culture of war'[50] in which he engaged as a boy. An out-of-bounds air raid shelter served as a base 'from which to play war games': '"Dagga-dagga-dagga-dagga-dagga" – machine gun fire. I'm not sure any of the kids played the part of Germans. We were all British "Tommies" … there seemed to be a different war film showing at local cinemas every week. I particularly remember seeing *The Dam Busters* and *The Colditz Story*. They were such exciting films … How

I wished I could have been in Colditz! It all seemed such fun – making fools of the Germans.'[51] Comics added to the heady mix: 'Most boys' comics in the 1950s carried one or more "war stories". Was it "Rockfist Rogan" in the Tiger comic who won the Second World War almost single-handedly? "Die, Fritz!" he would yell, before exterminating an entire Panzer Division.'[52] Waking up to the shift in consciousness caused by his changing position in the life course, Colin comments: 'How I wished, as a child, that I could have taken part in the war. But as an adult – how grateful I am that the timing of my birth excluded me from the horror of fighting.'[53]

In this world of Rockfist Rogans, some older male relatives evidently learned to exaggerate their role to fit the soldier hero model, or were perceived to be doing so. This too led to audience disinterest, particularly among girls. Eleanor, born in Wolverhampton in 1981, stated 'Grandad E was notorious for his "tales" of his time in the RAF. He had many a souvenir that he would delight in showing us ... [But] Nan reckoned she came closer to Germans in Wolverhampton than Grandad did in the desert!'[54] A line from a song by the folk singer Jake Thackray captures the tedium of repeated epic narratives: 'I'll be polite to your daddy/ ... I won't boo and hiss/ When he starts to reminisce/ ... The runs he used to score/ And how he won the war.'[55] Some young female audiences discouraged the 'how I won the war' stories of male relatives by giving more encouragement to mothers and grandmothers. 'Both of my granddads were in the army and served abroad', writes Wendy, born in 1972. 'But it has always been the Home Front that interests me, so I think I listened more intently to the stories of my nans.'[56] The gendering of audiences and its effects are not only about masculine consumption of the imagined thrills of the battlefront, but also feminine uptake of representations of the glamour and the drudgery of the Home Front which give access to a feminized version of the experience of war.[57]

There are other types of silence. Hannah (1969) referred to her recent discovery of the untold story of her great uncle's marriage to a German woman at the end of the war, in a context in which other war stories were an ever-present part of family life.[58] Such family censorship, sometimes prompted by nationalist and racist attitudes, is echoed in other accounts.[59] The moral outrage that informed it is part of the construction of the Second World War as an 'epic morality tale' (as Angus, above, put it) that was, as we have seen, fuelled by the popular war films and other representations of the 1950s. Explicit examples of the transmission of this stark morality were recalled by children and grandchildren who grew up regarding the Germans, or in some cases the Japanese, with implacable hostility.[60] This theme of enduring enmity to Britain's wartime enemies in post-war culture and everyday life was given satirical treatment in John Cleese's 'don't mention the war' episode of the sitcom *Faulty Towers*, first broadcast on 24 October 1975, itself part of a reflexive trend towards more critical attitudes towards war-derived xenophobia.[61]

A further type of silence relates more obviously to trauma. 'I remember being told not to mention the War to Granny because it made her upset' due to family losses in both wars, writes Rachel (1944).[62] Fiona (1943) believes that her stepfather had been in the Far East. 'Mum said he was but I certainly never heard him talk about it. That is the thing with that war … people did not want to talk about it perhaps because it was so horrific they wanted to put it out of their minds.'[63] Maybe so, but sometimes family censorship meant that hints leaked out that were all the more disturbing for their cryptic quality. Greta, born in 1953, writes that her mother's evasive references to 'bombs and aircraft overhead' and 'friends who went off to church one day and never returned', 'haunted me and gave me the horrors'.[64] Alison (1974) writes that much of her family's wartime experience was muted because it was emotionally disturbing. Thus she remembers her grandmother talking about evacuating her children, while those children themselves (her aunts and uncles) were silent on the subject: 'I think there may have been some unhappy experiences.'[65] Her grandfather served in Ceylon, and she remembers a photograph of him with a mongoose, as well as seeing the moonstones and opals that he brought home, but such material culture was left to speak for itself; there were no stories. Her partner's grandparents were 'more communicative'. However, there were still silences. 'One was apparently an army cook, the other apparently was among troops to liberate Belsen. My partner thinks that the second incident affected his grandfather a lot but no-one ever talks about it.'[66] Alison writes of what such occluded memories of the war meant to her: 'The general impression is of the war as part of an older, harsher period which younger generations are lucky to have avoided and which we are softer for.'[67]

The relief of concentration camps occurs more than once in these accounts, accompanied by statements to the effect that it was not or could not be talked about. In one case it disrupts an otherwise positive account of the family transmission of memories of the war and the pleasure the respondent takes in them. Pauline (1954) writes: 'The Second World has had a huge impact on my life both through childhood and adulthood. Memories of the war featured as part of my upbringing for as long as I can remember.'[68] She describes family conversations during 'high tea on Sundays' about what her parents and other relatives did for the war effort; she evokes vivid memories of the pill boxes and air raid shelters that littered the landscape in which she grew up in the 1950s and 1960s; Remembrance Day continues to play an important part in her life; she has visited war museums many times; she collects Second World War memorabilia; she is a *Dad's Army* fan; and she has watched war movies since her teens: 'as a teenager I remember seeing war films at the cinema with my mother who had been in the war'; and she has seen them again 'at least twice over the years when they were shown on television'.[69] Pauline's perception of Britain in the Second World War is optimistic: 'What stands out most for me is the camaraderie of everyone in the war, whether it be those away fighting or those on the home front. Everybody seemed to care about each other.' To Pauline these indirect memories contribute to her sense of composure: the war signifies British community and solidarity, a major dimension of the cultural representation of the war in Britain and British national identity at the time and since.[70] This view of the meaning of the war, however, was disturbed by Pauline's recent significant discovery while watching a film about the relief of Belsen by British soldiers with her mother. Pauline referred afterwards to 'how harrowing it must have been for those young men', whereupon her mother told her that her father 'was one of the marines who went to Belsen after the war to rebury the dead', expressing surprise that Pauline did not know this grim fact. Musing on her ignorance, Pauline states flatly that 'the only reason I have to explain it is that my father left my mother to start a new family when I was 15 and the opportunity never arose' – and never would, since her father was now dead.[71] The reassurance Pauline gained from the war talk of her childhood and teens, that had fuelled her enduring affection for the Second World War, was now destabilized, and the painfulness of the disruption was augmented by the link, in Pauline's reflections, between the emotional disturbance of the family break-up and the censored topic of the ghastly 'clean up' of a concentration camp. 'Remembering' the war for Pauline had become emotionally multivalent: it contributed to both her composure and her discomposure.

Some silences were almost absolute, and yet 'spoke'. For example, Ian, born in 1971, recalls the unvoiced but visceral transmission of traumatic memory in his family. Writing of the 'indirect effects' of the war on his life, Ian explains that his German mother was 'orphaned at the age of 5 or 6 years, father killed by Russians, mother killed by diptheria [sic]' and grew up near a death camp; his father was a British soldier in Germany in the 1950s; his paternal grandfather had been captured at Dunkirk and 'force-marched to a concentration camp somewhere'; his partner's father 'was a PoW of the Japanese for two years in South East Asia and suffered from the effects of disease and malnutrition he picked up there until his death a few years back'. Thus at family gatherings over the years 'WW2 was never far away', but Ian writes that, rather than making a 'huge impact' on his life, 'it is maybe more of an ache that comes and goes through my parents'.[72] Such largely non-verbal communication of traumatic experience is described in similar terms by Eva Hoffman, herself the child of Holocaust survivors, in her book on the legacy of the Holocaust: 'In my home, as in so many others, the past broke through in the sounds of nightmares, the idioms of sighs and illness, of tears and acute aches …'.[73] Second World War stories were not composed and articulated in such extended families, but the unspoken histories nevertheless had pervasive effects.

The life course and public discourses

The proliferation of references to the Second World War in post-1945 Britain, to which Eley refers, was, as we have seen, borne out by respondents. Representations on the public airwaves interacted with family stories which shaped indirect memory, whether evocations of the war circulated explicitly within families or were communicated through silences, and whether they engaged the imagination or were resisted because they did not fit expectations. Those born not just from the 1930s to the 1950s but also from the 1960s to the 1980s did not need to have experienced the war to 'remember' it. Among the cultural 'vectors of memory'[74] that respondents mention, one stands out because of the frequency of references to it. Many had read the diary that Nella Last, a Barrow housewife, sent to Mass Observation in monthly instalments from 1939 to 1966, part of which was first published in 1981 as *Nella Last's War* and republished in 2006.[75]

FIGURE 1.1 *Photograph of Nella Last. Courtesy of the Mass Observation Archive, University of Sussex*

Men as well as women refer to Nella Last, but while several men include her diaries in their lists of reading about the Second World War, few offer any reflective comments about her beyond, for example, '[it] really brings home the trials of ordinary people during wartime'.[76] One man explained that he had difficulties reading *Nella Last's War* which he attributed to his gender. Eric, a retired fire-fighter from Fleetwood, born 1940, writes of his pleasure in gaining an understanding of world geography and history from reading about the Second World War, but '*Nella Last's War*, which I read recently, on the other hand, needed me to compress myself into the story. Perhaps being male did not help, I have not the gift of reading too much "between the lines" especially in terms of relationships.'[77]

In contrast, there is a remarkable degree of consistency in the reflections of women on reading Nella Last in spite of widely divergent dates of birth and degrees of identification with the popular memory of the Second World War. While many refer to loving the domestic detail and the 'reality' of Nella's diary, reflective comments coalesce around the idea of war as a force for change in women's lives. Pamela, born in 1946, writes of reading *Nella Last's War* and thinking that 'for many women the Second World War was liberating, up until then they were the housewife, there to meet the needs of the husband and family, never questioning the husband's authority.'[78] Susan (1952) writes that 'a narrow housewife's life like Nella's in a not very happy marriage was transformed by paid and charitable war work'.[79] Pauline (1954) writes how 'the one thing that stood out for me was the independence Nella experienced as a result of the war and how she wasn't keen to give it up at the end'.[80] Samantha (1978) said 'it was the story about personal and social transformation that was of interest to me'.[81] Joanne (1983) writes, 'I loved Nella's sense of quiet determination and growing sense of self in the diary.'[82] Just two men comment in similar terms on Nella: one is disabled, the other homosexual. 'The war proves to be a liberation for her. Freed from her domestic role by going out into the wider world to "do her bit", she grows as a person', writes Peter (1963), who refers to 'being disabled'.[83] Timothy (1978), who describes himself as gay, reflects on his interest in the 'small personal stories of the war … particularly the odd, liberating effects they can have', and gives as an example 'Nella Last and the non-domestic life the war effort gave to her'.[84] Why did Nella Last appeal in these ways to women, and to men whose life experiences did not conform with those of the majority of men? How do generation and life course inflect the reading of such a document?

Nella Last (1890–1968) was in her late forties when she began her MO diary. She lived in the shipbuilding town of Barrow in north-west England, and was married to a self-employed carpenter/joiner.[85] For Nella, writing her wartime diary was an act of self-validation at a low point in her life. She began it in response to MO's appeal in 1939 to send in monthly war diaries. She describes herself in the first instalments, with reference to her occupation and age, as 'Housewife, 49'. The diary is an intimate document about running her household in wartime; her anxieties concerning her sons, particularly the younger one, Cliff; and her difficulties with her uncommunicative, stay-at-home and controlling husband. Nella also vividly brings to life the voluntary work that she took up during the war and the people she worked with at the Women's Voluntary Service Centre and the Red Cross shop in Barrow. She conjures, with remarkable although untutored skill, the distinctive ordinariness of the life of a lower-class woman in a northern British town in the extraordinary circumstances of war.

The appeal of Nella Last to MO panellists is not mysterious. MO itself reports that people who enjoy reading MO publications are inspired by them to join MO's present-day panel and write for it.[86] Nella Last's diaries are mentioned by women in particular, as in the case of one born in the 1960s who writes: 'Nella Last is my kind of hero, she's the reason I write this stuff to you. I imagine she inspired plenty of people to get writing.'[87] Thus Nella, like other MO diarists, acts both as a prompt to remember or imagine the Second World War and as a spur to write for MO. Her published diaries indicate that recording the everyday life of an ordinary woman, burdened by various constraints and oppressions, is a worthwhile undertaking: it is not hard, it seems, for women of all ages, as well as for men who experience day-to-day marginalization, to identify with Nella and feel validated by her. 'Reading', as Matt Houlbrook has argued in relation to a different historical context, offers 'one resource through which to engage in the messy work of negotiating emotional and psychological conflict, composing an acceptable sense of self and forging a better life.'[88] Writing for MO, in the past as James Hinton has noted,[89] and in the present, was and is a way of expressing all of the above.

Reading and remembering are further complicated by the changing position of individuals in the life course, which coincides with shifts in popular discourses concerning the meanings of the past and the present. Ann Curthoys has elucidated this process by comparing the meaning of reading Simone de Beauvoir's autobiographies as a young woman in the 1960s and as an older one in the late 1990s: 'So much has changed. What was new and scarcely imaginable then is being lived everyday in all its messy detail by a multitude of women.'[90]

We have some remarkable evidence of how these things affected one reader's response to Nella Last, as a figure with whom to identify and a vector of memory. Dorothy Sheridan, MO Archivist from 1974 until 2010, wrote in 1998 that when she first 'met' the 49-year-old Nella in the pages of her then unpublished diary, which Sheridan read in 1974, she reacted to her negatively. Sheridan was at that time 26 and responded to Nella as a member of an older generation who was 'pious and judgmental', 'snobbish and superior' and woefully immersed in domestic minutiae. Sheridan revisited the diary 23 years later in 1997, by which time Sheridan herself was 49, the same age as Nella when she started her MO diary, while 'rather annoyingly, Nella ha[d] stayed the same age'.[91] Sheridan realized that her perceptions had changed. She felt that the diary was 'moving and insightful', and that Nella's accounts of domesticity were combined with astute social and political analysis. In short, Sheridan found herself now identifying with Nella, especially with her 'struggles over ageing and femininity' in the context of the war. Sheridan concludes by drawing on the concepts of multiple identities and shifting standpoints: not only did Nella have many personae, but readers' relationships with the subjects of texts are variable and they change over time.[92] Even though Sheridan could never be part of the same generation as Nella Last, her perceptions of this wartime woman shifted profoundly between the two points in her life course.

Sheridan emphasizes the mutability of her relationship with Nella, but, as Ann Curthoys suggests, other things alter too. Not only are the subjects and the readers of life-writing possessed of multiple identities which mutate, but, as scholars of dialogics insist, the wider cultural discourses in which a text is read also develop.[93] Notably, since 1981, when Nella's diary was first published, the feminist idea that 'the personal is political' has entered popular culture. Thus it has become increasingly possible since the 1970s to read Nella's domestic preoccupations, her concerns about her sons, and her account of her difficult relationship with her husband, not as the private obsessions of a middle-aged menopausal woman, but as the kinds of things all women go through, that are central to gender dynamics, and that matter on the road to the achievement of gender equality.

There has been a further mediating factor. Nella Last's wartime diary has been dramatized for television, and many respondents who had read *Nella Last's War* had also, or alternatively, seen *Housewife, 49*, first broadcast in 2006. Profile Books republished the diaries in that year, and attribute the record sales of over 100,000 copies directly to the television show.[94] *Housewife, 49* was written by the British comedian and actress Victoria Wood who herself plays Nella. Wood's intervention is important in two ways. First, she succeeded in interpreting Nella Last for a popular audience in 2006, while a male television director, Richard Broad, one of the two editors of *Nella Last's War*, had failed 26 years earlier. Broad planned a television show of some sort in 1980, but rejected the idea because of what he saw as the abundance of domestic minutiae and the paucity of dramatic events in the narrative.[95] Wood, in contrast, made an interesting and popular drama in 2006 out of Nella's domesticity and social relationships in the relatively uneventful context of wartime Barrow. This was partly because of Wood's own comic persona, built since the 1980s on self-deprecating humour about the everyday concerns of a large, unglamorous woman from Northern England, which commands huge affection from British audiences. It is also the result of shifting cultural values to which popular feminism has contributed, which validate both 'the story of a middle aged woman in crisis' and the idea that 'the war opened the door for her a little', to quote Wood herself.

Victoria Wood portrays Nella sympathetically as the anxious wife of a silent, grumpy and unsociable husband, who cares deeply about both her husband and her sons, has trouble fitting in with the wealthier volunteers at the WVS, but finds satisfaction, happiness and a new purpose in life and sense of self through her voluntary war work. Wood does not flinch from portraying Nella as rather domineering towards her sons, as well as having limited experience of life and lacking awareness, in particular, of her younger son's homosexuality.[96] The respondents to the 2009 directive who felt that, as a result of the war, Nella Last was subject to a 'transformation' were responding not only to the diary itself, but also to Victoria Wood's representation of Nella, which itself contributes to the shifting discourses concerning both what it means to be a woman and what the Second World War means in today's world.

Conclusion

The concept of 'generation' is important in perceptions of the Second World War: people use it to claim membership of imagined communities characterized by respect for, and a sense of obligation to, participants in the Second World War, and to differentiate themselves from others assumed to lack these feelings. Engagement with the memory of the war is varied: strong identification does not characterize everyone; some feel detached or even alienated from popular discourses concerning the war. However, these patterns do not coincide neatly with the decades in which people were born; it is not the case that temporal distance from the events of the Second World War has weakened the impact of its memory with each succeeding generation; the popular memory of the Second World War does not map onto 'history' in the sense of the chronological march of time in any obvious way.

The memory of the war is not always conducive to 'composure' but is often negative and unsettling, and engagement is frequently occluded by family censorship. There are several explanations for such 'silences', of which a preference to look to the future rather than dwell on the past, though it may seem the most obvious, is not entirely satisfactory. Gendered expectations, themselves conditioned by gendered popular representations of the Second World War, have discouraged the transmission of some types of memory and encouraged others over time. 'Speaking silences' resulting from shame, grief and trauma also communicate powerful messages – albeit largely non-verbal ones – about the war within families.

'Remembering' the Second World War even if one did not live through it, or did so only as a child, has certainly been characteristic of those living in Britain since 1945, but it is not a simple matter of each generation being locked in understandings that were on offer when they were young. On the contrary, responses to texts alter during the life course as imaginative engagement with the past mutates, conditioned by changing personal, political and cultural contexts. Again, this is gendered. Almost paradoxically, it creates remarkable consistency across age groups in the take-up of particular versions of the memory of the Second World War. Explanations for the absence of pronounced generational layering lie in part in the constant cultural renewal of the memory of 'the war' through, for example, films, television and literature, in the light of current ways of viewing the world – to which Mass Observation itself makes significant contributions. They also lie in the practices of 'imaginative investment, projection and creation'[97] that characterize family talk, reading, viewing and writing, and that have given rise in Britain since 1945 to a seemingly constant process of the generation and regeneration of the memory of the Second World War.

Notes

1   Calder, A. (1969), *The People's War: Britain 1939-1945*. London: Jonathan Cape; Marwick, A. (1968), *Britain in the Century of Total War*. London: Bodley Head; Rose, S. (2003), *Which People's War? National Identity and Citizenship in Wartime Britain, 1939–1945*. Oxford: Oxford University Press; Field, G. (2011), *Blood, Sweat, and Toil: Remaking the British Working Class, 1939–1945*. Oxford: Oxford University Press.

2   Eley, G. (2001), 'Finding the people's war: film, British collective memory, and World War II'. *American Historical Review*, 106, 818–38. Here pp. 818–19.

3   See, for example, Connelly, M. (2004), *We Can Take It!: Britain and the Memory of the Second World War*. Harlow: Pearson Longman; Evans, M. and Lunn, K. (eds) (1997), *War and Memory in the Twentieth Century*. Oxford: Oxford University Press; Hurd, G. (ed.) (1984), *National Fictions: World War Two in British Films and Television*. London: BFI; Paris, M. (ed.) (2007), *Repicturing the Second World War: Representations in Film and Television*. Basingstoke: Palgrave Macmillan; Ramsden, J. (1998), 'Refocusing "The People's War": British War Films of the 1950s'. *Journal of Contemporary History*, 33(1), 35–63.

4   Noakes, L. (1998), *War and the British: Gender, Memory and National Identity*. London: I. B. Tauris; Summerfield, P. (1998), *Reconstructing Women's Wartime Lives: Discourse and Subjectivity in Oral Histories of the Second World War*. Manchester: Manchester University Press; Summerfield, P. and Peniston-Bird, C. (2007), *Contesting Home Defence: Men, Women and the Home Guard in the Second World War*. Manchester: Manchester University Press.

5   Hirsch, M. (2008), 'The generation of postmemory', *Poetics Today*, 29(1), 103–28. Here p. 106.

6   Madge, T. and Harrisson, C. (1939), *Britain by Mass-Observation*. Harmondsworth: Penguin, 1939, 9. See also Stanley, N. S. (1981), 'The Extra Dimension: A Study and Assessment of the Methods Employed by

Mass-Observation in its First Period, 1937–1940', Unpublished PhD thesis, Birmingham Polytechnic CNAA; Hinton, J. (2013), *The Mass Observers: a History 1937–1949*. Oxford: Oxford University Press; Hubble, N. (2006), *Mass Observation and Everyday Life: Culture, History; Theory*. Basingstoke: Palgrave MacMillan; Jeffery, T. (1978), *Mass Observation – A Short History*. Centre for Contemporary Cultural Studies, University of Birmingham; Summerfield, P. (1985), 'Mass-Observation: social research or social movement?' *Journal of Contemporary History*, 20, 439–52.

7   For example, Garfield, S. (2004), *Our Hidden Lives: The Everyday Diaries of a Forgotten Britain 1945–1948*. London: Ebury Press; Garfield, S. (2005), *We are at War: the Remarkable Diaries of Five Ordinary People in Extraordinary Times*. London: Ebury Press.

8   Such criticisms are addressed in Sheridan, D. (2008), 'The Mass-Observation Project 1981-2008. Background Report'. Unpublished ms., Mass Observation Archive.

9   Thomson, A. (1995), 'Writing about learning: using Mass-Observation educational life-histories to explore learning through life' in J. Swindells (ed.), *The Uses of Autobiography*. London: Taylor and Francis, 163–74; Noakes (1998), 75–102; Kushner, T. (2004), *We Europeans? Mass-Observation, 'Race' and British Identity in the Twentieth Century*. Aldershot: Ashgate, 103–45.

10   Ibid., 256.

11   Mass Observation Project, Directive, Spring 2009.

12   Sheridan, D. (2007), 'The Mass Observation Project. Director's Report'. Unpublished ms., Mass Observation Archive, December.

13   The only serious absence is of members of ethnic minorities.

14   See Summerfield, P. (2004), 'Culture and composure: creating narratives of the gendered self in oral history interviews', *Cultural and Social History*, 1(1), 65–93; Roper, M. (2000), 'Re-remembering the soldier hero; the composure and re-composure of masculinity in memories of the Great War', *History Workshop Journal*, 50, 181–205; Summerfield, P. (2000), 'Dis/composing the subject; intersubjectivities in oral history' in T. Cosslett et al. (eds), *Feminism and Autobiography: Texts, Theories, Methods*. London: Routledge, 91–106.

15   Mannheim, K. (1928), 'The problem generations' in Kecskemeti, P. (ed.) (1952), *Essays on the Sociology of Knowledge*. London: Routledge and Kegan Paul, 276–322.

16   Abrams, P. (1982), *Historical Sociology*. Shepton Mallet: Open Books, 227–66.

17   Wohl, R. (1979), *The Generation of 1914*. Cambridge, MA: Harvard University Press, 2.

18   Wohl, (1979), 210; Roseman, M. (ed.) (1995), *Generations in Conflict: Youth Revolt and Generation Formation in Germany 1770–1968*. Cambridge: Cambridge University Press; Von der Goltz, A. (2011), 'Generations of 68ers: age-related constructions of identity and Germany's "1968"'. *Cultural and Social History*, 8(4), 473–90.

19 M3190 M, 1959; G3126 M, 1941; B3252 M, 1945; S2207 F, 1952. All references to MO respondents are to their replies to MOP, Directive, Spring 2009. MO preserves anonymity by identifying each respondent by a letter and number. I am also indicating gender and date of birth. I have given respondents pseudonyms for readability.

20 G3752 M, 1959.

21 B3010 F, 1964.

22 E4111 M, 1940.

23 D2585 F, 1943.

24 See Summerfield, P. (2009), 'Film and the popular memory of the Second World War in Britain 1950-1959', in S. Grayzel and P. Levine (eds), *Gender, Labour, War and Empire: Essays on Modern Britain*. Basingstoke: Palgrave Macmillan, 157–75.

25 D2585 F, 1943.

26 S2207 F, 1952.

27 S2207 F, 1952.

28 M2986 F, 1956.

29 M2986 F, 1956.

30 G3752 M, 1959.

31 G3752 M, 1959.

32 Cubitt, G. (2007), *History and Memory*. Manchester: Manchester University Press, 200.

33 A3434 F, 1965.

34 S4002 F, 1978.

35 S4002 F, 1978.

36 C4102 M, 1964.

37 B4424 M, 1971.

38 W3994 F, 1972.

39 S4002 F, 1978.

40 Gregory, A. (1994), *The Silence of Memory: Armistice Day 1919–1946*. Oxford: Berg.

41 D826 F, 1950.

42 V3767 M, 1938.

43 B3252 M, 1945.

44 A3884 M, 1968.

45 V3767 M, 1938; A3884 M, 1968.

46 Passerini, L. (ed.) (1992), *Memory and Totalitarianism*. Oxford: Oxford University Press, pp. 1–18.

47 Thomson, A. (1994), *Anzac Memories: Living with the Legend*. Melbourne: Oxford University Press Australia; Summerfield (2004); Abrams, L. (2010), *Oral History Theory*. London: Routledge.

48 B1654 M, 1931.

49 M3190 M, 1958.

50 Paris, M. (2000), *Warrior Nation: Images of War in British Popular Culture*. London: Reaktion Books.

51 C3603 M, 1944.

52 '*Rockfist Rogan*', *a boxer and then RAF pilot*, appeared in the pages of *Champion*, a picture story paper, from 1938 to 1955, and subsequently in *Tiger* until 1960. Other male respondents (e.g. A4127 M, 1962) refer to the shaping of their playground games by similar comics featuring the Second World War especially those published by D. C. Thompson, such as *Commando* (1961–continuing) and *Warlord* (1974–86).

53 C3603 M, 1944.

54 E3977 F, 1981.

55 Jake Thackray (1967), 'Lah-Di-Dah'. N.W.R. Music Publ. Co. Ltd. Thackray was born in 1938.

56 W3994 F, 1972.

57 E3977 F, 1981.

58 F3137 F, 1969.

59 For example, S3845 M, 1966.

60 For example, F1634 F, 1943.

61 'The Germans', Series 1, Episode 6 of 'Fawlty Towers', script by John Cleese and Connie Booth, directed by John Howard Davies. BBC1, 24 October 1975.

62 R1227 F, 1944.

63 F1634 F, 1943

64 G2640 F, 1953.

65 S3844 F, 1974.

66 S3844 F, 1974.

67 S3844 F, 1974.

68 F2949 F, 1954.

69 F2949 F, 1954.

70 See, for instance, most of the British black and white war films of the 1940s and 1950s, especially the campaign films and prisoner-of-war escape films. Later British films and television shows about the Home Front, such as 'Dad's Army' (BBC, 1968–77), 'Family at War' (ITV, 1970–2), 'Yanks' (1979), 'Hope and Glory' (1987) and 'Land Girls' (1998), re-invoke the 'we're all in it together' spirit.

71 F2949 F, 1954.

72 B3111 M, 1971.

73 Hoffman, E. (2004), *After Such Knowledge: Memory, History and the Legacy of the Holocaust*. New York: Public Affairs, 10.

74   Rousso, H. (1991), *The Vichy Syndrome: History and Memory in France since 1944*. Cambridge, MA: Harvard University Press.

75   Broad, R. and Fleming, S. (eds) (1981), *Nella Last's War: a Mothers Diary*. Bristol: Falling Wall Press. Republished 2006 as *Nella Last's War: the Second World War Diaries of Housewife, 49*. London: Profile Books.

76   D4101 M, 1960; B3227 M, 1967.

77   E4111 M, 1940.

78   P1796 F, 1946.

79   S2207 F, 1952.

80   F2949 F,1954.

81   S4002 F, 1978.

82   P4347 F, 1983.

83   F4395 M, 1963.

84   T4426 M, 1978.

85   Broad and Fleming (1991); see also Hinton, J. (2010), *Nine Wartime Lives*. Oxford: Oxford University Press.

86   Sheridan, D. (2007), 'Mass-Observation Project: Director's Report', 3.

87   R4286 F, 1966.

88   Houlbrook, M. (2010), '"A pin to see the peepshow": culture, fiction and selfhood in Edith Thompson's letters, 1921-1922'. *Past and Present*, 207, 215–49. Here p. 249.

89   Hinton (2010), 1–20.

90   Curthoys, A. (2000), 'Adventures of Feminism: Simone de Beauvoir's autobiographies, women's liberation and self-fashioning'. *Feminist Review*, 64, 3–18. Here p. 15.

91   Sheridan, D. (1998), 'Getting on with Nella Last at the Barrow-in-Furness Red Cross Centre: romanticism and ambivalence in working with women's stories'. *Women's History Notebooks*, 5(1), 2–10. Here p. 2.

92   Sheridan (1998), 3–4.

93   See, for example, Hirschkop, K. and Shepherd, D. (eds) (1989). *Bakhtin and Cultural Theory*. Manchester: Manchester University Press.

94   Correspondence with Anna-Marie Fitzgerald and Lisa Owens, Publicity Managers, Profile Books, 17 July 2012. The sales figure includes *Nella Last's Peace* (2008) and *Nella Last in the 1950s* (2010), edited by P. and R. W. Malcolmson. *Nella Last's War* (which Profile took over from Falling Wall Press in 2006) alone sold 63,000 copies between 2006 and 2012.

95   Conversation with Richard Broad, London, 1980.

96   Malcolmson, P. and Malcolmson, R. W. (2008), *Nella Last's Peace: the Post-war Diaries of Housewife, 49*. London: Profile Books, 287–8.

97   Hirsch (2008), 107.

Key texts

Broad, R. and Fleming, S. (eds) (1981), *Nella Last's War: a Mother's Diary*. Bristol: Falling Wall Press. Republished in 2006 as *Nella Last's War: the Second World War Diaries of Housewife, 49*. London: Profile Books.

Curthoys, A. (2000), 'Adventures of feminism: Simone de Beauvoir's autobiographies, women's liberation and self-fashioning'. *Feminist Review*, 64, Spring.

Eley, G. (2001), 'Finding the people's war: film, British collective memories and World War II'. *The American Historical Review*, 106(3), 818–38.

Gregory, A. (1994), *The Silence of Memory: Armistice Day 1919-1946*. Oxford: Berg.

Hinton, J. (2013), *The Mass Observers: a History 1937-1949*. Oxford: Oxford University Press.

Hirsch, M. (2008), 'The generation of postmemory', *Poetics Today*, 29(1).

Hoffman, E. (2004), *After Such Knowledge: Memory, History and the Legacy of the Holocaust*. New York: Public Affairs.

Kushner, T. (2004), *We Europeans? Mass-Observation, 'Race' and British Identity in the Twentieth Century*. Aldershot: Ashgate, 103–45.

Mannheim, K. (1928/1952), 'The problem of generations', in P. Kecskemeti (ed.) (1952), *Essays on the Sociology of Knowledge*. London: Routledge and Kegan Paul, 276–322.

Paris, M. (2000), *Warrior Nation: Images of War in British Popular Culture*. London: Reaktion Books.

Passerini, L. (ed.) (1992), *Memory and Totalitarianism*. Oxford: Oxford University Press.

Ramsden, J. (1998), 'Refocusing "the people's war": British war films of the 1950s'. *Journal of Contemporary History*, 33(1), 35–63.

Roper, M. (2000), 'Re-remembering the Soldier Hero: the Composure and Re-composure of Masculinity in Memories of the Great War', *History Workshop Journal*, 50, Spring, 181–205.

Roseman, M. (ed.) (1995), *Generations in Conflict: Youth Revolt and Generation Formation in Germany 1770-1968*. Cambridge: Cambridge University Press.

Summerfield P. (1985), 'Mass-observation: social research or social movement?' *Journal of Contemporary History*, 20, 439–52.

—(2000), 'Dis/composing the subject: Intersubjectivities in oral History', in T. Cosslett *et al.*, *Feminism and Autobiography: Texts, Theories, Methods*. London: Routledge, 91–106.

—(2004), 'Culture and composure: creating narratives of the gendered self in oral history interviews'. *Cultural and Social History*, 1(1), 65–93.

Thomson, A. (1995), 'Writing about learning: using mass-observation educational life-histories to explore learning through life', in J. Swindells (ed.), *The Uses of Autobiography*. London: Taylor and Francis, 163–74.

Von der Goltz, A. (2011), 'Generations of 68ers: age-related constructions of Identity and Germany's "1968"'. *Cultural and Social History*, 8(4), 473–90.

Wohl, R. (1979), *The Generation of 1914*. Cambridge, MA: Harvard University Press.

CHAPTER THREE

'War on the Web'

The BBC's 'People's War' website and memories of fear in wartime in 21st-century Britain

Lucy Noakes

In June 2003 the British Broadcasting Corporation (BBC), the British state broadcaster, launched a new, interactive, online project called the 'People's War'. Responses to advertisements for people to record their wartime experiences on the website were overwhelming: by the time the site closed to new submissions in January 2006, it had received 47,000 written pieces and 15,000 images.[1] In order to enable veterans who were not familiar with computer technology to participate, the BBC recruited 2000 volunteer 'story gatherers' working from libraries, daycare centres and museums to help older people upload their material to the website. Partnership with the Department of Culture, Media and Sport enabled the BBC and the charity Age Concern to recruit 'outreach officers' to encourage participation from 'hard to reach' groups, and material was collected at commemorative events such as the many tea parties and air shows that marked the anniversary years of 2004 and 2005. The very size of the response to the project, organized by the national broadcaster and aided by the involvement of national and local government, charities and voluntary organizations, demonstrates the significance of the memory of the Second

World War in early twenty-first-century Britain, both for individuals, for families and for the state. This chapter utilizes some of the 'stories' entered on the website to consider the extent to which the electronic space of the internet enables the articulation of previously marginalized experiences of wartime; in this case, memories of fear.

The 'People's War' website can be understood as one of a range of 'sites of memory' which represented and commemorated the Second World War in early twenty-first-century Britain.[2] Pierre Nora, whose work on French nationhood developed the concept, argued that collective forms of identity, such as the national, could be analysed through an examination of sites of memory such as monuments, museums, memorials, rituals, public acts of commemoration and celebration, archives and classrooms.[3] As Jay Winter has argued, these various sites of memory can be understood as aspects of a 'memory boom', a phenomenon in which individuals, communities and societies return to the past as a means of anchoring themselves in a rapidly changing and unstable present.[4] In Britain the two 'total wars' of the twentieth century appear again and again across a range of representations and institutions, forming a central aspect of the memory boom in British culture. This has been paralleled and enabled by concomitant developments in digital memory. A revolution in media and communication technology has taken place over the last two decades, with the growing accessibility and ubiquity of the online world as a site for information, debate, representation and communication. Electronic sites of memory thus exist alongside traditional sites where wars are represented, commemorated and memorialized. For example, numerous British cities have websites that list and commemorate civilian deaths under aerial bombardment, often designed to accompany newly unveiled memorials to the civilian dead of war.[5] Unlike the traditional sites of memory listed above, websites can be created by anyone with access to and knowledge of the relevant software. Websites such as the 'People's War' provide a new 'site of memory' where representations of the past circulate, are articulated and can be argued over. Because they are 'open' to anyone with an internet connection, they potentially allow a wider range of memories to be represented than are apparent in traditional sites of memory.

Memory and the internet

Electronic sites of memory, or 'websites of memory', differ in a number of important ways from more traditional sites. First, when compared to most material sites of memory, such as memorials and museums, websites appear to be more transient, as they are rarely designed to be a permanent physical embodiment of a shared memory of a period or an event. They exist in a technologically defined temporality, and although, like museums, they can be created as a response to a perceived need to provide a space where memories can be publicly shared, and like memorials, as a space where acts of remembrance can take place, their virtual nature means that they are both less permanent than these physical sites of memory and potentially more accessible, 'open' to visitors with an internet connection at any moment in time. As researchers from a variety of disciplines have suggested, time is not a fixed quantity, but is rather shaped by culture, society and technological change.[6] Contemporary means of communication have acted to change the experience of time and space, as information can be shared around the globe in seconds. This technologically driven collapsing together of past and present, of our sense of space and our changing perceptions of time, is one of the features which define the experience of life in late modernity or post-modernity. Some scholars have suggested that the internet provides a particularly reflexive, transnational site for the expression and transmission of cultural memory; for example, Yochai Benkler contends that the internet makes users more 'self reflective and critical of the culture they occupy'.[7] Against this must be set the sense of fluidity and of constant and rapid change associated with modernity, which has contributed to the 'memory boom' as people strive for a historically grounded, stable sense of identity. In a swiftly changing present, this sense of stability can be found through a reassertion of a shared past, whether that past be a family history, the shared history and traditions of a neighbourhood or region, or the shared sense of the past found in national identities.[8] Internet users then appear just as likely to use websites as a platform for the expression of assertive national identities and nationalisms as they are to form new, transnational identities.[9] Indeed, as Erikson has argued, it appears that 'nations thrive in cyberspace' and that the internet has become 'a key technology for keeping nations together'.[10] 'Websites of memory' thus have a complex connection to our contemporary sense of time and space, and our collective relationship with the past. They are central both to the changing sense of time and space in contemporary society and to our attempts to reconnect with a sense of the past as a means of grounding ourselves within a rapidly changing and confusing world.

Second, they differ from other sites of memory in their physical, material form. War memorials and museums that commemorate and remember wars have a built form and a physical presence in a geographic space. They are often physically imposing, designed with an eye to posterity.[11] The material form that a website takes is very different. It is not a physical space but an electronic one, usually experienced via a small computer screen. Some make a conscious attempt to emulate traditional sites of remembrance, electronically replicating the carving of names of the dead into a stone memorial. The tactile element of visiting a memorial and tracing a name, as seen in commemorative practice at the Vietnam Veterans Memorial in Washington DC, is obviously unavailable to the website visitor, although the act of typing in a name or a story fulfils a similar function, linking the individual in a physical sense to the site. The Virtual Wall, a website which acts as an electronic version of the Washington memorial, combines the tropes of traditional remembrance, listing the names of the dead on a 'skin' which has a granite-like appearance, similar to a war memorial, with an electronic version of the practice of leaving gifts and letters by the Vietnam Memorial Wall, as individuals visiting the site can post messages to, and memories of, the dead.[12] Whilst museums, memorials and websites can all be understood as shared public spaces where acts of remembering and commemoration can be carried out by individuals, the experience of the visitor to the website is very different to that of the visitor to the museum or memorial. The public–private boundary is blurred in a different way: the visitor to a memorial or museum may experience a private emotion in a very public setting, whereas the website user who chooses to post a message may initially experience the website privately but enters into the public sphere by the act of posting. Whilst websites may often be created collectively, their virtual nature, and the ways they are usually accessed, via personal computers, means that they are often experienced individually, not as a site at which a community comes together in remembrance.

Third, websites are potentially more open and participatory than other, more traditional, sites of memory. Famously, *Time* magazine's 'Person of the Year' in 2006 was 'you', connoting the users of Web 2.0. This referred to the rapid transformation of the internet over the past few years, changing from an electronic space where the power relations of the material world are replicated, to a space where software has enabled the proliferation of decentred, individually created and often interactive websites such as blogs, social networking sites and file-sharing sites. Popular websites, such as the BBC's, often invite contributions from visitors, and while these might be edited or deleted, they provide a potential space for the recording and reception of otherwise marginalized or dominated viewpoints. For example, online comment on the *Guardian*'s website in 2009 following a leading article on the importance of D-Day, included criticism of the post-war state, description of the British bombing of Dresden in 1945 as a war crime and claims that veterans had been 'let down' by post-war immigration.[13] The internet thus provides a space for memories of and perspectives on the Second World War which are rarely seen in more formal sites of memory.

The very existence of the numerous websites that provide a space for the representation and articulation of memories of warfare demonstrate both the importance of war as a period in individuals' lives – as a time when people often feel that they are 'living through history', and which they thus often tell and retell stories about, and also the importance of periods of warfare and conflict in cultural memory, as times that are seen as significant for a community, society or nation. The BBC's 'People's War' website exists as a space where the dominant cultural memory of the war, which positions it as a pivotal event in British history and a defining moment in the articulation and mobilization of the shared mores and values which are still widely understood as being central to a shared national history and identity, interacts with more personal individual or family memories of the war, which may not always accord with the dominant narrative. As such, it provides an opportunity to consider the extent to which the participatory nature of the internet provides a challenge to the hegemonic nature of cultural memory, opening up public space to a variety of conflicting and oppositional voices that have previously been marginalized.

The 'People's War' website

Stories submitted to the site were divided into 64 separate categories, ranging from the largest, 'Childhood and Evacuation', 'British Army' and 'Family Life', to the smaller categories of 'Women's Volunteer Groups', 'Propaganda' and 'Concentration Camps'. Many stories were cross-referenced and could be accessed through several separate themed categories. The largest number of stories, 14,336, are listed under 'Childhood and Evacuation', reflecting the demographics of the contributors, whilst the smallest category is that accorded to 'Women's Volunteer Groups', with just 21 accounts. The decision not to check stories for historical accuracy was taken early on in the project. The website states that:

> The wartime generation in particular saw the BBC as a trusted supplier of 'the truth' … However, the BBC was keen to gather wartime memories precisely because it represented the user's perception, rather than received historical fact … What this site demanded was a record of how the wartime generation remembered those years: testimony in their own words; subjective interpretations that described 'what it was like', not what happened.[14]

The BBC thus made use of its status in British culture as a reliable source for objective and factual news and information, and stated its wish to 'open up' the existing, dominant narratives of the war to include more subjective reflections upon and memories of the period. A key aim of the website project was to incorporate a wider range of personal memories of the war than is normally visible in sites of wartime cultural memory. This was reflected in the comments of some of the contributors recorded on the site, such as the Herefordshire farmer who remarked that 'I didn't realise you'd want stories from the likes of us – I didn't go to fight.'[15]

The BBC collected stories for the website between 2003 and 2006, a period when, as Janet Watson's chapter in this volume demonstrates, numerous wartime anniversaries were publicly commemorated. The public visibility of the war may well have encouraged individuals to reflect on their personal experiences and memories, and to engage with the website's project of public memory and representation. Popular memory theory provides us with a methodological tool with which to analyse the processes by which individuals articulate memories of their own experiences within a public sphere. In this model, cultural memory is formed hegemonically: representations in the public sphere limit or encourage the articulation of personal memories, whilst these dominant representations must have some resonance with the majority of those who experienced the war in order to gain dominance.[16] 'Public' and 'private' memories thus act to shape one another. Those with difficult, discordant memories of the war years, such as conscientious objectors, may struggle to articulate their memories on the larger public stage, confining the articulation of their experience largely to smaller audiences who share their beliefs. Only 36 stories by conscientious objectors were entered on the website, one man commenting that the 'memory has remained a challenge ever since'.[17] Others utilized language and images which have become embedded in the cultural memory of wartime, such as 'the lights were going out all over Europe' and 'it was indeed their finest hour' in stories which, in many other ways, expressed memories that were marginal to the dominant discourse. Contemporary beliefs and values also shape the ways in which memories are articulated: the anniversaries of D-Day and VE Day in 2004 and 2005 both stimulated waves of entries on the website, while the London tube and bus bombings in July 2005 also appear to have prompted individuals to write about their experiences under bombardment. The dominant cultural memory of a particular period or event is thus fluid, open to a degree of re-interpretation and re-imagining. The remainder of this chapter will examine stories about three 'signal events' of the war, the Blitz, Dunkirk and D-Day, and consider whether the website provided a means for those with both civilian and military experiences that did not sit easily within dominant cultural memory of these events to find a wider audience.[18]

Civilian fear in the Blitz

One of the defining emotional responses to warfare, yet one which is remarkable for its marginality to the dominant cultural memory of the Second World War in Britain, is fear. While fear may produce a physical response in those who experience it, an embodied sensation, the expression of this response is often cultural; fear is expressed through language and culture as well as through the body, drawing on contemporary means of understanding the emotion in order to give voice to it in a way that others will comprehend.[19] Diaries and letters written during the war, and some autobiographical pieces written since, do make mention of the fearfulness felt by many in wartime. Betty Holbrook, who served with the Auxiliary Territorial Service on an anti-aircraft battery in East London, described one woman who 'threw herself on the floor of the hut, screaming and trying to dig a hole in the floor with her bare hands' when a V1 bomb fell nearby.[20] Captain Thomas Flanagan, a soldier with the 4th Battalion King's Own Scottish Borderers who was invalided out of the army with 'shell shock', described shaking 'all over with fear', a response which 'simply took over my body' when he saw yet another dead body while under fire in 1945.[21] In contrast to our perception of the fearfulness of combatants in the trenches of the First World War, expressions of fear as described by Holbrook and Flanagan have been marginal to both representations of the war at the time, and since. While rarely completely absent, fear has often been represented as a minority response to the conditions of wartime Britain. Wartime films like *In Which We Serve* (1943) represent the expression of fearfulness as shameful; an understandable emotion that had to be mastered if one was to do one's duty in wartime.[22] Post-war fiction, such as *The Cruel Sea* (1951), likewise recognized the existence of fear amongst those who experienced war, but again emphasized its incompatibility with wartime service and citizenship.[23] More recent representations have replicated this pattern. For example, the 'Blitz Experience' in the Imperial War Museum, London, emphasizes collectivity and stoicism under bombardment over and above the more fearful responses, which were sometimes recorded.[24] Film and television representations of the 1944 D-Day landings, whilst giving space to the trauma and fear of battle, focus on the bravery and comradeship of troops landing on the Normandy beaches.[25] In all of these representations, fear is portrayed as a personal, even selfish emotion, one that has to be controlled in order to experience the comradeship and collectivity that dominate narratives of the War. Subsequent representations and memories of the 'people's war', such as those found on the BBC's website, thus often marginalize or even silence memories of individual fearfulness. In this, they are shaped by wartime notions of fear as much as by popular memory of the war as a collective experience.

Doctors, psychiatrists and civil servants planning for warfare in the 1930s all expected to see widespread fear and panic amongst civilians under bombardment. Inter-war imaginings of a future war pictured vast air raids on urban areas, with tens of thousands of tons of explosive being dropped alongside poison gas on the terrified and panicking populations below.[26] As early as 1923, authors were predicting the transformation of London into 'one vast raving bedlam', while by 1935 novelists were imagining apocalyptic visions of 'waves of hysterical humanity' trampling one another in an attempt to reach underground shelters.[27] Plans were laid for the treatment of 'some 3–4 million cases of acute panic, hysteria and other neurotic conditions during the first six months of air attack', while civil defence workers were advised to deal with individuals showing symptoms of hysteria with 'a bucket of water or a severe box on the ears' as a short-term measure to prevent panic spreading.[28] Particular groups were thought to be more likely than others to show fear under bombardment. Claims that Jewish shelterers had panicked and caused the 1943 disaster at Bethnal Green Underground Station, when 173 people died, echoed earlier predictions that 'the foreign folk in the crowded East End', in particular the 'Jewish element', were the most likely to react to aerial bombardment with 'an unreasonable panic'.[29] This representation of fear and hysteria as somehow foreign to British people built on a narrative which existed alongside and pre-dated the predictions of panic and hysteria under bombardment, and which suggested that, with good planning and leadership, the British people would be well placed to withstand bombardment. This was articulated in *The Times* in 1937, where it was argued that the absence of hysteria was what 'impressed foreign observers at the Jubilee more than any other', and was apparent in the 1940 Ministry of Information film *London Can Take It!*, which described a city where 'there is no fear, and no panic' under bombardment.[30] A September 1940 report in *The Times* on the impact of the Blitz on East London made much of the 'wonderful spirit and fortitude' that civilians were displaying, a Bermondsey doctor commenting that she had not seen 'a case of hysteria or panic'.[31] The *Daily Mirror* reported on men and women in a pub in a badly bombed area of London singing '"Bless 'em all" at the top of their voices' as another raid began.[32] Civilian fear under bombardment was often understood as 'un-British', but also feminine. A Mass Observation Report on civilian morale written for the Ministry of Information in October 1940, a month after the Blitz on London began, claimed that 'women are far more depressed and upset than men. Their morale was always worst, but now it is much worse than men's', whilst an advert for Phyllosan, a nerve tonic, took the form of a letter from a 'middle aged woman' who described herself as 'not strong' and 'having lost much sleep through the present unsettled conditions'.[33] Mass Observation went on to suggest that those who found life under bombardment the most difficult also often had 'a strong, often secret, desire for immediate peace', while a psychiatrist's report on panic in civilians emphasized that, while 'breakdowns' were 'uncommon', they tended to occur in 'predisposed persons who have long suffered from emotional instability, neurotic symptoms and so on'.[34] Steadfastness and fortitude beneath the bombs were qualities that came to be seen as embodying a desirable and peculiarly British response to this new form of warfare; while many did display the 'courage, humour and kindliness' that Molly Panter-Downes observed in her reports for the *New Yorker*, those with a less robust response to bombardment were widely understood to be failing in their duty as wartime citizens.[35]

Given the emphasis on courage under bombardment during the war, it is perhaps unsurprising that expressions of civilian fear are fairly rare in stories submitted to the 'People's War' website. One story, submitted by a man who had already published a memoir of his experiences as an evacuee, described the physical manifestation of fear during a V1 rocket attack. In a submission entitled 'The Age of Fear' the author recounted how 'fear tightened my stomach muscles and the pounding of my heart vibrated through my body' when a rocket landed nearby. He went on to describe 'shaking' and how his legs 'turned to jelly'.[36] However, even a story such as this, which foregrounded the physical sensations of fear felt by a child in wartime, contained them within a wider narrative that emphasized adventure and childhood mischief, going on to explain how the near miss he experienced gave him the idea of secretly signing up for his school's evacuation as a means of avoiding his sisters as much as avoiding bombardment. Other contributors drew on widely shared discourses of the war to frame memories of fear under bombardment, one woman describing her sense of 'fear and trepidation' when the air raid siren sounded, and 'going through hell' in the public shelter that her family used, but highlighting the 'defiant good humour' of Londoners who 'were all in it together'.[37] Another woman recounted her *sangfroid* during the Blitz, but went on to tell how the V2 rocket campaign caused her 'nerves' to 'go to pieces ... worrying for my baby, my family, about being buried under piles of debris'. Nevertheless, like the previous contributor, she emphasized the 'blitz spirit', explaining how 'the civilians carried on ... everybody tried to help each other, they were friendly to strangers, they looked out for each other'.[38] Although air raids were one of the most popular categories under which people recorded their wartime experiences on the website, very few of the contributors wrote about any fear that they or others may have felt.

Popular memory theory would suggest that the articulation of personal memories which do not sit comfortably with the dominant cultural memory of an event becomes ever more difficult. A reluctance among wartime civilians to express fear under bombardment has been replicated in many post-war popular representations, ranging from the 1953 film *Those People Next Door* to John Boorman's autobiographical *Hope and Glory* (1987). Unlike military veterans entering stories on the website, civilians who experienced bombardment did not have veterans' associations to ally themselves with. These organizations operate in a manner similar to the 'fictive kinships' of the bereaved that Jay Winter has identified in his work on remembrance of the First World War.[39] They provide support, solace and companionship, an audience for memories that may be marginalized on the wider public stage and a forum through which dominant discourse can be mediated and contested. Without such mediating bodies, individuals with memories of the past that do not sit comfortably within dominant discourse, such as those whose memories of bombing are dominated by fear, can find it harder to express these memories, even on an 'open' site of memory such as the 'People's War' website. The importance of civilian morale, a loosely defined term that attempted to measure civilian responses to warfare and assess the population's willingness to continue with the war effort, resulted in a conflation of good citizenship with courage and stoicism, and may well have led to a reluctance to express fears by those feeling frightened. Many mastered their fear, and those who simply could not stand the bombing often left the cities, trekking out to the surrounding countryside at night or evacuating themselves more permanently. Consequently, those using communal shelters were increasingly less likely to be sharing the experience of bombing with those giving voice to their fears as the war progressed. Unlike soldiers under military discipline, the traumatized civilian retained some degree of autonomy. Among those who remained in the blitzed cities, a desire not to show fear in front of others was commonplace. As the American journalist Eric Sevareid observed while spending a night in a covered trench shelter, 'there was terror – but not panic. One could panic in his heart, but two together could not show it, nor a hundred in a group.'[40] The social taboo on expressing fear and panic in wartime shaped the many post-war representations of the Blitz in which the courage, cheerfulness and communal spirit that many did display under bombardment took centre stage.[41] These representations have, in turn, provided those who underwent bombardment with a set of images and a language through which to recount this experience.

Combatant fear in wartime: Dunkirk and D-Day

In contrast, popular representations of combat have shifted in focus during the post-war period, moving from an emphasis on stoicism and collective feeling in the immediate post-war decades to a more nuanced exploration of the feelings and emotions of the individual combatant in more recent times. As knowledge of the long-term psychological effects of combat on the individual has developed through work on Post-Traumatic Stress Disorder (PTSD), an understanding of the impact of fear on the combatant has become more widespread, reflected in popular literature, medical and political policy, journalism and visual representations of warfare.[42] In order to consider this shift, and to explore the management and expression of fear amongst those contributors to the website who experienced combat, it is necessary to briefly examine the ways in which the wartime military and the medical profession understood fear.

A conference convened by the Ministry of Pensions in 1939 considered how best to treat and compensate servicemen suffering from 'war neuroses', a term which was largely replaced by 'combat fatigue' during the war. The conference saw war neuroses as the expression of 'the effects of fright or terror' and concluded that 'emotional reactions induced by fear, danger or shock, and the effects of fatigue or war strain were of only temporary duration and soon disappeared if immediate and suitable treatment were given'. It recommended that enlistment procedures should identify men who had previously suffered with 'illness of a neurotic or psychological nature' and perhaps exempt them from front-line service.[43] In an echo of the First World War, two different, often opposed, approaches dominated. The first was the psychiatric approach to nervous breakdown that treated symptoms medically, with the use of drugs and sometimes surgery, seen in the work of William Sargant and his colleagues at the Sutton Emergency Hospital. The second was the psychoanalytic approach, utilized by analysts working at the Tavistock Clinic. Between these twin poles operated a range of approaches to, and treatment of, men suffering from combat fatigue. All of these shared in common with one another the overarching aim of returning men to service, and a widely stated belief that some men, described by Eliot Slater as displaying 'a feebleness of will and purpose', were predisposed to break down under the stress of combat.[44] They also all saw combat fatigue as the outward expression of, and failure to master, fear. While the experience of industrialized warfare in the First World War had weakened the belief that battle would be exciting and enjoyable, and led to an increased expectation that most combatants would experience fear, it was still expected that the majority of servicemen would control this emotion. As one author argued, 'even the bravest of men can feel afraid. The only difference between a brave man and a coward is the fear of the one is controlled whilst the fear of the other is uncontrolled.'[45] Fear in battle might be ordinary; the expression of fear through war neurosis was not.

Some of the conditions under which men were expected to serve seem to have been more likely than others to produce the symptoms of combat fatigue. The War Office estimated after the war that between 5 per cent and 30 per cent of all military casualties were psychiatric.[46] Following the retreat from Dunkirk in 1940 approximately 10 per cent of all casualties were found to be suffering from combat fatigue whilst approximately 14.6 per cent of soldiers evacuated from the combat zone in the first 16 days following the D-Day invasion of 1944 were psychiatric casualties.[47] The RAF used the pejorative term 'Lack of Moral Fibre' (LMF) to describe men who were rendered unable to fly or to perform combat duties effectively. The stigma of being declared LMF may have meant many men who were suffering from combat fatigue continued to fly, unwilling to be 'branded a coward' by admitting the extent of their illness.[48] For men in the army, however, the term 'combat fatigue' distinguished them from both civilians suffering with 'war nerves' and airmen displaying LMF. Conveying a sense of exhaustion rather than inadequacy, the very terminology used may have made it easier for men recalling their wartime experiences to reflect on fear felt under fire.

In the immediate post-war years, however, popular representations of combat only rarely included portrayals of fear. Instead, a stoic response to wartime conditions dominated the British war films, which were the most widely shared representation of the war in the first two post-war decades.[49] Films such *Reach for the Sky* (1956), *Carve Her Name with Pride* (1958) and *Dunkirk* (1958) took well-known individuals or events of the war and retold them in a manner which often re-inscribed them with a stoicism that effectively marginalized more fearful emotions.[50] The social, cultural and political shifts of the 1960s brought about a gradual change in the ways that fear appeared in popular representations of warfare. After Vietnam, and in response to the shifting terrain of gender politics and renegotiated models of masculinity, the archetypal soldier hero was no longer the fearless or phlegmatic character so visible in British and American war films of the 1940s and 1950s. The emphasis on the collective, on the duty of the individual to the wider community, so central to wartime films and still dominant in the immediate post-war period, was replaced by narratives that explored individual responses to warfare, and in particular to the conditions of battle.[51] In these representations, fear is normalized; it is the expected response of the individual caught up in conflict. In more recent representations of wartime combat such as *Atonement* (2001, 2007), *Saving Private Ryan* (1998) and *Band of Brothers* (2001), combatants typically articulate their fear but overcome it.[52] These representations of key European battles of the Second World War, Dunkirk and the D-Day landings, present audiences with the anguish and horror of combat yet ultimately frame this within a narrative that emphasizes the bravery and valour of the combatant, and the justness of their cause. While some veterans of these battles recorded on the 'People's War' website their memories in the language of the 1950s war films, one man for example using a gentle humour to recount the 1940 retreat to Dunkirk as a 'walk to the beach' which was 'not without incident as the Luftwaffe had taken a violent dislike to our presence and vented their spleen with some gentle bombing and strafing', others drew on the more graphic and visceral images of battle associated with the later representations.[53]

One veteran of the D-Day assault on Juno beach described a shattered assault craft as 'a bloody mess' with 'two bodies ... hanging from the side, where they had been blown by the force of the explosion'. He went on to detail the horror and 'carnage' of those landings, describing his feelings as 'like a coiled spring' and 'a bit numb and scared, and not ashamed to admit it'. This brief mention of fear, however, is contained within an overall focus on the valour of the men under fire, who fought their way up the beach and eventually through Normandy.[54] Similarly a 19-year-old infantryman recalled being 'so scared I got down on my hands and knees and then onto my stomach', but concluded his memoir of D-Day and its aftermath by describing his pride at being a part of the operation.[55] Others utilized the stoic discourse; a radio operator parachuted into Normandy on 5 June 1944 described a village that was 'on fire, end to end', commenting laconically that 'Things were a bit uncertain, to say the least'.[56] As a psychiatrist writing in 1944 reflected, men who were part of an active, successful invasion force were perhaps more able than those who came under fire in a military retreat to contain their individual fear within the wider, shared emotions of excitement, belief in victory and shared high morale.[57] Men recalling their participation in the Normandy landings some 70 years later were able to draw on the dominant cultural memory of D-Day which recognized fear and horror, but framed these within a wider emphasis on bravery, sacrifice and victory in a just cause.

Veterans of Dunkirk were less able to draw on a discourse that emphasized victory and valour than those who recounted their experiences of the Normandy landings. Despite Dunkirk's iconic position in British popular culture, which foregrounds the snatching of a victory from defeat, and the role of the flotilla of 'little ships' which assisted the Royal Navy in the evacuation of troops from the Dunkirk beaches, the cultural memory of Dunkirk has long been less secure, and more open to contestation, than the memory of D-Day. As Penny Summerfield has argued, 'the construction of the memory of Dunkirk ... was full of contradictions and differences of emphasis.'[58] Contributors to the 'People's War' website who had been present at the retreat were less able to utilize the language of victory and sacrifice than contributors recalling D-Day. In contrast, the Dunkirk retreat was described variously as 'a tiring and nerve straining business' and a 'nightmare', while fear was again described via a description of its physical symptoms, with men describing 'feeling pretty shaken' when bombers passed over and 'fear and helplessness' leaving men on the beach 'speechless'.[59] Unlike the D-Day stories, men recalling Dunkirk emphasized the chaos and panic on the beaches as they waited for rescue. Arthur Turner, a young military policeman whose job it had been to maintain order on the beachhead, recalled trying to board a Navy ship towards the end of the evacuation with the words 'that's when the panic started'.[60] Stories like Arthur's, which often emphasized the patience and resilience of men waiting for evacuation under bombardment, almost always included descriptions of chaos and confusion. Eric Cottam, who was to lose his left foot and his right leg in the retreat, commented that 'this war was not the one I'd imagined'. He continued:

> I had pictures of an entire command with trucks, troops, vehicles, tanks and so on. We couldn't see a thing in the street so we didn't know what was going on ... we were isolated from the battalion, so we were on our own, obeying orders to go here, there and everywhere.[61]

For many of the men who experienced the retreat at Dunkirk the dominant narrative of the 'little ships', and a victory snatched from defeat, could not effectively contain their memories of fear, uncertainty and chaos.[62] Although the actions of individual men and the stoicism of troops waiting on the beaches were often reflected upon, the sense of pride in a worthwhile sacrifice, so present in the D-Day stories, was almost entirely absent.

The ways that individuals with memories of these three signal events of the war wrote about fear appear to be shaped as much by the ways these events are remembered and represented today as by individual experience. While veterans of D-Day were able to describe fear within a wider narrative that emphasized valour and victory, descriptions of Dunkirk were often marked by a bitterness and a sense that the soldiers present at the retreat were let down by a lack of organization and poor planning by the military and political elites. Both groups of military veterans, however, were able to describe fear in battle without undermining an overall sense in most narratives of the bravery and determination displayed by combatants under fire. In contrast, veterans recalling their experiences of aerial bombardment were far less able to describe any fear they may have felt. Without access to the language of combat fatigue during the war, and widely remembered as displaying stoicism in the post-war years, those recalling life under bombardment often emphasized humour, fortitude and collectivity rather than fear, terror and horror in their stories.

Conclusion

The stories recorded on the 'People's War' website are part of the 'cultural circuit', the model of cultural production and consumption which sees meaning-making as an ongoing process, in which consumers of products and texts, such as those which convey the meanings of the Second World War in twenty-first-century Britain, are both active 'decoders' and producers of meaning. The veterans who submitted stories to the website were both responding to representations of the war that were already in circulation, and becoming part of cultural production themselves. The BBC had the stated aim of 'turning the audience into content generators', drawing on the stories entered on the website in dramatized documentaries about Dunkirk and D-Day broadcast in 2004.[63] Stories on the website, though, were not only shaped by the experiences being recounted there, but by public representations of the war that were already in existence. While military veterans had some access to representations of the war that showed Dunkirk and D-Day as events in which most combatants felt but overcame fear, civilians who experienced bombing had far less access to such representations. Already lacking the language of 'combat fatigue' as a means of articulating and containing fear under bombardment, civilian veterans' stories were also limited by dominant understandings of Britain in the Blitz. When suicide bombers attacked the London transport network in July 2005, comparisons between the attack and the Blitz of 1940/1 were immediate and omnipresent. Sir Ian Blair, then Metropolitan Police Commander, commented that 'if London can survive the Blitz, then it can survive four miserable events like this', whilst the *Daily Mirror* called on its readers to 'adopt the famous Blitz spirit', quoting Minister for Veterans Doug Touhig's call to 'keep up the spirit' which was shown in the 'grim days between 1939 and 1945'.[64] Although there were representations of the Blitz in circulation that did give voice to civilian fear, these were overwhelmed by celebrations of 'the Blitz spirit'.

Although websites like the 'People's War' enable individuals to record memories of the war which may not 'fit' comfortably with the dominant cultural memory, wider social processes of remembering are at work that limit both the language with which these are expressed and the very act of expressing them. The Second World War is a particularly powerful memory in Britain, one that remains important to constructions of national identity and a national past. Mobilized time and again as a symbol of what it means to be British, to position oneself as outside of this cultural memory is to position oneself outside of a still dominant, though increasingly contested, sense of British national identity. Whilst the way that the war has been remembered and represented has of course changed since 1945, shifting from the 'people's war' of the 1940s to the Churchillian rhetoric of the 1980s to an embodiment of the values associated with the 'war on terror' of the early twenty-first century, it has retained its central role in British national history and identity.[65] The discourse of a 'good war' has remained central to the shifting cultural memory of the war throughout the post-war period. This 'good war', it appears, provides a limited space through which military veterans can express their fear in battle, containing this within discourses of military heroism and a just cause so prevalent during the war and today, but less space for recognition of the fear that the 'stoical' British civilian may have experienced under bombardment.

The author would like to thank Hazel Croft and Rebecca Searle for comments on this chapter.

Notes

1   BBC, 'WW2 People's War. An archive of World War Two memories – written by the people, gathered by the BBC'. Available online at http://www.bbc. co.uk/history/ww2peopleswar/.

2   For discussion of some other public 'sites of memory' see Peniston-Bird, C., 'The people's war in personal testimony and bronze', Houghton, F., 'The "Missing Chapter"', and Watson, J. K., 'Total war and total anniversary', Chapters 4, 8 and 9 respectively in this volume.

3   Nora, P. (1989), 'Between Memory and History. Les lieux de memories'. *Representations*, 26, 7–25.

4   Winter, J. (2006), *Remembering War. The Great War Between Memory and History*. New Haven: Yale University Press.

5   See, for example, http://www.plymouthdata.info/Second%20World%20 War-1941-Blitz.htm and http://www.thejwarrens.pwp.blueyonder.co.uk/ bathblitz/blitzroll.htm/.

6   See Baert, P. (1992), *Time, Self and Social Being*. Aldershot: Avebury; Giddens, A. (1991), *Modernity and Self Identity*. Oxford: Polity.

7   Benkler, Y. (2006), *The Wealth of Networks. How Social Production Transforms Markets and Freedoms.* New Haven, CT: Yale University Press, 15.

8   Anderson, B. (1983), *Imagined Communities.* London: Verso; Samuel, R. (1994), *Theatres of Memory. Volume One: Past and Present in Contemporary Culture.* London: Verso.

9   Drinot, P. (2011), 'Website of memory: The war of the Pacific (1879–84) in the global age of YouTube'. *Memory Studies,* 4(4), 370–85.

10   Erikson, T. H. (2007), 'Nationalism and the internet'. *Nations and Nationalism,* 13(1), 1–17. Here p. 1.

11   Duncan, C. and Wallach, A. (1980), 'The universal survey museum', *Art History,* 3(4), 448–69.

12   http://www.virtualwall.org/.

13   http://www.guardian.co.uk/commentisfree/2009/jun/06/dday-anniversary-second-world-war/.

14   BBC, 'WW2 People's War': 'Project'. Some stories were edited before being entered on the site, but there were no changes made to fact or content.

15   BBC, 'WW2 People's War': 'Storygathering'.

16   Ashplant, T. G., Dawson, G. and Roper, M., 'The politics of war memory and commemoration: contexts, structures and dynamics', in T. Ashplant, G. Dawson and M. Roper (eds) (2000), *The Politics of War Memory and Commemoration.* London: Routledge, 3–86.

17   Spray, B., 'A matter of conscience', BBC, 'WW2 People's War'.

18   Rose, S.O. (2003), *Which Peoples War? National Identity and Citizenship in Wartime Britain, 1913–1945.* Oxford: Oxford University Press, 1.

19   For recent studies of the expression of fear in wartime see Bell, A. (2009), 'Landscapes of fear: wartime London 1939-1945'. *Journal of British Studies,* 48(1), 153–75; Bourke, J. (2005), *Fear: A Cultural History.* London: Virago; Pattinson, J. (2007), *Behind Enemy Lines: Gender, Passing and the Special Operations Executive in the Second World War.* Manchester: Manchester University Press; Roper, M. (2009), *The Secret Battle: Emotional Survival in the Great War.* Manchester: Manchester University Press.

20   B. Holbrook, 'No medals for us'. Imperial War Museum (IWM) Department of Documents (DD), 95/27/1, 76.

21   Captain T. H. Flanagan, 'Tom's War', IWM, DD, 87/19/1, 109.

22   *In Which We Serve* (dir. David Lean, 1943). The sailor who leaves his station during an attack, played by Richard Attenborough, is fatally injured in a later attack, but is reassured by his Commanding Officer (Noel Coward) that he will tell his parents that he 'did his duty' before he died.

23   Monsarrat, N. (1951), *The Cruel Sea.* London: Cassell. For a discussion of the film adaptation of the novel see Summerfield, P. (2011), 'Divisions at sea: class, gender, race and nation in maritime films of the Second World War'. *Twentieth Century British History,* 22(3), 330–53.

24   Noakes, L. (1997), 'Making histories: Experiencing the Blitz in London's

museums in the 1990's', in M. Evans and K. Lunn (eds), *War and Memory in the Twentieth Century*. Oxford: Berg.

25 *Saving Private Ryan* (dir. Steven Spielberg, 1998), *Band of Brothers* (TV Mini Series, HBO, 2001).

26 See Grayzel, S. R. (2011), *At Home and Under Fire. Air Raids and Culture in Britain From the First World War to the Blitz*. Cambridge: Cambridge University Press.

27 Fuller, J. F. C. (1923), *The Reformation of War*. London: Hutchinson, 150; Stokes, S. (1935), *The Air Gods' Parade*. London: Arthur Barron, 121.

28 Harrisson, T. (1978), *Living Through the Blitz*. Harmondsworth: Penguin, 41; Bennett, J. F. (1940), *Psychological Casualties in Air Raids and Their First Aid Treatment*. London: S.P.C.K., 14.

29 See Bourke, (2005), 237–8; Air-Commodore Cherlton, *War Over England*, cited by Fuller, J. F. C. (1937), 'The air defence of London and our great cities'. *The English Review*. 64(2), 168–81. Here p. 168.

30 *The Times*, 2 February 1937, 13; *London Can Take It!* (dir. Harry Watt and Humphrey Jennings, 1940).

31 *The Times*, 27 September 1940, 6.

32 *Daily Mirror*, 21 March 1941, 1.

33 Mass Observation (MO), File Report (FR) 447, *Weekly Report from Mass Observation*. 3; *The Times*, 19 September 1940, 2.

34 MO, FR 447, *Weekly Report from Mass-Observation*. 3; Walker, H. (1940), 'Panic states in civilians'. *British Medical Journal*, 1 June, 887.

35 Panter-Downes, M. (1972), *London War-Notes, 1939-1945*. London: Longman, 105. For more on citizenship and aerial bombardment see Noakes, L. and Grayzel, S. R. (2012), 'Defending the home(land): gendering civil defence from the First World War to the war on terror', in A. Carden-Coyne (ed.), *Gender and Conflict Since 1914*. Basingstoke: Palgrave Macmillan, 29–40.

36 Allwright, A., 'The age of fear', BBC, 'WW2 People's War'. For this contributor's memoir, see Allwright, A. (2002), *A Stranger and Afraid*. Bristol: BeWrite Books. Jones, T., 'Excitement and fear as a young lad', BBC, 'WW2 People's War', has a similar narrative structure.

37 Styon, J., 'Air raids in London', BBC, 'WW2 People's War'.

38 Lawrence, M., 'My aunty Mary's wartime memoirs', BBC, 'WW2 People's War'.

39 Winter, J. (1999), 'Kinship and remembrance in the aftermath of the Great War', in J. Winter and E. Sivan (eds), *War and Remembrance in the Twentieth Century*. Cambridge: Cambridge University Press, 40–60.

40 Sevareid, E. (1946), *Not So Wild A Dream*, cited in Stansky, P. (2007), *The First Day of the Blitz*. New Haven, CT: Yale University Press, 51.

41 Noakes (1997).

42 For discussion of PTSD, see Hunt, N. (2010), *Memory, War and Trauma*. Cambridge: Cambridge University Press.

43 *The Times*, 1 January 1940.

44 Slater, E. (1943), 'The neurotic constitution. A statistical study of two thousand neurotic soldiers', *The Journal of Neurology and Psychiatry.* 6(1 and 2), 3–16. Here p. 1.

45 Copeland, N. (1942), *Psychology and the Soldier*. London, p.75, cited in Bourke (2005), 211.

46 Cited in Jones, E. and Wessely, S. (2001), 'Psychiatric battle casualties: An intra and interwar comparison', *British Journal of Psychiatry*, 178, 242–7. Here p. 243.

47 Ibid., 244.

48 Cited in Shephard, B, (2000), *War of Nerves. Soldiers and Psychiatrists 1914–1994*. London: Cape, 286. See Shephard for a discussion of the difficulty of attaining accurate figures for levels of combat fatigue in Bomber Command, 286–7.

49 Eley, G. (2001), 'Finding the people's war: British collective memory and World War II', *American Historical Review*, 106(3), 818–38.

50 *Reach for the Sky* (dir. Lewis Gilbert, 1956); *Carve Her Name With Pride* (dir. Lewis Gilbert, 1958); *Dunkirk* (dir. Leslie Norman, 1958). It should be noted of course that some representations of the war in the 1950s could be understood as producing a critique of stoicism. *Bridge on the River Kwai* (dir. David Lean, 1957) and *The Cruel Sea* (dir. Charles Frend, 1953) are of especial interest here.

51 This can be seen most clearly in the body of 'Vietnam films' produced in Hollywood in the 1970s and 1980s, which often combined a vaguely critical perspective on US foreign policy with a sympathy for the young men who were sent to war. For an interesting critique of these films see Klein, M. (1990), 'Historical memory, film and the Vietnam era', in L. Dittmar and G. Michaud (eds), *From Hanoi to Hollywood: The Vietnam War in Hollywood Film*. New Brunswick: Rutgers University Press, 19–40.

52 McEwan, I. (2001), *Atonement*, London: Jonathan Cape; *Atonement* (dir. Joe Wright, 2007); *Saving Private Ryan* (dir. Steven Spielberg, 1998); *Band of Brothers* (TV Mini Series, HBO: 2001).

53 Middleton, R., 'To arms!', BBC, 'WW2 People's War'.

54 Clarke, R. A., 'My D-Day', BBC, 'WW2 People's War'.

55 Littlar, B., 'Bob Littlar's D-Day: 2nd Battalion King's Shropshire Light Infantry', BBC, 'WW2 People's War'.

56 Gray, C., 'D-Day, Normandy, 1944: Burying the dead', BBC, 'WW2 People's War'.

57 Anderson, C. (1944), 'Psychiatric casualties from the Normandy beach head', *The Lancet*, 12 August, 218–21. Here p. 218.

58 Summerfield, P. (2010), 'Dunkirk and the popular memory of Britain at war, 1940-1958', *Journal of Contemporary History*, 45(4), 788–811.

59 Davey, A., 'Falling back to Dunkirk: 7th MAC British Expeditionary Force', BBC, 'WW2 People's War'; Barker, F., 'Five days at Dunkirk', BBC, 'WW2 People's War'.

60 Turner, A., 'Arthur Turner's Dunkirk', BBC, 'WW2 People's War'.

61 Cottam, C., 'Eric Cottam's Dunkirk', BBC, 'WW2 People's War'.

62 For the creation of the 'Dunkirk myth' see Priestley's BBC Radio broadcast of 5 June 1940. Priestley, J. B. (1940), *Postscripts*. London: Heinemann, 1–4.

63 'Project', BBC, 'WW2 People's War' *Dunkirk* and *D-Day 6.6.1944* were both originally broadcast on the BBC in 2004 as part of the commemoration of the Second World War.

64 *Daily Express*, 9 July 2005; *Daily Mirror*, 9 July 2005.

65 See Hurd, G. (ed.) (1984), *National Fictions: World War Two in British Film and Television*, London: BFI for a discussion of the ways that this memory has shifted over the post-war period.

Key Texts

Ashplant, T. G., Dawson, G. and Roper, M. (eds) (2000), *The Politics of War Memory and Commemoration*. London: Routledge.

Bourke, J. (2005), *Fear: A Cultural History*. London: Virago.

Drinot, P. (2011), 'Website of memory: The war of the Pacific (1879-84) in the global age of YouTube'. *Memory Studies*, 4(4).

Eley, G. (2001), 'Finding the people's war: film, British collective memories and World War II'. *The American Historical Review*, 106(3).

Grayzel, S. R. (2011), *At Home and Under Fire. Air Raids and Culture in Britain From the First World War to the Blitz*. Cambridge: Cambridge University Press.

Harrisson, T. (1978), *Living Through the Blitz*. Harmondsworth: Penguin.

Hunt, N. (2010), *Memory, War and Trauma*. Cambridge: Cambridge University Press.

Hurd, G. (ed.) (1984), *National Fictions: World War Two in British Film and Television*. London: BFI.

Nora, P. (1989), 'Between memory and history. Les lieux de memoire'. *Representations*, 26.

Priestley, J. B. (1940), *Postscripts*. London: Heinemann.

Rose, S. O. (2003), *Which People's War? National Identity and Citizenship in Wartime Britain, 1939-1945*. Oxford: Oxford University Press.

Shephard, B. (2000), *War of Nerves. Soldiers and Psychiatrists 1914-1994*. London: Cape.

Summerfield, P. (2010), 'Dunkirk and the popular memory of Britain at war, 1940-1958', *Journal of Contemporary History*, 45(4).

Winter, J. (1984), *Remembering War. The Great War Between Memory and History*. New Haven, CT: Yale University Press.

CHAPTER FOUR

The people's war in personal testimony and bronze

Sorority and the memorial to The Women of World War II[1]

Corinna M. Peniston-Bird

Sixty years after the end of the war, a memorial to The Women of World War II was unveiled in Whitehall. It offers 'an abstract interpretation of the contribution of the women to the war efforts' [sic], depicting 'the hats, coats, handbags, overalls, gas masks and other women's attire of the time'.[2] The memorial is 'abstract' because this clothing is uninhabited, it hangs, discarded, on a plinth. The description makes no allusion to the fact that the 17 representations of 'women's attire of the time' include the uniforms of the three auxiliary services, as well as a variety of civilian roles.[3] The controversy over this remit and design lasted the eight years from inception to unveiling, and beyond.[4] Yet the memorial draws upon British memories of service and the Home Front, in which the concept of the 'people's war' – defined by Angus Calder as 'the sense that rich and poor, civilians and fighters, were "all in it together", that privilege was or should be in abeyance and that even conscripted effort had a voluntary character' – remains a dominant historical discourse.[5] In retrospective personal testimonies, innumerable accounts subscribe to the construction of the war as a period when the whole nation voluntarily united in defence of Britain and its values, and when the contribution of the Home Front was as significant as that of the military.[6] The memorial emphasized a collective identity based on gender, however, not role or nationhood. This focus proved problematic for members of one constituency in particular: female veterans. The contention over the implication of parity of service in the auxiliary forces and on the Home Front contributes to the on-going historical debate over the limitations of wartime collective solidarity and reveals the complexities of the gendered hierarchy of status of wartime roles in shifting post-war constructions of the conflict.[7]

The impetus around the turn of this century, to memorialize before all survivors are dead and the young do not know what they are to remember, offers a pathway into the evolution of the construct of the 'people's war'. This chapter explores the archives of the charity 'The Memorial to Women in World War II Fund', established in 1998,[8] for 'the promotion of good citizenship by the provision and maintenance of a memorial to commemorate the contribution made by women in wartime occupations during World War II.'[9] These include four large boxes containing letters written to the charity by men and women, individuals and interest groups from across the world; and the letters written by the charity in response, and regarding fund raising, planning and profile-raising activities.[10] The charity cannot be faulted on its sincere commitment to the project, its resilience and creativity when encountering repeated obstacles, and its willingness to enter into dialogue with its critics, with some success.[11] Thus this complex history left a rich archive. Women's memoirs were also donated to the Imperial War Museum Documents Department from an associated programme entitled 'Experiences'.[12] On the themes of war service and sorority, I also draw upon the narratives of the BBC's 'People's War' website. Between June 2003 and January 2006, the BBC asked the public to contribute their memories of the war to an archive that finally comprised 47,000 stories.[13] These provide a relevant counterpoint as they overlap with the period when many of the letters were written to the charity. The past and the present met when participants in the war recalled their memories for a present-day audience, and the public and the private collided in the battle over what the memorial should remember, and how.

The origins and development of the project

The controversy surrounding the memorial is entwined with the original vision for it. The inspiration came from a veteran of the Auxiliary Territorial Service (ATS). In February 1997, Helen Jean Crawley (née Cameron) (1925–2010) wrote to Major David Robertson about the dearth of memorials to British servicewomen. Resident in Canada from 1957, Crawley still considered herself 'a daughter of England'. She had served with the 93rd Search Light Regt R.A. between 1942 and 1946, 'the only searchlight regt in the world in 1942 managed entirely by women, and

I'm so very proud to have served'.[14] Crawley was convinced that, 50 years since the end of the war, there should be a memorial to the British service-women and nurses 'who served and died for freedom'. She was inspired by the Canadian Brant County War Memorial Park, which houses a Cenotaph dedicated in 1933 and which was expanded in 1954 to commemorate the fallen of the Second World War and the Korean War.[15] The original design by Walter Seymour Allward, the sculptor of the Vimy Ridge Memorial in France (unveiled in 1936), had included a group of bronzes to represent 'Humanity', consisting of a wounded youth, a resolute mother, a figure praying and crippled field artillery. Insufficient funding prevented their completion, but the original intention was not forgotten. In September 1992 seven bronze statues were unveiled, commissioned from the Canadian sculptor Helen Granger Young.[16] Three male statues to the left of the cenotaph and the inscription 'They gave their lives for humanity' represent the men of the Canadian Navy, Army and Air Force. Four female statues to the right represent the parallel female organizations and a Nursing Sister of the Royal Canadian Medical Corps. The intention was to commemorate not only those who died but those who served.

Frustrated by the lack of any comparable memorial in Great Britain, Crawley launched a letter campaign. Her missives to the Queen, the Prime Minister, Tony Blair (Prime Minister at the time), and the Conservative MP Sir Edward Macmillan (Teddy) Taylor had not elicited encouraging replies, but in 1997 she wrote to Major Robertson. After retiring from the Royal Artillery in 1989, Robertson had taken up an appointment with the Civil Service, working for the Ministry of Defence in York. In 1993 he had been asked to advise on the protocol for a Regimental Dinner Night that an ATS veteran, who had served with the Royal Artillery on the Anti-Aircraft Batteries, was organizing as a reunion. This reunion was a huge success, and Robertson became President of the Royal Artillery Association Branch for the Auxiliary Territorial Service whose members, like Crawley, had served with the Anti-Aircraft Command (Ack-Ack), and who met regularly until dwindling numbers brought the reunions to an end in 2004.[17] Jean Crawley's letter fell on fertile ground; Robertson was intrigued by the fact that there were no war memorials in the United Kingdom specifically dedicated to women.[18]

Initially Crawley and Robertson shared the same vision.[19] A fact-sheet disseminated to garner support stated:

> It is intended to commission three bronze sculptures, standing about 5'3", depicting each of the Women's Services from World War 2. These will be mounted together on a suitable stone base with an inscription to all the Women who did so much towards that blessed victory. An estimate for the commission is about £75,000, and it is hoped to have it sited somewhere in Central London.[20]

Four factors changed the original plan. The first stemmed from the research conducted to confirm Crawley's complaint, in which Robertson discovered that, although female casualties were included on British war memorials, 'there were far more women involved with the War effort than the Armed Services, in fact ... some 7 million, rather than the 640,000 Ladies from the Services.'[21] Britain was the first country to conscript women in 1941 into both industry and the auxiliary forces. Between 1942 and 1945 nearly 125,000 recruits were called up into the women's auxiliary services, serving alongside volunteers. Over two and a half million more women were brought into or returned to the work force compared with 1939 figures.[22] The numbers involved made Robertson question whether the memorial should only represent a minority or be more inclusive. He put the expansion of the remit to the Ack Ack Command Association, who agreed that the memorial should acknowledge the work of all the women of the war, not merely those in uniform.[23]

The second factor reinforcing this shift was the reaction received by the Memorial Fund Charity from the general public, public figures and the media. From 1998, it was inundated by letters from men and women advocating the inclusion of women in every role imaginable, including the NAAFI, the Land Army and the Timber Corps, the Royal Observer Corps, the Police, Fire, and Ambulance Services, Air Raid Precautions, the Women's Voluntary Service, the Air Transport Auxiliary, the Junior Air Corps, the Girls Training Corps, the River Emergency Service, munitions workers, railway workers, nurses and doctors, prisoners of war and internees, carers for husbands or sons wounded in service, and those in reserved occupations exempted from conscription owing to the significance of their occupation to the war effort, such as members of the civil service. Individuals also wrote on behalf of female relatives defined by experience not role. The veteran N-L- wrote from Dorset:

> [M]y ex ATS friends and I are so pleased about the memorial. Don't forget the young mothers struggling with babies, rationing, absence of men folk and the bombing. They were true heroines. My mother had three of us in the Forces, one just started work, two at school and two babies.[24]

This desire for public recognition can be placed in the context of the momentum for wider commemoration fostered by the anniversaries of 1995 and 2000, the latter with a particular focus on the Home Front; by the sense that time was running out if women who had lived through the war were to see their contributions acknowledged; and by the evolution of the hierarchies of remembrance of service: it was not until 1998 that Bevin Boys marched on Remembrance Day and not until 2000 that Land Girls did.[25] As a growing number of constituencies received recognition for their roles in the war, the desire for acknowledgement of other roles grew, with a concomitant sense of entitlement to inclusion in the celebration of service within the war effort and resentment at unjust omission.

The third factor was the impetus the Charity rapidly gained beyond its original instigators. Hugh Bayley (MP for York and a vice-patron of the Charity) raised an Early Day Motion in the House of Commons (no 351, 27 October 1997) which attracted 280 signatures from across the House. By the beginning of 1998, the Princess Royal had agreed to become vice-patron and Betty Boothroyd, then Speaker of the House of Commons, to be a patron. By June 1998, the Charity had raised around £10,000.[26] It was decided to hold an open competition with a design brief to acknowledge the part *all* women played on *all* fronts, placing no emphasis on any one occupation, service or individual. The judging panel included Judith Collins, Head of Modern Sculpture at the Tate Gallery, the sculptor Phillip King, the then President of the Royal Academy, and James Butler, another eminent sculptor.[27] This composition ensured the choice would be made on the basis of artistic merit, rather than the expectations of the instigators or interested parties. The panel awarded the commission to two sculptors, combining the plinth by John Mills and the top piece by Anthony Stones, which, like Mills's rejected statue, depicted a woman and children in an air raid.[28] This version was never to be erected.[29] The Charity was inundated with complaints as soon as the winning combination was publicized.

It was not this public response which proved decisive for the final design. When the artwork and maquette were submitted to the City of Westminster Council for planning permission, the Public Art Advisory Panel (meeting on 29 January 2002) agreed with one of the criticisms the design had provoked: that the top piece favoured one organization – anti-aircraft precautions – and that the two sculptures sat uncomfortably as a composition. They recommended that a re-submission be made of Mills's plinth alone. The final factor in the shift from the original figurative vision was thus on the basis of artistic merit. As Robertson wrote to one of the critics, 'Whilst you may find the artwork unexciting I can assure you a statue of three servicewomen on top of a plinth, which I personally find admirable, would fail to pass mustard [sic] on any Planning Application as unimaginative.'[30] Stones's design was dropped and the plinth was levelled off with a simple geometric design. At the Major Planning Applications Committee meeting on 25 July 2002, Westminster City Council supported a location in Whitehall, despite opposition to the design from their art panel. The final decision was made on 20 August 2003.[31] Various sagas followed, involving bids for funding, planning applications, siting problems, and public campaigns for and against the design. Eight years after Crawley's initial letter, the 'plinth' memorial was finally unveiled by the Queen on 9 July 2005, the day before the joint VE and VJ celebrations.

Controversy

In many ways the plinth achieves its goals. It respects the location, its scale clearly subservient to the Cenotaph, its geometric levelling-off deliberately reminiscent of Lutyens's design. It avoids the perils of over-specificity and can thus claim inclusivity – for example, the nurse's uniform suggests the role, but not any specific organization. Bronze figures would have raised the issues of inclusivity and selection, the challenge of aesthetics, of expense (at £25,000 each) and of originality in an area already replete with statuary.[32] The final design avoids prioritizing any one service over another: the viewer can approach the memorial from any angle and is drawn to walk around it, with no sense of any suggested hierarchy. Its message of selfless collective service is emphasized by the fact that the hooks bearing the clothing are invisible, Mills expressing thus his belief that women had made these contributions with little external support.[33] It draws upon resonant wartime and peacetime constructions of the 'people's war', particularly regarding the importance of every contribution to the war effort. Its focus remained consistent after the initial shift to the representation of the latter, and, despite external pressures, the project was not reconfigured to include the women of the First World War, or to foreground the Queen Mother, who died in 2002.[34] In brief, the memorial fulfilled the remit set by the charity in 1998. Why, then, was it so controversial?

First, the support for the project at each stage must be acknowledged, as evidenced by the correspondence,[35] the stream of donations, the willingness of individuals and groups to fight for the memorial, for example by berating Westminster Council,[36] and requests for tickets to the unveiling.[37] To give a sense of the range and scale involved, in the consultations with the Council in July 2002 support came from English Heritage, the Westminster Society, the British Land Army Society, the Women's Auxiliary Air Force Association, Queen Alexandra's Royal Army Nursing Corps Association, the First Aid Nursing Yeomanry, as well as 35 letters of support from or on behalf of ex-servicewomen. Conversely, three individuals wrote five letters of complaint, advocating a memorial specifically for ex-servicewomen, and suggesting a separate memorial for 'semi or non-military personnel'.[38] The Women's Royal Army Corps Association (incorporating the ATS and QMAAC) found the explanatory texts ill-informed and patronizing. This had some justification: the description of the top figures of a female ARP warden protecting children was 'here is a woman in man's clothes, doing a man's job', and of the plinth, 'When the Women were called by their Country they came [forward in their millions] and did what was asked of them. Now the war is over they have hung up their war garments and returned from whence they came.'[39] Despite Robertson's best efforts, through the pages of *The Lioness*, the house journal of the WRAC Association, for example, opposition from the local branches of the Association persisted: some branches demanded (and received) their donations back on the ground that they felt they had been misled,[40] and the Association sent no representatives to the unveiling. Robertson defended Mills's design by suggesting that angry veterans were motivated by a false sense of their own superiority, pointing out that they had raised only £7000, although each penny had been appreciated, and that it was inappropriate to suggest that one contribution had more worth than any other.

The objections came in two main waves: when the combined design was first publicized in 2000, and again in 2004 when the successful 'plinth only' design gained publicity. Media coverage, in particular in *This England: the patriotic quarterly for all who love our green and pleasant land* (popular with the ex-pat community), the *Daily Telegraph*, the *Daily Mail*, Peri Langdale's film *Lest we Forget* (first aired in 2000; Langdale subsequently became a trustee), *Songs of Praise* for Remembrance Sunday in 2001, and Betty Boothroyd's fundraising on *Celebrity Who Wants to be a Millionaire?* (25 December 2002), also provoked veterans to put pen to paper.[41] One letter suggests the tone and range of these criticisms:

Dear Sir,

I do not know Mr John Mills or Mr Anthony Stones – indeed I do not want to know them. I can only hope they will never be allowed to construct another memorial – if this is the best they can do – they should get out before they mess up any others.

This memorial to women at war is utterly disgusting. I think we deserve to be remembered by something that depicts who and what we were – but to be remembered by a coat hanging on a peg! – I cannot understand how they reached such a stupid way to depict us.

As regards to the lady up above – messing about with the children – she could probably get home every night – we weren't that lucky. But *this* is a memorial to *us*, the women of the services – if he cannot think up something better than this – then get someone else for goodness sake.

It's ironical – soldiers, sailors and airmen all get statues that are deserving of them – *we* get the greatcoats on a peg. *We* also had a war – many of us on fighter Stations didn't exactly enjoy being bombed – we didn't either particularly enjoy the cold Nissen huts – didn't very much enjoy being miles away from nowhere – but we did it – and we pulled out all the stops to make *sure* we were good.

Get rid of these 2 characters – send them back to school – ideas, imagination, common sense – they don't possess any of these – *please* get cracking with a memorial worthy of all of us.

J.B.

PS The Canadians have a super memorial showing all 3 services – perhaps they could learn something from them.[42]

As this emphatic expression of outrage reveals, female military service was aligned to that of men and clearly distinguished from civilian contributions to the war effort. As suggested here, critics were inspired by the expectation of figurative representations of the women's services (with or without additional representation of civilian roles); they attacked explicit details of both designs, and the relationship between them; and they challenged the temerity of the Charity, the sculptors and Westminster City Council in believing that individuals of the wrong gender or age and without direct experience of World War II had the right to make choices on women's behalf.[43] Veterans were frustrated by their lack of influence, their inability to determine the outcome despite their sense of ownership over the memorial, and their awareness of how their community had responded to the design.

Parity of service?

I concentrate here on one category of complaint: the erosion of the difference between auxiliary and civilian contributions.

One of the most vociferous and energetic critics was Joy Bone, who had volunteered for the ATS in 1943 aged 17. Her main objection was the suggestion of parity of roles simply because the memorial commemorated women:

> A sharp distinction has always been made by officialdom between military and civilian status, and I see no reason why that distinction should cease to be observed now, simply because the service people involved are women and not men. *That* is why I am so critical of the chosen design.[44]

She denied that she or any other veterans considered their contributions superior, but emphasized the desire for recognition of their 'special *Military Status* – as had always been accorded to men in the Armed Forces without question. It has nothing whatsoever to do with the nature of the work they did in relation to the equally important war time duties undertaken by other women.'[45] Bone went so far as to lodge a formal complaint with the Equal Opportunities Commission, and declared in the *Daily Mail*, 'If approval *is* given for this particular memorial – the main purpose of which is to commemorate wartime civilians – it plainly should not be sited in Whitehall. Whitehall has long since been widely recognised as a strictly military zone.'[46] M-W- also raised the issue, not only in terms of memorials to men, but also the location:

> I do feel that women who served in the armed forces should be counted equal to the men who served, and should be recognised as such, with

their own memorial, and I would think that you [Robertson] as an ex-serving officer would understand this. We do not see in Whitehall a combined memorial to service men, miners, farm workers, munition workers etc, although all did a sterling job.[47]

The sense of discrimination on grounds of gender was emphasized by the departure from the precedent established by memorials to servicemen, a precedent strongly defined by the tropes of commemoration established in the wake of World War I, which tended to favour tradition over innovation.[48] The location was mobilized both by supporters of the monument and by its detractors, suggesting a shared understanding of its significance albeit with contradictory conclusions drawn. As the application for planning consent emphasized, Whitehall was not only 'the symbol and seat of political power', but also had powerful associations with war through the buildings, monuments and rituals located there.[49]

The final site for the location of the memorial lies between the Cenotaph and the statue of Field Marshall Earl Haig. It stands outside the Ministry of Defence, and adjacent to three World War II Field Marshals (Alanbrooke, Montgomery and Slim). The Cenotaph is of course more than a monument, it is also the focus of military parades, most significantly the Remembrance Day parade in November, which has itself been the source of disputes over appropriate inclusions and order. The Charity had to tread carefully around the issue of siting its Memorial near the Cenotaph: it sought to draw upon the Cenotaph's significance and resonance while avoiding the accusation of diminishing them. A site on the Victoria Embankment had been rejected because it 'would hold no particular significance to the invaluable work done by our Women ... In siting the Memorial we must also be very aware of inadvertently offending the sensitive and high profile issues of equality and gender.'[50] Conversely, according to Robertson, 'its placement in line with the Cenotaph is ideal because it is the only location that speaks a similar vocabulary'. A site near the heart of government, 'along one of the main processional routes, close to memorials of considerable commemorative significance reflects the degree of acknowledgement sought by the proposers.'[51] The organization thus sought enhancement of its message through proximity: status by association. The application for planning consent claimed there would be a valuable dialogue between the two memorials and their immediate surroundings. Robertson argued the Memorial could not be seen as being in competition with the Cenotaph: 'it is intended to complement it, in the same way as men and women are not "in competition", but are complementary.'[52]

The military connotations of the location, however, could not overcome the reservations expressed by correspondents challenging what they perceived as the gender discrimination of Mills's design; indeed they reinforced them. Correspondents asked whether the Army, Navy or Air Force would ever be commemorated in such a way; if there was a memorial to servicemen representing them by coats and hats (Dorothy Jones, the founder of the WAAF Association, wrote: 'We had a fight on our hands then to be accepted by the men as part of the Forces, what a pity we are still having that same fight to be accepted as ex-Service Women as against hats and coats'[53]); why women had to be associated with and represented by fashion ('let it be females, not old fashions on parade'[54]), and whether 'any British service men share their memorials with civilians'.[55] The latter was a rhetorical question: the answer in the affirmative is largely only in the case of those memorials – usually plaques, not figurative representations – which commemorate in the broadest possible terms all those of a specific locality who served, or gave their lives.[56]

The wartime hierarchy of service clearly maps onto post-war commemorative practices. Service continued to be valued, in ascending order of status, on a spectrum defined at one end by death and danger, proximity to action, degree of self-sacrifice, and overt and obvious connection to the war effort. For women, there is the added component of proximity to males ranked according to the same spectrum. It is no coincidence in this context that some of the most vociferous critics of the Memorial had served in the searchlight units or anti-aircraft batteries, acknowledged by historians as the closest women came to the combat end of the spectrum.[57] These women had a particularly strong sense of their unique proximity to action, their role in combating the enemy; and from 1941 they could have served in mixed batteries. Jutta Schwarzkopf argues that these 'mixed batteries formed a kind of enclave, not only within wartime society at large, but also inside the military', one whose members were intensely loyal to each other and who felt their roles separated them from those, particularly civilians, who could not possibly understand their experiences.[58] But for other critics also, while the discrepancies between commemorative practices honouring male and female service were challenged, the gulf between the experiences of auxiliaries and civilians was a matter of some emphasis.

Competitive sacrifice

Challenges to the design focused on the comparative sacrifices of comfort, liberty and home life, which H-H- also sought to see expressed as a visual hierarchy:

All ex-service personnel are well aware of the efforts of the non-military population who contributed to the war effort. The difference of course is that those of us who were in the services swore an oath of allegiance and were required to serve for the duration. The civilians, however worthy, were free to leave their positions if and when they chose and they were not governed by military regulations. Many were not required to leave their homes as we did, and live in some very difficult conditions. As well, the pay civilians received for their work was many times that of service personnel. Perhaps their efforts could be mentioned on the plinth.[59]

Such constructions did not recognize the restrictions on civilians (who were not free to leave their positions if and when they chose) and sought to emphasize the distinction between military and industrial service, despite conscription applying to both. Civilians and auxiliaries competed to establish who had experienced the greater hardships. A former subaltern in the ATS (R.A.) described how 'Our living conditions on the Essex mud marshes were appalling to say the least, as I am sure you know. No symbolism there, just gritty endurance and determination. I am proud to have been one of them.'[60] Conversely, civilians wrote inverting the hierarchy of suffering. E-F-, a civil servant in the Air Ministry in the war, wrote to draw Robertson's attention to the women in reserved occupations who had had to endure the bombing, and work long hours followed by civil defence duties – in E-F-'s case, guarding her place of work. She emphasized both danger and compulsion:

We were not allowed to join the forces or nursing services. We dodged the bombs, V1s and VIIs getting to and from work. Some were killed in heavy night air raids or spent sleepless nights in air raid shelters, but expected to be at our place of work the next day.
We had very little social life in the evenings, or at week-ends, while many of our sex were enjoying their postings in less hazardous places.[61]

S-R- also wrote to both Robertson and Boothroyd protesting against the objections by her local WRAC branch and defending the Charity's choice to include civilians. She covered similar themes as R-A-: long hours, danger, hard living conditions and lack of fun. Her narrative also draws attention to the theme of thwarted service: she had wanted to join the WAAF, but was sent instead to an aircraft factory, where her work had included making 'the bombs for the dam busters raid' – that is, work of significant importance to the war effort. Such narratives countered the implications of the opinion that civilian roles were reserved 'for those not suited for the armed services', emphasized compulsion (conscription was not unique to the military) and challenged the status of military uniform alone in determining the value of contributions to the war effort.[62]

We worked long hours 12 hr shifts and extra on a Saturday at this time when experiments were going on for the bouncing bomb. This is just an example of what 'civilians' did and we were often in danger when the factories were bombed. I appreciate that many ATS served on ACK ACK guns but *many* had only menial jobs – cooks – domestic office and general admin. What they don't seem to accept is that we *served* too.

We were billeted out, no choice of sometimes poor standard accommodation – paying for our board out of meagre wages – we were governed by strict conscript [rules] – we could not leave our job – only approved leave allowance per year – penalties if we went absent – and could be prosecuted. ... I had no choice and it is very hurtful that we 'civilians' are being made to feel like second class citizens by the attitude of the services.[63]

Some veterans agreed that civilians had had a harder time. As regular correspondent P-M-J- (ATS) wrote:

I know quite a few women are disappointed that the main figure is not a service person, but I think it is admirable that it is not. The public know what service personnel went through but one of the objects of the memorial is to remind them that civilians often suffered more than we did and I do my best to emphasize that.[64]

This competition for the hierarchy of suffering was not one that could be won, nor was it one that could successfully compete with the unassailable respect granted to male sacrifice in commemorative practices. One compromise solution was to suggest alternative designs, the favoured solution being four or five figures, three of whom represented the auxiliary services,[65] which constituted the design veterans felt, with some justification, they had been led to expect.[66] When the clothing was inhabited, the juxtaposition of uniformed and civilian women was acceptable, but when women were represented merely through their outer garments, this was perceived as a gross insult. It foregrounded gender in two ways: the representation of women through clothing and the departure from commemorative precedents. An alternative proposal was two separate memorials, in which case the civilians' memorial could also commemorate the men of the Home Front. As Joy Bone pointed out:

I seem to recall that men too, of all ages (who, for various reasons, were not accepted by the Armed Forces) were also to be found actively employed, jointly with such women, in exactly the same fields. Therefore, instead of proposing a memorial dedicated to *all* women (both military and non-military), it would surely make better sense to have a separate Memorial dedicated to all those, both men and women, within this second group?[67]

The latter did in fact already exist. A gender-blind memorial reading 'In gratitude to God and to commend to future generations the self-sacrifice of all those who served on the Home Front in the Second World War' had been unveiled in 2000 in the grounds of St Michael's Cathedral in Coventry, a telling location. The lack of explicit recognition of the contributions made by male civilians on the Home Front clearly remained a vexatious issue, however. In January 2001, for example, the Vice President of the Bevin Boys Association, Warwick Taylor, wrote to Robertson to suggest that, 'in all fairness', Bevin Boys should be 'equally named on such a memorial' which could be dedicated to 'the Men and Women of World War II'.[68] The Bevin Boys encompassed those men who were balloted (i.e. compulsory conscription), opted or volunteered for service in the mines, many of whom had a particular sense of grievance at their treatment both within and after the war. Elizabeth Grice described them in the *Daily Telegraph* as 'the misfits of the Second World War, never recognised as servicemen, often stigmatised as conscientious objectors and refused a war pension'.[69] More invisible still were the disparate men working on the Home Front: around five million men served in reserved occupations in 1940.[70] Their masculinity sits uncomfortably in the gendering of the Home Front, although specific roles (particularly those easily placed at the far end of the spectrum) are celebrated, for example in Mills's National Fire Fighters Memorial (1991/2003). The Bevin Boys Association's desire for inclusion on this memorial supports the contention that a memorial emphasizing *all* roles on the Home Front should not be gendered, and that there was a perception of greater parity of contribution between men and women on the Home Front than between women in the auxiliary forces and in civilian roles.

Sorority

Veterans critical of the memorial design had no issue with the alignment of all civilian efforts, male and female, but challenged collectivity when it was applied only to women, and in all possible roles. One explanation lies with the manner in which individuals experienced the sense of togetherness that was implied by Mills's plinth and that remains such an important feature of the 'people's war'. After all, as Robertson's daughter Alison Sanders (Head of Office for the MP Adrian Sanders, her husband) commented: 'quite why service women are more entitled to a memorial than women who worked in factories or fire watched or worked on the land is beyond me – don't people hark back to the war as a time when we ALL pulled together?'[71] Given the strength of that construction of the war, why did this design so offend the key constituency it had set out to represent by depicting sorority on a national scale?

A brief study of the use of the term camaraderie in memoirs on the BBC's 'People's War' website is telling in this context.[72] When civilians, both men and women, speak of wartime camaraderie, it tends to be in the context of the nation at war, or specifically the locality, encompassing all those sheltering from the bombs, or neighbours sharing food. Mildred Jean Winnan, who was in school during the war, recollected the hardships of rationing and commented:

[B]ut we survived, were never hungry and when I think back to those days, life in the community was great everyone was kind – generous with little they had – a neighbour with a big family would always help out someone who had run out of butter or the like. There was such a great feeling of cameradery [sic]. We are all in this together feeling.[73]

As Penny Summerfield has demonstrated, within the rhetoric of 'all in it together' there were strong bonds within specific civilian groups, between factory workers, for example, based as much on exclusion (disliking the other shift, for example) as inclusion.[74]

When female veterans speak of comradeship or camaraderie it is almost always in the context of their sisters in the same service, not the nation at war as a whole. Jean Crawley's autobiographical emphases are revealing in this context.[75] Crawley shared her memories with the Memory Project of the Dominion Institute Digital Archive, offering a narrative of selfless service. In this she drew upon and challenged the conventional hierarchies of service, which accord the combatant male the highest position. Hers is also a narrative of collective service, defined above all by the women with whom she served. She had served in the ATS 'with the British Army, Royal Artillery', a point of some pride. After basic training she was transferred to a searchlight unit in North London where, 'because we took over from the men, we had to do ... I'll go as far as to say, a better job than the men, because we were women'. Crawley's pride in women's contributions was repeated later in the interview:

When Mr. Churchill said, 'Let the women come forward', we did. And 640,000 women were in the British Armed Forces during the Second World War. I don't think we even thought about whether we would die or get injured or anything like that, we just hung up our aprons, covered our typewriters, said good-bye to our families and went to war. And we were very, very proud to be a part of it.

For Crawley, unlike Mills, the key to the story was when civilian clothing had been left behind, for in many ways the uniform never had been – hence the perception of the design which emphasized discarded wartime identities as insulting. She finished by returning to the camaraderie that had existed between the women who had served together and that persisted to the present day:

As I say, we laughed together, we cried together, we looked after each other and that bond has never left me. There was just something there ... like a bright light that held us all together.[76]

Crawley's narrative is not unique. C-R- also wrote to describe 'the happiest days of my life, with the wonderful girls I met'.[77] In the letters written by individuals to the Charity, the theme of female friendships features strongly: individuals and their places of origin are listed by name, casualties and friends lost to time and space are remembered on appropriate occasions, and, as the reunions and cross references in the correspondence suggest, many friends had clearly remained in touch. H-H-, who wrote from Namibia, recalled:

> We were a wonderful group of women, mostly in late teens or early twenties, with a wonderful spirit of caring for each other. There were no quarrels, unkindness or spitefulness, I am so proud of the fact that I was one of this group and though I don't think I was a good soldier, too bolshie, I never have regretted that I was one of the Auxiliary Specialists Women Auxiliary Army Service.[78]

The theme of sorority also pervades the reminiscences in the Experiences collection: in contrast with the narratives sent to the Charity, these are more detailed, and often told for humorous effect. Together these sources suggest that, for servicewomen, in common with their male counterparts, the sense of a collective endeavour in war came from the camaraderie of joint service, and sorority from shared experience within their force. Their gender was not insignificant in this context, but their role was more so, an identification which the memorial challenged.

Conclusion

Women's appropriation of the term comradeship to describe relationships in their wartime organizations is one which has received some attention in the context of World War I and its aftermath – for example in Janet Watson's works, and Janet Lee's writing on sisterhood in the First Aid Nursing Yeomanry – when women drew upon the growing public rhetoric on male comradeship as a defining, redeeming experience of the war.[79] The BBC testimonies speak to its longevity, its continued appropriation by civilians of both sexes fighting their war on the Home Front, and by female veterans. But the camaraderie experienced within the ATS, WRNS and WAAF was located within that specific context. This should not be over-emphasized: women, like their male counterparts, were civilians in uniform and maintained peacetime relationships, as well as forging new ones in the forces. But as Lisa Handler discovered in her work on sororities as gender strategy, 'by seeing their sisterhood as an exceptional form of female friendship, sorority members separate themselves from women outside the sorority.'[80] The responses to Mills's memorial design reveal how the 'togetherness' of the war effort was experienced by different constituencies. It is not that the sense of exclusivity challenged the notion of 'all in it together', but the understandings of the boundaries of the imagined community of the 'all' were not necessarily national, nor for that matter gender-inclusive.[81] Furthermore, in the competition for public acknowledgement and appreciation, despite the rhetoric of parity of service, the notion of the 'people's war' reinforced the vying for placement within a status hierarchy defined largely by conventional warfare (such as proximity to the enemy), precisely because of the range of roles of relevance to the war effort it had encompassed.

The heart of the controversy over the 'hats and coats' design lay in the ways in which it claimed and represented parity of service between civilians and military personnel, and how that theme was bisected by that of gender.[82] As the Friends of War Memorial's Trustees stated, 'the iconography proposed for the memorial is unlikely to be representative of the self-image of women who served (in whatever capacity) in the war, or to accurately reflect the impact of their experiences for other generations and for the future'.[83] For some women, the memorial neither sent an accurate message to the future, nor did it represent their past: 'You have demeaned us and trivialized what we did. It has taken fifty seven years to get to this point and by betraying us, you and the people who have decided on this design have made it totally worthless.'[84] Despite its aspirations, the memorial to the Women of World War II did not set in bronze *all* women's experience of the war.

Notes

1   This paper is dedicated to Amelie Kuroski and Isabell Peniston-Bird, cousins representing nations on either side of the conflict commemorated in this memorial.

2   *Women of World War II Memorial, Planning statement*, prepared by Giles Quarme and Associates, Chartered Architects. GQA 9397 January 2002, 44.

3   The brief for the maquette requested the inclusion of the WRNS, ATS, WRAF, Land Army, Nurses, FANY, Firefighters, Munitions Workers and a Housewife. At this stage ARP wardens were represented through the top figure. Major Robertson (henceforward DMR) to John Mills 27 June 2001. 1 Jan 01 YG/4700; Planning. All similar references reflect the filing system of the Charity 'The Memorial to Women in World War II Fund', in the possession of the author.

4   The art critic Richard Cork commented: 'I can't get why that was considered a good way to memorialise the women of WWII, to have empty coats. It doesn't say anything about their contribution and it rather underplays their role. It's very puzzling and quite annoying.' Cited in T. Geoghegan, 'How do you build a modern memorial?' *BBC News Magazine*, 6 August 2008.

5   Calder, A. (1995), 'Britain's good war?' *History Today*, May, 55–61. Here p. 56. The reworkings of the People's War have been a particular focus

through the media of film: see Eley, G. (2001), 'Finding the people's war: film, British collective memory, and World War II'. *The American Historical Review*, 106(3), 818–38; Hurd, G. (ed.), (1984), *National Fictions: World War Two in British Films and Television*. London: BFI Publishing; Summerfield, P. (2009), 'Public memory or public amnesia? British women of the Second World War in popular films of the 1950s and 1960s'. *Journal of British Studies*, 48(4), 935–57.

6   See, for example, the BBC's 'WW2 People's War' website, as well as further chapters in this collection, including those by Frances Houghton, Lucy Noakes, Penny Summerfield and Janet Watson.

7   See, for example, Connelly, M. (2004), *We Can Take It! Britain and the Memory of the Second World War*. Harlow: Pearson Education Limited; Noakes, L. (1998), *War and the British Gender, Memory and National Identity*. London: I. B. Taurus Publishers; Ponting, C. (1990), *1940: Myth and Reality*. London: Cardinal Books; Rose, S. O. (2002), *Which People's War?: National Identity and Citizenship in Wartime Britain, 1939–1945*. Oxford: Oxford University Press.

8   Registered No: 1069791 under the Charities Act 1960.

9   Wording suggested by the Charity Commission to DMR, 26 March 1998, 01 February 1997 YG/Admin/17/1/1 One ATS Members of AA Comd – Memorial; Planning and Erecting.

10   As I can no longer seek their permission to cite their words, I have anonymized individuals, but the public players in this narrative retain their names. All emphases in quotations are as in the originals.

11   J-H-, for example, on receiving DMR's explanation of the memorial, wrote back: 'It sounds wonderful. I think I was totally wrong and I look forward very much to seeing the real thing.' 10 December 2001, YG/4701 Jan 02; Fundraising.

12   This project was part of a goal to merit Heritage Lottery Funding, but was not necessary when the Charity received the grant from the National Heritage Memorial Fund of £934,115 (82 per cent of the cost of £1,134,115).

13   Online at http://www.bbc.co.uk/history/ww2peopleswar/

14   Dominion Institute Digital Archive.

15   Online at http://www.brantwarmemorials.com/memorials-of-brant-county/the-brant-war-memorial/

16   Young had sculpted the Tri-Service Memorial in commemoration of the contribution of the Commonwealth Women's Forces to the World Wars I and II (Winnepeg, 1976). Online at http://www.carfac.mb.ca/profile/hgranger/ and http://www.caamagazine.ca/caadvice_articledetail.aspx?ContentId=382

17   DMR described this to Mike Grey, Westminster Council, 8 November 2000. YG5506 Two; Planning and Erecting.

18   DMR to Jean Crawley, 14 May 1997 (Jean Crawley File, henceforward JCF).

19   Information Sheet, 1997. 01 Feb 1997 YG/Admin/17/1/1 One.

20   Factsheet (1997) (JCF).

21 DMR to Baroness Finlay of Llandaf, 3 Dec 2003; 1 Jan 03 YG/4700; Planning.

22 Howarth, J. (2001), 'Women at war', in I. C. B. Dear and M. R. D. Foot (eds), *The Oxford Companion to World War II*. Oxford: Oxford University Press, 997–1002.

23 1 Jan 03 YG/4700; Planning.

24 N-L-, 16 March 2001, Experiences, Imperial War Museum Documents.

25 See the Bevin Boys Association webpage, http://www.seniorsnetwork.co.uk/bevinboys/index.htm/; Kramer, A. (2008), *Land Girls and their Impact*. South Yorkshire: Remember When, 176.

26 DMR to Manager, Legal Department, General Accident Life, 22 June 1998. 01 July 97 Yg/Admin/17/1/2 Part One; Fundraising.

27 Jan 2002 YG/4701; Fundraising.

28 DMR to Mrs H-, 5 December 2001. 1 Jan 2001 YG/4701, Women of WW2 Memorial; Fundraising.

29 For further discussion see Peniston-Bird, C. M. (2012), 'War and peace in the cloakroom', in S. Gibson and S. Mollan (eds), *Representations of Peace and Conflict*. Basingstoke: Palgrave.

30 DMR to S. P. Nield, Brg (Ret'd), Vice President, WRAC Association, 1 Jan 02 YG/4700; Planning.

31 Giles Quarme, 11 July 2003, 1 Jan 03 YG/4700; Planning.

32 DMR to John Mills (hereafter JM), 27 June 2001; 1 Jan 01 YG/4700. Planning. There are over 300 statues and monuments located in Westminster.

33 JM, interviewed by the author (CPB), May 2005.

34 Patricia Hewitt, Hansard, House of Commons, 2 May 2002, Oral Answers, 1046.

35 See, for example, DMR to Mrs B-M-, 23 May 2002: 1 Jan 02 YG/4700; Planning.

36 'I ask you to look around your chamber as you argue amongst yourselves[;] would your Mother or your Grandmother be proud of you?' This pertained to the requirement to submit a new application for planning consent, which would have delayed the unveiling. 7 March 2005. 1 Feb 05 YG/4700; Planning.

37 The Charity contacted multiple veterans' associations, but struggled to invite appropriate civilians.

38 1 Jan 03 YG/4700. Planning. At the end of the year (same file), DMR noted the Council had received over 800 individual letters and many petitions with thousands of signatures supporting the Charity's case. DMR to Mr D., 26 November 2003.

39 Cited for example by DMR to Mrs B-H-, 5 December 2001. 1 Jan 01 YG/4701; Fundraising.

40 Their £100 donation was returned to the Eastbourne branch. 12 April 2003. 1 Jan 03 Yg/4701; Fundraising.

41 'I am also delighted to say that as a result of the Telegraph piece showing a picture of the maquette, we had a quick flurry of donations to the funds.' DMR to BB, 2 November 2001.

42 J-B- (not Joy Bone) to DMR, undated but Nov 2001. 1 Jan 01 YG/4701; Fundraising.

43 The secretary of the Colchester branch complained: 'the trouble we feel is because the people who are handling this are of this day and age, and have never experienced the efforts of living through a war let alone take an active part in it.' Reported by Bob Russell, MP for Colchester, to DMR, 20 February 2002, 1 Jan 02 YG/4700; Planning.

44 Joy Bone (JB) to British WLA Society, 23 June 2002, and to Friends of War Memorial. 25 June 2002. JBF.

45 JB to Cyril Demarne Esq. OBE, father-in-law of John Mills. 25 August 2003. JBF. Demarne published his wartime memoirs in *The London Blitz – A Fireman's Tale* in 1980, followed by *Our Girls – A Story of the Nation's Wartime Firewomen* in 1995.

46 JB to the *Daily Mail*, 6 August 2003. See also her article (2007), 'The Memorial to the Women of World War 2'. *Women's History Magazine*, 55, 28–31.

47 M-W-, New South Wales. 24 April 2002, YG/4701 Jan 02; Fundraising.

48 For analysis of the appeal of classical, religious and romantic motifs, see Winter, J. (1995), *Sites of Memory, Sites of Mourning: The Great War in European Cultural History*. Cambridge, Cambridge University Press.

49 The UKNIWM lists twelve memorials in Whitehall excluding that to The Women of World War II.

50 1 Jan 01 YG/4700; Planning.

51 25 July 2002. Classification: For General Release. Proposal: Erection of a memorial to the Women of World War II on axis with the Cenotaph. Held in 1 Jan 03 YG/4700 HQ York Garrison: Memorial to Women of WW2; Planning.

52 DRM to Giles Quarme, 11 March 2002, in 1 Jan 02 YG/4700 Women of WW2 Memorial; Planning.

53 Dorothy Jones to DMR, 13 November 2001. 1 Jan 01 YG/4701; Fundraising.

54 M-G- to DMR, undated but November 2001. 1 Jan 01 YG/4701; Fundraising.

55 M-F- (ex-Ack Ack, France) to DMR, 17 August 2003, 1 Jan 03 YG/4701; Fundraising.

56 See, for example, the framed list of roles undertaken by locals displayed in the entrance to the church at the Port of Menteith; within the body of the church is a memorial to the dead.

57 DeGroot, G. J. (1997), 'Whose finger on the trigger? Mixed anti-aircraft batteries and the female combat taboo'. *War In History*, 4(4), 434–53.

58 Schwarzkopf, J. (2009), 'Combatant or non-combatant? The ambiguous status of women in British anti-aircraft batteries during the Second World

War'. *War and Society*, 28(2), 101–31. Here p. 127. See also Stone, T. (1999), 'Creating a (gendered) military identity: the Women's Auxiliary Air Force in Great Britain in the Second World War'. *Women's History Review*, 8(4), 605–24.

59   H-H- to DMR (Alberta), 15 April 2002. YG/4701 Jan 02; Fundraising.

60   A-E- to DMR, 20 April 2002; YG/4701 Jan 02; Fundraising.

61   To DMR, 11 November 2003, 1 Jan 03 Yg/470; Fundraising.

62   'Although the role of an Air Raid Warden was imperative, in many cases it was a volunteer position, for those not suited for the armed services, and these women could go back to their homes after an air-raid.' P-H- (BC, Canada) to DMR, 4 Feb 2002, YG/4701 Jan 02; Fundraising.

63   YG/4701 Jan 02; Fundraising. Also to BB, Jan 17 2003, 1 Jan 03 Yg/4701; Fundraising.

64   P-M-J- to DMR, 20 Jan 2002, 1 Jan 02 YG/4700; Planning.

65   See, for example, A-E- to DMR, 20 April 2002; YG/4701 JAN 02; Fundraising.

66   The Charity's headed notepaper depicted three uniformed women, and Jean Crawley had done much to disseminate her original vision. See, for example, the letter written by Barbara W. Reeves, Chairman, Colchester Branch, ATS Association to DMR: 'Who made the decision to change the proposed Memorial from three ex-servicewomen as on the original letter headings, to the current design which is no longer viable?' 30 August 2002, 1 Aug 2002 YG/4700; Planning.

67   JB to DMR, 12 February 2002. JBF.

68   Warwick H. Taylor to DMR, 19 Jan 2001, 1 Jan 01 YG/4700; Planning.

69   Elizabeth Grice, 'Bevin Boys: "Most of us couldn't wait to get out"', *Daily Telegraph*, 26 March 2008.

70   See the BBC Fact File on Reserved Occupations, available online at http://www.bbc.co.uk/ww2peopleswar/timeline/factfiles/nonflash/a6652019.shtml/

71   25/09/04 Pink folder: Letters Re: Whitehall/Embankment Re: 25 September 2004.

72   Noakes, L. (2009), 'The BBC "People's War" website', in M. Keren and H. R. Herwig (eds), *War, Memory and Popular Culture: Essays on Modes of Remembrance and Commemoration*. North Carolina: McFarland, 135–49.

73   BBC 'WW2 People's War': Childhood in Penryn, A4122398.

74   Summerfield, P. (1998), *Reconstructing Women's Wartime Lives*. New York and Manchester: Manchester University Press, 168–72.

75   Crawley on the Dominion Institute Digital Archive for The Memory Project.

76   Crawley on the Dominion Institute Digital Archive. The emphasis on sorority is underlined by the captions for the accompanying photographs.

77   C. M. H. R. to DMR, 14 May 1998. 01 July 97 Yg/Admin/17/1/2 Part One. HQ York Garrison. ATS members of AA Comd – Memorial Fundraising.

78   H-H-, 1st Heavy Battery. 3 December 1997, to DMR. 01 July 97 Yg/Admin/17/1/2 Part One; Fundraising.

79 Watson, J. K. (2004), *Fighting Different Wars: Experience, Memory and the First World War in Britain*. Cambridge: Cambridge University Press; Lee, J. (2008), 'Sisterhood at the front: friendship, comradeship, and the feminine appropriation of military heroism among World War I First Aid Nursing Yeomanry'. *Women Studies International Forum*, 31(1), 16–29.

80 Handler, L. (1995), 'In the fraternal sisterhood: sororities as gender strategy.' *Gender and Society*, 9(2), 236–55. Here p. 253.

81 On the self-construction of women's service see Summerfield, P. and Peniston-Bird, C. (2000), 'Women in the firing line: the Home Guard and the defence of gender boundaries in Britain in the Second World War'. *Women's History Review*, 9(2), 231–55, and Pattinson, J. (2011), '"The thing that made me hesitate …": re-examining gendered intersubjectivities in interviews with British secret war veterans'. *Women's History Review*, 20(2), 245–63.

82 Referred to as such, for example, by Mr George North, writing in complaint from Canada to Her Majesty, Queen Elizabeth II; the Prime Minister, Tony Blair; and Dr Mike Gray, Dept of Planning, Westminster City Hall. No date; 1 Jan 03 YG/4701; Fundraising.

83 Friends of War Memorials to Mr C. Powell, Director of Planning and Transportation, Westminster City Council. 28 February 2002; 1 Jan 02 YG/4700; Planning.

84 J-S-,4 August 2002; 1 Aug 2002 YG/4700; Planning.

Key texts

Abousnnouga, G. and Machin, D. (2011), 'Visual discourses of the role of women in war commemoration: A multimodal analysis of British war monuments'. *Journal of Language and Politics*, 10(3), 322–46.

Calder, A. (1995), 'Britain's good war?' *History Today*. May, 55–61

Connelly, M. (2004), *We Can Take It! Britain and the Memory of the Second World War*. Harlow: Pearson Education Limited.

Noakes, L. (1998), *War and the British: Gender, Memory and National Identity*. London: I. B. Tauris.

Peniston-Bird, C. (2012), 'War and Peace in the Cloakroom: The Controversy over the Memorial to the Women of World War II'. S Gibson & S Mollan (eds), *Representations of Peace and Conflict*. Palgrave Macmillan, Basingstoke.

Ponting, C. (1990), *1940: Myth and Reality*. London: Cardinal Books.

Rose, S. O. (2002), *Which People's War? National Identity and Citizenship in Britain, 1939-1945*. Oxford: Oxford University Press.

CHAPTER FIVE

'When are you going back?'

Memory, ethnicity and the British Home Front[1]

Wendy Ugolini

In November 2004, the *Coventry Evening Telegraph* reported that a 'row' had erupted over the decision by the Lord Mayor, John Gazey, to order the removal of a Remembrance Installation artwork that incorporated images of a local Sikh ex-serviceman. Positioned within the Council House as part of the local authority's 'Peace Month' celebrations, the artwork incorporated two photographs of 85-year-old veteran Sawarn Singh, who had served with the British forces in Africa, the Middle East and Burma, and had lived in Coventry since 1957. The row touched upon contested notions of war, citizenship and commemoration, with the Mayor objecting, in particular, to the assertion by the exhibition curators that the vast majority of ex-colonial veterans living in Britain do not receive official invitations to attend annual remembrance ceremonies.[2] This dispute, played out in the pages of the local newspaper, serves to underline how there is still a need within Britain to embed the experience and memory of the two world wars into 'a more multiracial and international framework'.[3] As Paul Ward emphasizes, the predominant discourse of the Second World War in Britain, privileging community and togetherness, constructs 'the "people" as socially and ethnically homogenous, not just in the 1940s but across the decades since'.[4] Indeed, the fact that thousands of Indians and West Indians served in the British armed forces in 1939–45 'hardly registers in public memory of the war'.[5] The war also brought to Britain a large contingent of European refugees and prisoners of war, many of them Polish,[6] yet the contribution of 'white' ethnic groups in wartime Britain also tends to be overlooked within the cultural memory of the war. Focusing on the narratives of two groups who served and subsequently settled in Britain, male West Indian RAF volunteers and Polish servicemen, this chapter examines the commonalities between the experiences of black and white migrant groups in wartime and the ways in which their presence in Home Front Britain has been remembered, highlighting the limitations of Britain's wartime imagined community. Acknowledging the 'virtually unrepresented and undiscussed intersection of nationality and ethnicity' on the home front, this chapter explores the narrated experiences of migrant groups from their position of marginality within Britain's cultural memory of the Second World War.[7]

From war to *Windrush*: West Indian experience

Jose Harris suggests that, in terms of future cultural change, the single most significant social occurrence of the war was the temporary migration into Britain of West Indian workers and servicemen, many of whom returned after the war as permanent settlers.[8] On the British Home Front, volunteer workers travelled from the West Indies and East Africa to support the war effort, including 1000 technicians and factory workers in Merseyside, 1200 Honduran foresters in Scotland and over 10,000 Caribbean servicemen who joined the RAF.[9] Added to this mix was the arrival of 130,000 black GIs as part of the US army's invasion force.[10] Work by Gavin Schaffer, Marika Sherwood and Neil Wynn[11] highlights the governmental anxiety that surrounded the notion of a 'heightened' black presence in wartime Britain, which in itself suggests a selective amnesia about the existence of Britain's own black population – which had reached 15,000 by 1939.[12] Instead, there was a tendency to problematize the arrival of black troops. Schaffer notes how, even in the midst of war, 'racial ideas of white difference and superiority continued to shape white British reactions to black workers and soldiers.'[13] In particular, fears of racial mixing – miscegenation – which had been most forcibly expressed during the 1919 anti-black riots in British seaports in the aftermath of the First World War, continued to undermine white responses to black communities in Britain.[14] Sherwood argues that discrimination against blacks – known in contemporary parlance as the 'colour bar' – was 'rampant' in wartime British society with hotels, boarding houses, landlords, pubs, dance halls, swimming pools, sporting associations and even people in air raid shelters attempting to exclude blacks.[15] A survey undertaken by Mass Observation in October 1943 found that, while most respondents expressed disapproval of 'colour prejudice', there were still those who commented, 'I'm prejudiced against coloured people', 'I don't like them blacks', and 'I shouldn't like any daughter of mine to marry a coloured person'.[16] In her study of British Honduran lumbermen who were sent to three Scottish camps in 1941 as imported workers, Sherwood exposes the institutional resistance within departments such as the Ministry of Supply towards the idea of 'coloured labour recruited into the UK'.[17] Anxieties about interracial sex also underpinned objections by local dignitaries such as the Duke of Buccleuch, who wrote to Harold Macmillan, Under-Secretary of State for the colonies, in August 1942: 'Does the Colonial Office have any policy about their association with white women? ... Personally I dislike this mixture of colour and regret that it should be allowed with no discouragement.'[18] The lumbermen were placed in barely furnished, unheated barracks in isolated areas with insufficient amenities, betraying an official mindset which proved reluctant to countenance the presence of a colonial workforce on British soil and which ultimately achieved the partial repatriation of the foresters within two years.[19]

This first half of this chapter focuses on the narratives of West Indian men who volunteered to serve in the wartime Royal Air Force (RAF), a cohort whose experiences have since been immortalized in Andrea Levy's award winning novel, *Small Island* (2004), also dramatized by BBC TV in 2009.[20] Martin Francis has noted the potency of this wartime connection with the RAF that enables Caribbean migrants to access the potent myth of the heroic wartime flyer, and, implicitly, their right to be accepted as an integral part of the British narrative of war.[21] On 10 October 1939, the British government announced the lifting of the 'colour bar' in the Armed Services for the duration of the war, stating that 'British subjects from the Colonies and British protected persons who are in this country, including those who are not of pure European descent, are to be on the same footing as British subjects of pure European descent as regards voluntary enlistment in the armed forces.'[22] However, Sherwood underlines the 'speciousness' of this announcement, pointing out that, by not lifting the specific requirement that recruits must be British-born subjects of British-born parents, the Royal Navy, the Royal Air Force and the Army officer corps essentially hoped to avoid having to accept any black recruits, as they 'obviously presumed that there would be no Black British subjects with British-born parents'. This example of the armed services' 'sophistry', she argues, effectively operated to exclude many of those the government had publicly intimated it would accept.[23] Tony Kushner concurs that the effective existence of a wide-ranging colour bar in Second World War Britain still needs to be 'subject to sustained memory work within the armed services and British society as a whole'.[24] Schaffer has demonstrated how a belief in black inferiority shaped policy towards the use of Empire war volunteers, citing a 1942 report by the Secretary of State, James Grigg, which argued: 'While there are many coloured men of high mentality and cultural distinction, the generality are of a simple mental outlook ... In short they have not the white man's ability to think and act to a plan.'[25] However, Schaffer believes that policy towards black volunteers was somewhat more enlightened in the RAF, pointing to research undertaken in 1945 on the performance of 422 West Indian aircrew and 3900 black ground personnel which concluded: 'Selected West Indian personnel have on the whole proved themselves fully capable as individuals of holding their own as Pilots and members of aircrew.'[26]

It should be recognized that official and popular memories of the West Indian presence in wartime Britain cannot be readily disentangled from the post-war complexities of Britain's response to Caribbean migration signalled by the arrival of 492 men from Jamaica aboard HMT *Empire Windrush* in June 1948.[27] Paul Ward sees the paradox of the Second World War being that, while it encouraged migration, at the same time 'it created a new sense of a socially cohesive British identity' which remained largely colour-blind.[28] Chris Waters suggests that, after 1945, against the backdrop of post-war imperial decline and attempts to reconfigure the meaning of citizenship in a new multi-ethnic Commonwealth, questions of race became central to questions of national belonging in Britain. In the 1950s particularly, discussions about the rapid increase of 'new Commonwealth' migration to Britain could not be wholly separated from discussions of what it now meant to be British, and attempts to regain the sense of wartime national unity encouraged the construction of Caribbean migrants as the internal 'dark stranger'.[29] Paul Gilroy agrees, noting that since 1945 the life of the nation has been dominated by an inability to acknowledge the profound change in circumstances that followed the end of Empire and consequent loss of imperial prestige. This reluctance to confront this history feeds into the construction of postcolonial people as 'unwanted alien intruders without any substantive historical, political or cultural connections to the collective life of their fellow subjects.'[30] In contrast to the almost complete absence from national consciousness of Britain's postcolonial conflicts in Malaya, Korea, Kenya, Suez and Cyprus, the Second World War continues to act as a privileged point of entry into national identity and self-understanding.[31] Gilroy decries Britain's unhealthy obsession with the Second World War, noting how an enduring emotional investment in the 'luck, pluck and resilience' which supposedly characterized wartime Britain is epitomized by 'the perennially troublesome crowd at England football matches humming the theme tune from *The Dambusters*' or the iconic wartime planes which appear in ceremonial flypast at national commemorative events.[32] He sees the continuous re-calibration of this 'particular mythic moment of national becoming and community' being utilized as a touchstone of togetherness which implicitly critiques the multicultural present.[33]

Within this context, as Matthew Mead notes, 'freeing the imaginary of the Second World War from its conjunction with an exclusionary "white" British or English national identity is no small undertaking.'[34] From June 2008 to March 2009, the Imperial War Museum in London hosted a highly publicized exhibition, 'From War to Windrush', which aimed to tell 'the personal stories of the involvement of Black men and women from the West

Indies and Britain in the First and Second World Wars'.[35] Significantly, the museum identified the presentation of military service narratives as the most fitting way to celebrate the 60th anniversary of the arrival of the *Empire Windrush*. This acknowledgement, that two-thirds of the men entering Britain on the iconic ship in 1948 had served in Britain during the war,[36] tacitly reinforces the link between military service and citizenship rights. It also reflects how many ethnic groups in Britain use evidence of wartime participation and military service as a way of asserting their right to be incorporated into the meta-narrative of 'the British at war'.[37] Cultural theorists working on the interdisciplinary project, *photoCLEC*, have provided a particularly illuminating analysis of 'From War to Windrush'.[38] The displays appeared across two galleries positioned either side of the museum's main entrance, with the first gallery looking at experiences in the West Indies and the second examining life in Britain.[39] Researcher Mead believes that the situating of the exhibition at the museum entrance represents an intentional 'interruption of its institutional context' which aims to subvert the 'whiteness' of Second World War imagery in the popular imagination. Mead records the observation of an Imperial War Museum education officer that, when shown a photograph of a black Second World War pilot, classes of largely black British schoolchildren tend to assume they are being shown the photograph of an actor.[40] While commending the museum's attempt to make the contributions of black men and women more visible, Mead notes that the traditional presentation of the exhibition material tended to conform to audience expectations rather than challenge them. For example, the gallery highlighting the experience of black servicemen and women was dominated by a series of large, backlit portrait photographs of uniform scale and tone, each showing the head and shoulders of the subjects, most often wearing military uniforms. Fundamentally, Mead argues, the display was effective due to cultural familiarity with the soldier portraiture form and the ability of the exhibition visitors to read this photographic genre.[41] Thus, while the remit of the exhibition constituted a 'forceful rewriting of the Second World War imaginary in Britain and created a powerful iconography of black belonging', it ultimately failed to unsettle or expand upon the prescribed national narrative.[42] The containment of a vision of black belonging in wartime within 'From War to Windrush' thus serves to privilege the historical stability of Britain's imagined community.[43]

Kushner has noted similar shortcomings within two other landmark exhibitions attempting to commemorate the role of wartime colonial servicemen: the Ministry of Defence's 'We Were There' (2001)[44] and the RAF Museum's 'Diversity in the RAF' (2009), which he classifies as examples of 'official heritage construction' for public consumption.[45] While the latter exhibition acknowledges earlier discrimination against those not of 'pure European descent', these admissions of past prejudice are most commonly framed within a 'redemptive ending' where the focus is on the lifting of the colour bar at the start of the Second World War.[46] This compulsion to tell a positive history, Kushner argues, leads to the glossing over of the ambivalent responses to both colonial soldiers and British-born individuals regarded as possessing African, Asiatic or Oriental 'blood' in the British armed forces during the war.[47] The desire to show loyalty and sacrifice has meant that the continuation of racism, especially during Britain's 'finest hour', has been largely downplayed.[48] Indeed, the mythology of Britain as a tolerant, decent nation perpetuates the notion of racism as a problem of other countries, as something fundamentally un-British.[49] Kushner notes how prominence is given to the positivist testimonies of West Indian veterans such as Billy Strachan, who became an acting squadron leader: 'I didn't come here as a West Indian. I came to England and joined as an Englishman. I never encountered any racism.'[50] In their examination of the ways in which the experiences of immigrant groups have been 'remembered' in Britain, Kathy Burrell and Panikos Panayi identify the understandable desire amongst ethnic groups 'to provide alternative histories of immigration and to open up understandings of the past beyond official national narratives'. Yet they also caution that this type of popularized 'history-making' often leads to over-simplistic or celebratory accounts of migrant histories: 'in the rush to create positive, attractive histories the complexities of immigrant experiences are lost' and experiences of racism often sidelined.[51]

'You're treated as a favourite teddy bear'[52]: narrative accounts

Reflecting upon the on-going struggle to accept the credibility of a multicultural vision of postcolonial Britain, Martin Francis stresses the need to go beyond the dominant myths to ensure that 'the stories behind it are retold in their unabridged versions'.[53] Whilst he accepts that the experiences of non-white aircrew have been largely erased from the dominant cultural memory of the wartime RAF, he also believes there is a danger that, when deploring the 'monoracial refashioning' of the wartime period, we overlook the individual subjectivities of the veterans themselves, many of whom felt a sense of pride in their wartime achievements.[54] For the purposes of this research I accessed four recorded interviews with male West Indian veterans held at the Imperial War Museum and one from the 1993 'Voices of London' exhibition hosted online by the Museum of London. Joanna Bornat points out that historians need to be careful when approaching the secondary analysis and interpretation of previously archived oral material, urging sensitivity to 'the social and historical contexts of data, both original and subsequent when revisiting interview material'.[55] The interviews accessed at the Imperial War Museum were carried out between 1987 and 1994 and appear primarily to have been undertaken with those who had served in the British armed forces during the war and who then returned to settle in post-war Britain, with at least one interview taking place in the headquarters of the West Indian Ex-Servicemen's Association.[56] Thus there is a distinct narrative arc to this dataset which focuses on motivations for enlistment, wartime experiences and encounters, with a key focus on return to Britain – often on *Windrush* – and the prejudice encountered in the immediate post-war era. A fresh interrogation of these archived recordings enables the historian to move beyond the simplicity required by exhibition sound bites to recover some sense of the complex and contradictory nature of male West Indian veteran wartime experience. It would appear that these testimonies were not collected with the 2008 exhibition specifically in mind, and for that reason they include memories which do not fit so easily into official representations. Alan Wilmot, born in Jamaica in 1925, served initially as a seaman aboard HMS *Hauken* in the Caribbean before serving with RAF Air Sea Rescue in Britain as an aircraftsman from 1944 to 1947. In recalling his arrival in Britain, Wilmot underlines the levels of ignorance he encountered amongst British people, which drew upon entrenched notions of racial inferiority:[57]

> My first impression of Britain was a bit of a surprise because we thought more or less that, being a part of the British Empire, that people here *knew* about us but we realised that they didn't have a clue. When you said you were from Jamaica, they said 'What part of Africa is that?' Once you are black or dark skinned they assume right away that you are from Africa ... They couldn't understand what we were doing in Air Force uniform, how we got in, how we passed the tests ... At first, I thought they were taking the Mickey but after, I realised it wasn't Mickey taking; it was just that they didn't have an idea about us because in school all our curriculum was nothing about the West Indies. It was all Europe. We could tell you the different towns, the different cultures and everything but they knew nothing about us.
>
> Q: What kinds of things were they asking?
>
> A: The first thing they used to ask, if we lived in trees? If we had a wash? They couldn't understand being dark, how we are always having a wash and all that. They just couldn't figure it out for a while.[58]

This motif of the ignorant, uneducated inhabitants of the Motherland is also present in the narrative of another RAF veteran, William 'Billy' Strachan. It serves to highlight the newcomer's perceived shock at the lack of reciprocity within the colonial relationship, as well as placing the West Indian narrator in a position of civilized superiority, subtly inverting the power dynamics within these remembered wartime encounters. Strachan was born in Kingston, Jamaica, in 1921, the son of a tobacco company manager who encouraged his family to stand up for 'God Save the King' at the end of BBC radio broadcasts and who felt 'proud to be British'. Strachan travelled to Britain to volunteer in 1940:

> I went along to Adastral House, having walked from Tottenham Court Road ... and I spoke to the guard who I now know was a corporal, but I thought he was head of the Air Force or something. I said to him, 'I'd like to join the Air Force' – I'll never forget this – he said to me, 'Piss off'. Here am I dressed in rather lightweight colonial stuff in March, fairly cold – I think he thought I was drunk or a lunatic or something. I said, 'I want to join the Air Force.' I persisted and as he began to revile me to try to get me away, a more senior rank, I think it was a sergeant, came along and asked what was going on and I tried to tell this sergeant. He intervened because he was in charge of the corporal, and he said, 'You don't join the Air Force here, you're trying to take the Mickey out of us? This is the head office of the Air Ministry.' But in my logic at that period, where else do you join the Air Force but at the Air Ministry?
>
> He said, 'Where do you come from?' and I said, 'Kingston.' He said 'There's a recruiting station at Kingston down in Surrey.' And I said 'It's a Kingston, Jamaica.' I remember this – he didn't know where Jamaica was. And as he stood there quite mystified, I said 'I don't come from Kingston, Surrey, down the road, I come from Kingston, Jamaica.' A young, Hooray Henry-type officer came past and he overheard this argument, and he said, 'Oh you're from Jamaica – one of our colonial friends. Welcome.' He said, 'I did geography at university and I've always been impressed with you West Africans. Come in.' And thanks to his supreme ignorance, I was dragged in.[59]

While the British Nationality and Status of Aliens Act (1914) stated that, 'Any person born within His Majesty's dominions and allegiance' was in effect a 'natural born British subject',[60] the work of scholars such as Laura Tabili emphasizes the continual struggle men of colour faced in the ensuing decades to establish themselves as British subjects rather than aliens. The meaning of what it was to be 'coloured' or black was constantly reformulated in the process of state policymaking in the interwar period, especially in relation to the colonial seafaring labour force, so that racial difference was increasingly construed as *prima facie* alien status.[61] Both the above narratives highlight the ways in which British subjects from the colonies were received as somehow 'alien' to British culture. An incident during an early RAF physical training session in Blackpool caused a further jolt in Strachan's own self-identity as a proud Briton and highlights the continual renegotiation of his British status once in England:

> A man called Corporal Hyles was in charge of us, an ex-Bertram Mills clown I remember. Like most clowns [he was] extremely gymnastic and fit. So, he looked at us and, in the usual traditional way a corporal looks

at a bunch of new recruits, he said, 'Now I want you all running on the spot.' And these blokes creaked into action. I, because of my sporting background in school, seemed to run the most regularly. He said 'Right, I'm making you my deputy. Darkie, come over here. You're deputy in charge of the squad.' In terms of Jamaican society, I'd always been called 'red man', which means not black. I'd never been called 'Darkie' in my life before. I was shattered because darkie was a term of contempt. And I recall him saying that to me – 'Darkie, you are in charge of the squad.' Again, I had conflict in my mind. I was annoyed I was called 'Darkie', my chest swelled out because I was regarded as a man to be promoted second airman in the RAF.[62]

Another common motif within these veteran narratives was their comparative positioning in relation to the reception and treatment of black American troops in Britain. Historians such as Graham Smith and David Reynolds have concluded that black GIs were 'warmly welcomed in Britain' while white Americans who attempted to impose a colour bar in British towns were roundly condemned.[63] Schaffer agrees that many British soldiers and civilians felt outraged on behalf of black GIs and often became embroiled in fights to defend them from aggressive white American behaviour, but he stresses that these instances cannot be used easily as evidence of broader enlightened British attitudes towards 'race'. Often this British defence of black American soldiers stemmed from a disinclination to have values in Britain dictated by the US military and can therefore be attributed to anti-Americanism rather than instinctive anti-racism.[64] Wilmot's testimony highlights this dynamic. At the same time, by defining 'we' West Indians and black GIs as being on one 'side' and the British as the 'public' who come to their aid, he situates himself outside of the British national community:

There was quite a bit of violence. But the white Americans now they realised to keep away from the West Indians, you see? ... We just don't mess about because for a start, we weren't used to racism and to us, it's like putting a red cloth before a bull. That was our reaction. And the white Americans realised: keep away from those British army uniform guys, black guys. But the whole thing is: they couldn't understand how the white British public took onto the black fellas, the white Americans ... Because they were brought up into, that blacks were second class citizens. Over here the people didn't have that experience: we were new to them. There weren't any established racism like it was in America. So they just couldn't figure it out. Because at times when we had conflict the white British population was always on our side, would always help us to fight. I can remember that plainly. They were always helping us to fight because some of them didn't like the white American attitude, you know: that we come over here and we are in charge. The British public just couldn't take that. So, in any conflict they were always on our side.[65]

The testimony of Billy Strachan also underlines the fluidity of a wartime identity construction informed by the black American presence, his interview highlighting the fights between white Americans and blacks and pointing to British attitudes being 'as much against the American white as the American black'.[66] Reflecting on his wartime career, which he ended as a West Indian liaison officer, Strachan believed that it was mainly since 1943, when more blacks were recruited into the RAF, 'that you saw the racism really rear its head':

> One of the phenomena about black people in my experience and most of my colleagues in this country is wherever one black arrives anywhere he's always welcomed and treated well. Two they cope with but it's when three come that racism gets really sharp. Amongst black people – a number of my friends who've been here years and newcomers – we all share that view; that when you arrive in England, anywhere, as one black man you're treated as a favourite teddy bear, you're loved, feted. The war years were like that. [67]

This interview extract, endorsing a 'visibility' thesis, suggests that even during the war years limitations were inherent within the popular embrace of colonial servicemen.

'From when you were in uniform, it was a different thing'[68]

While these narratives of West Indian servicemen primarily situate experiences of racial antagonism within the post-war period, the cumulative sense from these testimonies is that they were tolerated 'for the duration only'. Kathleen Paul's work notes the paradox in the UK's policy towards different migrant groups in the post-war period where successive British governments spent a great deal of money attracting white European aliens to work in Britain while all the time 'resisting the independent migration to Britain of thousands of colonial citizens of colour'.[69] Sam King, born in Portland, Jamaica, in 1926, served in the Royal Air Force in Britain during the war and returned on the *Empire Windrush* in 1948. Having served as Mayor of Southwark in the 1980s, Mr King is frequently represented in exhibitions and formed one of the case studies at the 'From War to Windrush' exhibition.[70] In a Museum of London interview, he asserts that his military service, and decision to rejoin the RAF in 1948, enabled him to survive in the harsher post-war environment by knowing how to work 'the system'.

He recalls how, alongside his brother, he attempted to buy a large council property in London:

> I applied to the council from the air force. The council sent me back a letter, 'Thank you Corporal King' – I was a Corporal – 'for applying for a mortgage, but since you are from Jamaica, a colony, we would recommend that you go back to the colony'. They did! I had the letter for a long time. Now I took the letter to the man who was selling it, off Camberwell Road. And he was so disgusted that the council, a man in the air force – I went in my uniform with chevrons on – and he says, 'It's a disgrace' … He said, 'I will give you the mortgage but you must swear on the Bible' – they knew we were religious – 'swear on the Bible that you will pay'. And he gave us the mortgage, normal rate, and I don't have to tell you we paid and we paid quicker than the time.[71]

As Wendy Webster notes, in times of war 'attributed martial capability' plays a significant role in determining whether outsiders might be embraced by the British nation.[72] The RAF uniform conferred an approved martial identity on West Indians in wartime Britain. Once out of uniform, King acknowledges, it was a 'harder life' for former servicemen, with a concomitant loss of toleration:

> The people who knew me carried on, naturally, I was the same Sam King. But the people who didn't know me, yes they were different. For example, when we were in Manchester, a large amount of middle-class people during the war and after the war would ask for servicemen for Sunday dinner and things like that. If you were black or white they wouldn't mind … if you get there: 'Good afternoon Mrs Brown', 'Oh yes, come in' and they ask about the colonies and all that. If you were now a civilian going in their street and you were black, I don't think they would want you. But they would have you in for tea in the uniform, yes was different.[73]

The testimonies held at the Imperial War Museum which address post-war settlement in Britain dwell on similar themes: the coldness of the reception West Indians received on their return, from both former acquaintances and strangers in public spaces, and the difficulty in finding work other than menial positions. Robert Miles argues that the largely negative response of the government towards the arrival of British citizens from the colonies, whose migration was motivated primarily by the desire to work, can be attributed to the 'racialization' of potential sources of migrant labour which, in its preference for European 'aliens', increasingly displaced the formal significance of nationality laws and citizenship.[74] Alan Wilmot found the post-war environment 'frightening' and reflected upon the contrasting nature of his wartime and post-war identity in Britain:

[B]eing a civilian it was a complete different thing from in the services. Because in the services for instance, coming to London, you had the Union Jack club. You had other establishments where you could get a room, you could get a meal and everything but as a civilian you were just ... thrown to survive on your own. Unfortunately, I arrived back here near the Christmas, the 21st of December I arrived back here at Southampton and everything was closed down for the Christmas, right? And it was terrible, to really survive. You couldn't get a room; you couldn't afford a hotel and three of us ex-servicemen ... used to stick together. We used to hang around the dance halls and then at night we'd get the last tube, the end of the line tube and sleep on the train. Fortunately, most of the men there were ex-servicemen and they had sympathy and lent us blankets and all that and that's the way we survived.

The thing was: 'What you come back here for? The war's over. What you come back here for? Why didn't you stay at home?' That was the attitude ... I knew a few people around. I had said more or less that I would contact them but the reception was a bit quiet. Until we found our way around. For instance, you'd go into a pub and the pub would go dead quiet as you walked in. Because you are a novelty then. Let's face it, you are a novelty then. But the main thing was: 'Why have you come back here?'[75]

Rene Webb served as an airman with the RAF in both Jamaica and Britain from 1944 to 1945. Having originally volunteered because he was 'brought up to be British' and believed he had an obligation to fight as a member of the British Empire, Webb also struggled to establish a foothold in post-war London. Eventually he found work shunting on the railways, and then as a storekeeper:

I was terribly concerned at that time that people should have forgotten so easily ... during the war everybody was co-operating. I was terribly upset and concerned about it, when they began to call you names. I mean some of the many questions that were asked of me, one of the main ones was: 'When are you going back?' That annoyed me, because I've always believed that I was a part of the British Empire. I was prepared to pay the supreme sacrifice for coming here because we know we're going to a war and we could have got killed. In fact, many of my friends died fighting for that cause, and there have been many promise that were made to us – people like Mr Churchill and others made many promises to us that at the ending of the war, things would be much better than what it used to be. And I was terrible upset that people were now behaving in the way they were.[76]

These veteran narratives, focusing particularly on their post-war rejection by British society, serve to underline the fragility of wartime belonging and, instead, highlight the extent to which accommodation of their presence was often experienced as being 'for the duration only'.

The Clasp o' Frien'ship'? Polish troops in wartime Scotland[77]

Following the fall of France in June 1940, some 20,000 Polish servicemen, under the leadership of General Wladyslaw Sikorski, were evacuated to Scotland, and organized initially into the 1st Polish Armoured Division.[78] While the welcome the Polish 'allies' received in Scotland was generally felt to be warm, Allan Carswell notes that the preponderance of senior officers tended to provide a rather dandified, 'caricature image' of the Polish army: 'The immaculately turned out cavalry officer, complete with title, cigarette holder, briefcase, and eau de Cologne, became as much a part of the popular image of wartime Glasgow as air raid shelters and rationing.'[79] Indeed, the wartime characterization of Polish troops as 'a race of Casanovas who menaced the integrity of British womanhood'[80] often dominated representations. The novels and short stories of Scottish writer Fred Urquhart, for example, capture the transformative effect of the arrival of Norwegian sailors, Free French and Polish servicemen in Scotland, depicting a tumultuous wartime world of 'foreign sodgers' populating the streets of Edinburgh. Within Urquhart's picaresque stories, Polish troops, with their 'cheap-jack tricks and their hand-kissin' and all that palaver'[81] are largely framed in terms of the amorous response of local Scottish women, with the latter depicted as corrupted by the foreign presence: being 'chums a' bubbly wi' a Pole' or 'shop soiled' due to their liaisons.[82] Within these stories, composed during the war, the Poles are both infantilized, consorting with matronly, middle-aged lovers whom they call 'Mummy',[83] and highly sexualized, their surface politeness of pomade and clicking heels masking a predatory form of sexuality.[84] In his contemporaneous account, *Polish Invasion* (1941), journalist Ksawery Pruszyński, who was posted with Polish forces in Scotland, recounts the 'Sunday mediations' between a general, two chaplains and officers about why the Poles enjoy 'such an undeserved popularity' with Scotland's womenfolk. Their Scots landlord glumly pronounces that it is because they have 'learned how to be good liars in love', deceiving women with 'sweet words, the small attentions, flowers, flattery and unconcealed infatuation' and, due to their wartime status as faithful allies, their assurances of love are explicitly believed.[85] This latter point supports Wendy Webster's contention that Churchill's wartime rhetoric, by positively focusing on the martial masculinity of Polish servicemen, aimed to facilitate the acceptance of Poles as 'fellow Europeans' and bolster the idea that these 'valiant warriors' should be offered citizenship of the British Empire at the war's end.[86] Yet even during the war, there was some unease surrounding the formation of relationships with local Scottish women, and marriages were often opposed on the grounds of anti-Catholic hostility.[87] Furthermore, by 1942 attitudes towards the Polish presence were beginning to cool due to shifting geopolitical realities.

'Why Don't You Go Back?'[88]: narrative accounts

Since the German invasion of Russia in June 1941, a wave of pro-Soviet feeling had gripped the British nation, from popular iconography surrounding the avuncular 'Uncle Joe' Stalin, to the fundraising campaign for the 'Brave Russians' sponsored by the Prime Minister's wife, Clementine Churchill.[89] The presence of openly anti-Soviet Polish forces on British soil became increasingly problematic, especially in Scotland with its left wing traditions. At the war's end, the Labour government instituted a policy of controlled resettlement through the Polish Resettlement Corps, the Polish Resettlement Act of 27 March 1947 and the European Volunteer Workers (EVW) scheme.[90] Some 157,000 Poles now stationed in Britain decided to remain, of whom around 20 per cent resided in the central belt of Scotland.[91] This government action signifies the degree to which Polish settlers were superficially perceived as more acceptable migrant workers on the grounds of racial similarities; Webster notes how, within official discourse surrounding the labour recruitment of Poles, this group was primarily defined in terms of the white ethnicity they shared with Britons.[92] But official rhetoric had its limitations, with community historian Thomas Kernberg noting that few Polish servicemen were psychologically prepared at the war's end for the abuse they received from people amongst whom they had lived.[93] In August 1945, Peebles Town Council passed a resolution to speed up the return of Poles to their homeland; one councillor stated that they had overstayed their welcome and 'had plenty of money to burn'.[94] In 1946, miners in Fife organized a 'Poles Go Home' campaign, and the National Union of Miners Scottish Executive urged the government to remove all Polish troops from Scotland.[95] In her survey of Scottish press coverage of the Poles, Rachel Clements shows that by 1946 the media was presenting Poles in a deviant light, highlighting the criminality of Poles or their political mindedness, thus confirming their transformation from 'gallant heroes' to increasingly dysfunctional 'inconvenient foreigners'.[96] George Orwell picked up on this reversal in his *Tribune* column, recounting a conversation he overheard between two businessmen in a Scottish hotel in which they managed to blame Polish immigrants for coal shortages, unemployment and the housing problem, as well as the fact that they were 'very degraded in their morals'. Orwell equated this racial stereotyping to the anti-Semitism he had witnessed against British Jews during the war, highlighting the continuities in prejudice.[97] Equally significant was how the recurring mantra of 'Go back home' met by Caribbean servicemen also pursued the Poles who decided to settle in Britain after the war. One interviewee, recorded by the Kirklees Sound Archive in West Yorkshire in the 1980s, remembered:

> After the war there were some people in Scotland already, mostly politi-cally motivated, who used to – were hostile to us. And I remember an instant that a woman came to me as I was waiting in a queue at the bus station and she loudly said to me, 'Why don't you go back to Poland? Because of you I get a shilling less for my child.' There were a lot of the media which was ... we are not needed any more, we are all right when we are fighting for our and your freedoms – that was all right. But now some of them think that our usefulness has ceased, so we should go.[98]

Many Poles in Scotland articulated their personal post-war experience of racist attitudes as being tinged with sectarian hostility:

> Glasgow was a dreary place, and the people were generally distant and uncooperative. Many didn't like us at all. At work, in a machine-tool factory, some of the workers completely ignored me and the few other Poles employed there. We were obviously not wanted, also, appar-ently because we were Catholics. At that time, I was renting a shabby, ill-furnished room, and there were neighbours who sometimes shouted at me, 'Go back to Poland!' or 'When are you going back to your own country?' After a time, I was so pleased to leave 'Bonnie Scotland' behind for a better job in London.[99]

Yet significantly, like institutional representations of Caribbean wartime experience, the Poles in Britain tend to downplay or sideline these memories of exclusion. Mirroring trends within representations of West Indian service experience, the Polish community in Britain commemorates its wartime history within a one-dimensional militarized framework which disregards the multiplicity of personal experience. Indeed, the powerful male narrative of war, exemplified by the mushrooming of Polish Ex-Servicemen's Clubs in the post-war era, means that 'the historical identity of the community has been constructed disproportionately from the masculine image'.[100] In 1993, the Scottish United Services Museum at Edinburgh Castle hosted the exhibition 'For Your Freedom and Ours', with an accompanying booklet, which firmly adhered to a military narrative.[101] In 2011–12, there was a touring exhibition with similar title, 'For Our Freedom and Yours', which told the story of the 1st Polish armoured division, from their formation in Duns in 1942 to their campaigns in western Europe in 1944–5.[102] The most recent manifestation of this militaristic narration of the Polish wartime presence is the RAF Museum's online exhibition, 'The Polish Air Force in WWII', which 'tells the proud story of the Polish Air Force in the

Second World War'.[103] However, this privileging of martial masculinity within Polish memory work means that migrant women are generally marginalized in discourse surrounding refugees in Britain, as Kathy Burrell demonstrates in her study of the Polish community in Leicester. Indeed, this focus on the 'brave soldier' has generally led to the neglect of the complex histories of child deportees, of women fighting, of disabled men working in the refugee camps or of systematic rape by Soviet troops (and the realities of post-war lives in Britain with women often playing a lead role).[104] It also marginalizes those with mental health issues and denies the depth of unresolved pain caused by enforced deportation and exile experienced by Polish men who arrived in wartime Britain, identified in the work of Michelle Winslow.[105]

Conclusion

As Santanu Das acknowledges in relation to the First World War, while 'colonial non-white participants are slowly being wheeled in from the shadowy chambers of modern memory', much work remains to be done.[106] While there has been increasing recognition of the colonial contribution to Britain's war effort during World War Two, there is a tendency for formalized representations to celebrate rather than to critically analyse the wartime experiences of different black and minority ethnic groups. Furthermore, within museum settings, there are structural tensions between the demands of narrating the nation and the need to embrace the multicultural reality of post-colonial Britain.[107] However, while the experiences of black and white ethnicities continue to be positioned on the edges of Britain's self-narration about the Second World War, memory work will continue to be challenging. The two case studies of West Indian airmen and Polish servicemen demonstrate how both were the subjects of racialized stereotyping during the war itself, particularly on the grounds of their perceived sexual threat. Archived testimonies also stress the extent to which both groups confronted expressions of outright hostility in the immediate aftermath of the war, being rapidly re-configured as unwanted foreigners who ought to 'go back home'. Yet, both groups have also engaged in positivist official representations that commemorate their military contribution, and downplay the more negative aspects of their wartime histories in an attempt to gain a tentative foothold in the cultural memory work of Britain's war. Recorded personal narratives stored in archives across the UK provide a potentially rich mine of information that hints at the contradictory and multi-faceted nature of wartime memories, a complexity that tends to be airbrushed out of exhibitions which aim to commemorate migrant experience.

Notes

Thanks to Dr Matt Mead for advance sight of his paper: Mead, M. (2012), 'Plane Spotting, Military Portraiture and Multiculturalism in the Imperial War Museum', *Photography and Culture*, 5(3), 281–94.

1   Imperial War Museum (IWM) Sound Archive, 15285, Rene Webb, 1994. Wide Visions Productions/Channel 4.

2   Hazelton, L. (2004), 'Row erupts over artwork's removal'. *Coventry Evening Telegraph*, 19 November.

3   Das, S. (2011), 'Introduction', in S. Das (ed.), *Race, Empire and First World War Writing*. Cambridge: Cambridge University Press, 1–6.

4   Ward, P. (2004), *Britishness Since 1870*. London, Routledge, 124.

5   Cesarani, D. (1996), 'The changing character of nationality and citizenship in Britain', in D. Cesarani and M. Fulbrook (eds), *Citizenship, Nationality and Migration in Europe*. London: Routledge, 57–73. Here p. 96; Bousquet, B. and Douglas, C. (1991), *West Indian Women at War: British Racism in World War II*. London: Lawrence and Wishart; Visram, R. (2002), *Asians in Britain: 400 Years of History*. London: Pluto Press.

6   Harris, J. (1992), 'War and social history: Britain and the home front during the Second World War'. *Contemporary European History*, 1(1), 17–35. Here p. 35.

7   Gledhill, C. and Swanson, G. (1996), 'Introduction' in C. Gledhill and G. Swanson (eds), *Nationalising Femininity: Culture, Sexuality and British Cinema in the Second World War*. Manchester: Manchester University Press, 1–12. Here p. 8.

8   Harris (1992), 35.

9   Schaffer, G. (2010), 'Fighting racism; Black soldiers and workers in Britain during the Second World War', *Immigrants and Minorities*, 28, 246–65. Here p. 248.

10   Ibid., 246.

11   Schaffer (2010); Sherwood, M. (1985), *Many Struggles: West Indian Workers and Service Personnel in Britain (1939–1945)*. London: Karia Press.

12   Bourne, S. (2010), *Mother Country: Britain's Black Community on the Home Front 1939–45*. Stroud: The History Press, 11.

13   Schaffer (2010), 246.

14   Bland, L. (2005), 'White women and men of colour: miscegenation fears in Britain after the Great War', *Gender and History*, 17(1), 29–61.

15   Sherwood, M. (1985a), '"It is not a case of numbers": A case study of institutional racism in Britain, 1941–3', in K. Lunn (ed.), *Race and Labour in Twentieth Century Britain*. London: Frank Cass, 116–41, here 116.

16   Mass Observation Archive, File Report 1944, Fortnightly Bulletin (17), 11 October 1943. See Kushner, T. (2004), *We Europeans? Mass-Observation, 'Race' and British Identity in the Twentieth Century*. Aldershot: Ashgate, for a critical interrogation of Mass Observation as a source on 'race'.

17   Sherwood (1985a), 137.

18   Ibid., 126–7.

19   Ibid., 132.

20   Levy, A. (2004), *Small Island*. London: Headline Review. One of the key protagonists in Levy's book is a Jamaican RAF recruit, Gilbert Joseph, who returns to post-war Britain on *Empire Windrush*.

21   Francis, M. (2009), 'Men of the Royal Air Force, the cultural memory of the Second World War and the Twilight of the British Empire' in P. Levine and S. R. Grayzel (eds), *Gender, War and Empire: Essays on Modern Britain*. Basingstoke: Palgrave Macmillan, 179–96. Here 192. Francis argues that, although the RAF's wartime story promotes the cultural memory of the Second World War, it is also entwined with an equally powerful narrative of the end of empire.

22   Lambo, R. (1994), 'Achtung! The Black Prince: West Africans in the Royal Air Force, 1939-46', in D. Killingray (ed.), *Africans in Britain*. Ilford: Frank Cass, 145–63. Here p. 148.

23   Sherwood, M. (1985b), *Many Struggles: West Indian Workers and Service Personnel in Britain (1939–45)*. London: Karia Press, 7–8.

24   Kushner, T. (2012), ' "Without intending any of the most undesirable features of a colour bar": Race Science, Europeaness and the British Armed Forces During the Twentieth Century', *Patterns of Prejudice* 46 (3–4), 339–74. Here p. 339.

25   Schaffer (2010), 248.

26   Ibid., 250.

27   Webster, W. (1998), *Imagining Home. Gender, 'Race' and National Identity, 1945–64*. London: Routledge, 25.

28   Ward (2004), 124.

29   Waters, C. (1997), ' "Dark strangers" in our midst: discourses of race and nation in Britain 1947–63'. *Journal of British Studies*, 36(2), 207–38. Here, 208.

30   Gilroy, P. (2004), *After Empire: Melancholia or Convivial Culture?* London: Routledge, 98.

31   Ibid., 97.

32   Ibid., vii; 95.

33   Ibid., 95.

34   Mead (2012), 281.

35   Imperial War Museum, 'From War to Windrush' website. http://london.iwm.org.uk/server/show/conEvent.2377/.

36   Ward (2004), 124.

37   Ugolini, W. (2012), 'The embodiment of British Italian war memory? The curious marginalization of Dennis Donnini, VC', *Patterns of Prejudice*, 46, 397–415.

38   Mead, M., 'From War to Windrush: curating multiculturalism in the Imperial War Museum, London', PhotoCLEC.

Photographs, Colonial Legacy and Museums in Contemporary
European Culture website. http://photoclec.dmu.ac.uk/content/
war-windrush-curating-multiculturalism-imperial-war-museum-london/.

39 Mead (2012), 282.

40 Ibid., 286.

41 Mead, 'From War to Windrush'.

42 Mead (2012), 286.

43 Mead, 'From War to Windrush'.

44 RAF, 'RAF honours service by ethnic minorities', RAF 2001 News Archive,
www.raf.mod.uk/history/museumex.html/.

45 Kushner (2012), 345.

46 Ibid., 344.

47 Ibid., 369.

48 Ibid., 347.

49 Ibid., 370.

50 Ibid., 345.

51 Burrell, K and Panayi, P. (2006), 'Immigration, history and memory
in Britain', in K Burrell and P. Panayi (eds), *Histories and Memories:
Migrants and The History in Britain*. London: Tauris Academic Studies, 3–17.
Here p. 16.

52 IWM Sound Archive, 142/5/2, Billy Strachan, 1987.

53 Francis (2009), 193.

54 Ibid., 188.

55 Bornat, J. (2003), 'A second take: revisiting interviews with a different
purpose'. *Oral History*, 31(1), 47–53. Here p. 47.

56 Rene Webb's interview, IWM 15285, was recorded in the West Indian
Ex-Servicemen's Association in 1994 as part of the Channel 4 series, *What
Has Become of Us?*

57 See Schaffer, G. (2008), *Racial Science and British Society, 1930-62*.
Basingstoke: Palgrave Macmillan.

58 IWM Sound Archive, 31047, Alan Wilmot.

59 IWM, Billy Strachan.

60 Smith, R. (2008), 'The Black Peril: race, masculinity and migration during
the First World War', in L. Ryan and W. Webster (eds), *Gendering Migration.
Masculinity, Femininity and Ethnicity in Post-war Britain*. Aldershot:
Ashgate, 19–34. Here p. 23.

61 Tabili, L. (1994), 'The construction of racial difference in twentieth-century
Britain: the Special Restriction (Coloured Alien Seamen) Order, 1925'.
Journal of British Studies, 31(1), 54–98. Here p. 69.

62 IWM, Billy Strachan.

63 Smith, G. (1987), *When Jim Crow Met John Bull. Black American Soldiers
in World War II Britain*. London: I.B. Tauris, 118; Reynolds, D. (1995), *Rich*

Relations: The American Occupation of Britain 1942–1945. London: Harper Collins, 302–24.

64   Schaffer (2010), 251–2.

65   IWM, Alan Wilmot.

66   IWM, Billy Strachan.

67   Ibid.

68   IWM, Alan Wilmot.

69   Paul, K. (1997), *Whitewashing Britain. Race and Citizenship in the Postwar Era*. Ithaca: Cornell University Press, xii.

70   Mead (2012), 290.

71   Museum of London Oral History Archive (MOLOHA). Accession number 92.181. Interview with Sam King; interviewed by Rory O'Connell, 1992.

72   Webster, W. (2008), 'Britain and the refugees of Europe 1939–50' in L. Ryan and W. Webster (eds.), *Gendering Migration. Masculinity, Femininity and Ethnicity in Post-war Britain*. Aldershot: Ashgate, 23.

73   MOLOHA, Sam King.

74   Miles, R. (1993), *Racism after 'Race Relations'*. London: Routledge, 164–5.

75   IWM, Alan Wilmot.

76   IWM Sound Archive, 15285, Rene Webb, 1994. Wide Visions Productions/ Channel 4.

77   The *Clasp O' Frien'ship (Ogniwo Przyjalni)* was a bi-lingual weekly published in 1941–2 in Glasgow. Kernberg, T. (1990), *The Polish Community in Scotland*, Unpublished PhD thesis, University of Glasgow, 93.

78   Stachura, P. D. (2011), '"God, Honour and Fatherland": The Poles in Scotland, 1940–1950, and the legacy of the Second Republic', in T. M. Devine and D. Hesse (eds.), *Scotland and Poland: Historical Encounters, 1500–2010*. Edinburgh: Birlinn, 157.

79   Carswell, A. (1993), *For Your Freedom and Ours: Poland, Scotland and the Second World War*. Edinburgh: National Museums of Scotland, p. 7.

80   Zubrzycki, J. (1956), *Polish Immigrants in Britain. A Study of Adjustment*. The Hague: Martinus Nijhoff, 82.

81   Urquhart, F. (1951), *Jezebel's Dust*. London: Methuen, 128.

82   Ibid., 126; Urquhart, F. (1946a), 'Dirty linen', in *Selected Short Stories*. London: Maurice Fridberg, 107–15. Here p. 108.

83   Urquhart, F. (1946b), 'Mrs. Coolie-Hoo's Pole', in *Selected Short Stories*, London: Maurice Fridberg, 33–40. Here p. 40.

84   Urquhart, (1951).

85   Pruszyński, K. (1941), *Polish Invasion*. London: Minerva, 40–5.

86   Webster (2008), 35–6.

87   Carswell, (1993), 9–10.

88 KSA, interview 036PL, cited in Nocon, A. (1996), 'A reluctant welcome? Poles in Britain in the 1940s'. *Oral History*, 24(1), 79–87. Here p. 81.

89 Rose, S. O. (2003), *Which People's War? National Identity and Citizenship in Wartime Britain 1939-1945.* Oxford: Oxford University Press, 50.

90 Kernberg, (1990), x.

91 Stachura, (2011), 158.

92 Webster (2008), 'Britain and the refugees of Europe', 45.

93 Kernberg, (1990), 8.

94 Ibid., 223.

95 Ibid., 160.

96 Clements, R., 'Press reception of Polish migrants in Scotland, 1940–2010' in Devine and Hesse (eds.) (2011), 173–85. Here, 175–8.

97 Orwell, G. (1947), 'As I Please', *Tribune*, 24 January, reprinted in Orwell, G. (2001), *Orwell and Politics.* London: Penguin, 468–70.

98 KSA, interview 036PL.

99 Archive of the Research Centre for Modern Polish History (ARCMPH), Peter D. Stachura interview with Zbigniew Bienek (pseud.), A.1, 24 April 2003, cited in Stachura, 'God, Honour and Fatherland', 160–1.

100 Burrell, K. (2008), 'Male and female Polishness in post-war Leicester: gender and its intersections in a refugee community', in Ryan and Webster (eds) (2008), 71–87. Here 77.

101 Carswell, (1993).

102 See Pike, D., 'Wartime memories exhibition breaks all records', 5 October 2011. http://exploretheborders.com/wartime-memories-exhibition-breaks-all-records/

103 http://www.rafmuseum.org.uk/research/online-exhibitions/the-polish-air-force-in-world-war-2.aspx/

104 Burrell, (2008), 77.

105 Winslow, M. (1999), 'Polish migration to Britain: war, exile and mental health'. *Oral History*, 27(1), 57–64.

106 Das, (2011), 6.

107 Mead (2012), 290.

Key texts

Burrell, K. and Panayi, P. (eds) (2006), *Histories and Memories: Migrants and The History in Britain.* London: Tauris Academic Studies.

Devine, T. M and Hesse, D. (eds) (2011), *Scotland and Poland: Historical Encounters, 1500-2010.* Edinburgh: Birlinn.

Francis, M. (2009), 'Men of the Royal Air Force, the cultural memory of the Second World War and the twilight of the British Empire', in P. Levine and

S. R. Grayzel (eds), *Gender, Labour, War and Empire: Essays on Modern Britain*. Basingstoke: Palgrave Macmillan, 179–96.

Gilroy, P. (2004), *After Empire. Melancholia or Convivial Culture?* London: Routledge.

Kushner, T. (2004), *We Europeans? Mass-Observation, 'Race' and British Identity in the Twentieth Century*. Aldershot: Ashgate.

—(2012), '"Without intending any of the most undesirable features of a colour bar": Race Science, Europeanness and the British Armed Forces During the Twentieth Century', *Patterns of Prejudice*, 46(3–4), 339–74.

Mead, M. (2012), 'Plane Spotting, Military Portraiture and Multiculturalism in the Imperial War Museum'. *Photography & Culture*, 5(3), 281–94.

Paul, K. (1997), *Whitewashing Britain. Race and Citizenship in the Postwar Era*. Ithaca: Cornell University Press.

Schaffer, G. (2010), 'Fighting Racism: Black Soldiers and Workers in Britain During the Second World War'. *Immigrants & Minorities*, 28, 246–65.

Sherwood, M. (1985a), '"It is not a case of numbers": A case study of institutional racism in Britain, 1941-3', in K. Lunn (ed.), *Race and Labour in Twentieth Century Britain*. London: Frank Cass, 116–41.

—(1985b), *Many Struggles: West Indian Workers and Service Personnel in Britain (1939-1945)*. London: Karia Press.

Ward, P. (2004), *Britishness Since 1870*. London: Routledge.

Waters, C. (1997), '"Dark strangers" in our midst: discourses of race and nation in Britain 1947-63', *Journal of British Studies*, 36(2), 207–38.

Webster, W. (1998), *Imagining Home. Gender, 'Race' and National Identity, 1945-64*. London: Routledge.

—(2008), 'Britain and the refugees of Europe 1939-50', in L. Ryan and W. Webster (eds), *Gendering Migration. Masculinity, Femininity and Ethnicity in Post-war Britain*. Aldershot: Ashgate.

Wynn, N. A. (2006), '"Race war": Black American GIs and West Indians in Britain during the Second World War', *Immigrants and Minorities*, 24(3), 324–46.

CHAPTER SIX

Remembering war, forgetting empire?

Representations of the North African Campaign in 1950s British cinema

Martin Francis

In his powerful critique of how the imperial past has remained the crucial site of repression within contemporary British national memory, Paul Gilroy isolates the Second World War as an ongoing impediment to coming to terms with the nation's diminished status on the world stage. The dominant national myth of the Second World War, whether in its progressive (the patriotic communalism of the Blitz) or conservative (the romantic Toryism of Winston Churchill's speeches) manifestations, has continued to serve as the critical agent in 'making the journey out of Britain's imperial pre-eminence both bearable and liveable'.[1] Gilroy's insistence that the memory of 1939–45 has served to obscure the rapid and definitive demise of Britain's empire in the immediate postwar decades would seem to be borne out by popular memory of the British war effort against the Axis in North Africa between 1940 and 1943. The British military's campaign in Egypt, Libya and Tunisia has been characterized as essentially a European war, which, while it took place on the continent of Africa, involved fighting with European weapons against a European enemy. Moreover the fact that so many of its critical military encounters took place in the vast, apparently empty terrain of the Western Desert allowed the memory of the North African campaign to operate at a distance, not merely from the war in Europe but from previous British military campaigns on the African continent. In so doing, it was able to secure the status of a uniquely 'civilized' war, free from the taint of violence against non-combatants that had become such a dramatic feature of military conflict in metropolitan Europe (and Asia) in the first half of the twentieth century, but which had also long been integral to wars of Western colonial conquest and pacification, and, as the European empires disintegrated, to the final, bloody campaigns of colonial counter-insurgency.[2] Academic scholarship has done little to confront such popular understandings, and there is a striking contrast with studies of the Second World War in South East Asia that have made clear that the conduct and legacy of the war in that region was intrinsically entwined with the end of empire.[3]

In fact there is considerable justification for framing Britain's participation in the Desert War within the rubrics of race and empire. Space precludes a comprehensive catalogue of the myriad ways in which imperial tropes and references were woven into the fabric of the North African campaign, but a few selected examples indicate the broader picture. Egypt, whose successful defence (first against the Italians, and then against a combined German–Italian effort) was Britain's overwhelming strategic objective during the campaign, was (despite the nominal recognition of its independence in the 1936 Anglo–Egyptian Treaty) effectively a British protectorate, in which the British ambassador, Sir Miles Lampson, actively intervened in Egyptian parliamentary and court politics to ensure continued British authority.[4] Egypt's defence was in the hands of a military force that was distinctly imperial (as opposed to merely British) in character. Several senior commanders, notably Alexander, Auchinleck and Montgomery, hailed from the Anglo-Irish ascendancy, while others had extensive associations, not just with imperial warfare, but with imperial governance. Wavell, Commander-in-Chief in the Middle East, had begun his career as a junior officer in India, and was subsequently to become Viceroy, while Auchinleck's ill-fated time in command of the Eighth Army was book-ended by two stints as Commander-in-Chief in India.[5] It also should not be forgotten that the British war effort in North Africa (even after the arrival of Rommel's Afrika Korps in 1941) was predominantly directed against Italy, much of it taking place in Libya, an Italian colony, and a case could be made for regarding the Desert War as the final stage of an old-style imperial rivalry between two European maritime powers, which took place over the carcass of another empire (that of the Ottomans).[6] A large part of the 'British' forces stationed in North Africa during the war was actually made up of South Africans, New Zealanders and Australians, and also troops from India. Indeed several South Asian officers commanded battalions, and even brigades, during the campaign, notably Ayub Khan and Yahya Khan, who both later served as presidents of independent Pakistan.[7] The presence of

Indian troops in the Western Desert neatly encapsulates how the political, strategic and military imperatives of the British campaign in North Africa and its personal hinterlands were indisputably imperial in character.

The British public's dominant understanding of a campaign where continuous swings of the offensive pendulum made it difficult to establish a clear and legible narrative owed much, not to a Briton, but to the Australian war reporter Alan Moorehead, who in the postwar years authored a number of books that linked the British experience in Egypt to the wider histories of empire and exploration in Africa as a whole.[8] Indeed desert combat during the Second World War was repeatedly interpreted through the tropes of exploration and adventure, especially the irregular warfare associated with the Long Range Desert Group (LRDG), whose founder, Major Ralph Bagnold, was the quintessential imperial gentleman-adventurer, appropriating for military purposes the techniques and equipment originally developed for peacetime long-distance travel and desert navigation.[9] Men such as the charismatic founder of the Special Air Service, Major David Stirling, were compared to the fearless maritime adventurer-explorers who had supposedly been responsible for forging the British Empire. A biographer of Stirling, writing in the 1950s, insisted that the reason the British proved more effective at irregular desert warfare than their opponents was that 'it was natural that a great seafaring race should take easily to the huge uncharted wastelands. Sea and desert had much in common ... both offered the same sense of isolation, comradeship, exploration and adventure'.[10] If the Desert War allowed the refurbishment of the clichés and heroic myths of an earlier era of imperial adventure, it also encompassed the less attractive elements of Britain's empire story. In their different ways, the amiable contempt directed at their Egyptian hosts in the memoirs of British officers and the more overt abuse and violence directed at everyone from taxi drivers to King Faruq and his family by soldiers stationed in Cairo, provide testimony to the resilience of racially-grounded notions of Western superiority and oriental backwardness that had underpinned Britain's imperial dominion in its heyday.[11]

Race, empire and reassessing the 1950s British war film

How then to explain the relative absence of race and empire from British memory of the Desert War? Part of the explanation may lie in the relative absence of the North African campaign from a critical site of collective memory formation, the 1950s British war film. Once derided for their pin-headed triumphalism, unreflective nostalgia and social conservatism, films such as *The Dambusters* (1955), *Reach for the Sky* (1956), *The Colditz Story* (1955) and *The Cruel Sea* (1953) have, in the three decades since Andy Medhurst's iconoclastic intervention, been subject to a dramatic revaluation, serving as a surprisingly effective index of changing configurations of both class and gender in postwar Britain.[12] By contrast, race and empire have been adopted much less in interpretations of the British war movie genre. Moreover, war films set in North Africa have received virtually no attention, with the exception of that increasingly iconic text *Ice Cold in Alex* (1958), but, even here, the focus has been on the film's exposure of an increasingly frayed British masculinity as the 1950s drew to close, rather than on its relationship to the eclipse of British imperial authority.[13] Such an absence is, at one level, perfectly understandable. Films dealing with aspects of the Desert War often appeared to wholeheartedly embrace the premise of the 'empty desert'. *Sea of Sand*, a 1958 drama about a LRDG patrol cut off behind German lines, emphasized the 'searing heat and loneliness of the desert' without any acknowledgment of the indigenous peoples who called the Libyan interior home.[14] Similarly *Ice Cold in Alex* pitted three soldiers, a female nurse and an ageing military ambulance against a thousand miles of unforgiving desert.[15] In this struggle against the pitiless forces of nature, the physically unprepossessing (and alcoholic) British Captain Anson finds himself dependent on the monumental muscularity of South African Captain Van Der Poel. However, any reading of this relationship as a metaphor for the assertion of (white) colonial settler virility against a fading metropolitan power – the latter's authority fatally compromised by effete political leadership and the apparent inability to protect the mother nation's racial exclusivity – is ultimately voided by the fact that Van Der Poel turns out to be a false Springbok, a German officer in disguise. *Ice Cold in Alex* repudiates more conventional wartime national and gender differences to celebrate the collective bravery of a decidedly heterogeneous collection of individuals that incorporates a decidedly non-heroic version of the classic British officer, a woman and an enemy combatant, but, critically, has no space for the imperial (in this case, white settler) citizen. Here the erasure of empire appears unequivocal and uncontested.

However, two neglected cinematic texts from this era allow the possibility of bringing race and empire back into consideration when analysing the popular memory of the Desert War. *The Black Tent* (1956) is a fictional tale of a wounded British officer who hides out among the Bedouin tribesmen of the Libyan Desert and marries the sheik's daughter, before being killed in a guerrilla attack on an Axis column. *Foxhole in Cairo* (1960), by contrast, is based on a true story, the frantic search for a German spy in wartime Cairo in the critical period immediately prior to the battle of Alamein. Both movies were of limited artistic and dramatic merit, meeting with lukewarm responses from audiences and critics. However, as with their more illustrious cinematic peers, they offer a window into contemporary structures of feeling, at a time when the records that ultimately came to constitute more conventional archives were often reticent in recording the emotional dimension to both the memory of war and the more immediate trauma of decolonization. While cinema-going was losing out to new forms of leisure, notably television, throughout the 1950s, cinema admissions in the year *The Black Tent* was released still totalled 1,100 million, suggesting that film fully deserves its standing as the most frequented site for the creation and dissemination of popular memory of the Second World War.[16]

While data on box office returns for individual films remains unavailable, *The Black Tent* featured one of Britain's leading home-grown film stars, Anthony Steel, and its mix of action and romance presumably guaranteed respectable audience numbers, while *Foxhole in Cairo* drew on the presence of the dependable and popular James Robertson Justice to ensure widespread release and distribution. Both films were subsequently shown on television and have been re-released on disc, ensuring their dissemination across successive generations, and raising the intriguing scenario of 1950s wartime memorializing itself being subsequently remembered.[17] Moreover, the status of both films as indexes of popular memory can be raised further if a close reading of the content of the movies themselves is accompanied by due regard to their augmentation by adjacent literary texts. For example, *The Black Tent* was scripted by novelist Robin Maugham, who published a version of the story in *Chambers Journal* and included it in a later anthology of his writings.[18] *Foxhole in Cairo* both followed on from, and reinforced, the popularity of *The Cat and the Mice*, Leonard Mosley's journalistic account of the events featured in the film.[19] While *The Black Tent* and *Foxhole in Cairo* may be relatively minor players in the 'monumentalized apotheosis' of the Second World War in 1950s British culture, they offer a valuable point of access to the largely overlooked intersections between memory of the Second World War and the end of empire.[20]

At the very least, consideration of these two movies demonstrates the rewards of venturing beyond the cluster of celebrated and familiar classic war films (usually focused on an individual service or specialized unit within the military) that have, to date, received most coverage. An important recent study by Penny Summerfield has drawn attention to a previously overlooked number of 1950s war films that dealt with female wartime experiences, whether as heroines or victims. However, these films still retain many of the elements of the classic male-dominated war film, notably a quasi-documentary approach, a restrained emotional disposition, and the grounding of the story in real-life events and characters.[21] By contrast, there are films made in Britain during the 1950s that are also set during the Second World War, but that eschew many of the elements of the classic war film genre, and would repay proper historical attention. We need to widen our definition of the 'war film' to include movies such as *The Black Tent*, which, in their resort to melodrama, and their preference for stylized expressivity over documentary-style restraint, are clearly very different from films such as *The Dambusters* or even the woman-centred *Carve Her Name With Pride* (1958). *Foxhole in Cairo*, it is true, has much more affinity with the mainstream war film (or at least its counter-espionage sub-genre) but, unlike those texts, it shares with *The Black Tent* two critical motifs: the presence of issues of racial difference in an imperial–orientalist setting, and the disruptive impact of women and female sexuality on notions of male military obligation.

The latter of these two themes had more purchase in 1950s British cinematic culture than would be apparent from the ongoing fixation among historians on the festishization of male homosociability (and the parallel erasure of the feminine) in many of the classic war film narratives.[22] Carol Reed's *The Key* (1958), in which a succession of doomed Merchant Navy captains pass on their key to a flat – and its resident woman – to their successors in the event of being killed in action, combined documentary-style action sequences with straight human drama, romance and a disquieting element of the supernatural and macabre. Stella, the woman in question, is an ambiguous figure, presented as both a source of solace for men coping with fear and loneliness, and as a possible siren leading men to disaster. While the film was set in a down-at-heel seaside town, the casting of Sophia Loren, who played Stella as a sultry Italianate woman of mystery, ensured that the film's exotic and erotic thermostats were set at a decidedly higher level than those of *The Cruel Sea*.[23] The presence of Italy's most voluptuous *maggiorata* in a film ostensibly concerned with weary wartime tug-boat captains suggests that we may need to be a little more sceptical about how prevalent the high homosociability which characterized a select number of canonical war film narratives was in the wider cinematic culture that concerned itself with memory of the war. It also requires us to modify the conventional wisdom that films portraying the Second World War made in Britain in the 1950s were dominated by the tropes of national parochialism. Many continental European stars featured in British-made features (notable examples being Brigitte Bardot's appearance in the *Doctor* film series and Simone Signoret's incongruous presence in a gritty Yorkshire industrial town in *Room at the Top*), including films with wartime settings. *The Black Tent* featured Italian starlet Anna Maria Sandri in the role of Mabrouka, the Bedouin girl who provides the film's love interest. In *Foxhole in Cairo* the allure of the foreign and the exotic was satisfied by the casting of former Mexican ballet dancer Gloria Mestre as the Egyptian belly dancer (and German agent) Amina.

Incorporating *The Black Tent* and *Foxhole in Cairo* into an analysis of British war films of the 1950s can further two important ends. First, in contrast to Gilroy's assertions, it allows us to register how empire and its demise on the one hand and the cultural memory of the Second World War on the other were not posed as antithetical alternatives but were in fact intrinsically linked. Specifically, both films featured (albeit in caricatured form) the indigenous peoples of North Africa and exposed the precariousness of British imperial authority over them. *Foxhole in Cairo*, in particular, acknowledged Arab nationalism and the creation of Israel, the two historical forces which were to shape the Middle East in the aftermath of British disengagement from the region. Indeed its Egyptian setting did not merely recall the setting of Britain's greatest wartime military triumph – at Alamein in 1942 – but also raised less congenial associations, with Britain's most notable (post-) imperial humiliation, the Suez debacle of 1956. Second, the presence of empire in films set during the Second World War facilitated the incorporation into the negotiation between the memory of a wartime past and the post-war present of a number of additional issues – notably those relating to racial politics in the metropole, the increased visibility of both female heterosexuality and male homosexuality, or the levelling consequences of the welfare state – and, in so doing, call into question the 'temporal and geographic reductions' that beset much existing scholarship on modern British history.[24]

Repudiating the myth of the 'empty desert': *The Black Tent* (1956)

The Black Tent opens with Charles Holland walking in the gardens of his country mansion, part of the landed estate he has inherited from his brother David, an officer who was reported as 'missing, presumed dead' in the Western Desert in 1942. Charles is summoned to the Foreign Office, where he is informed that an undated promissory note, signed by his brother, has recently been handed into the British embassy in Tripoli. Charles travels to Libya in order to solve the mystery of his brother's fate. He traces the note to a Bedouin tribe, whose head, Sheik Salem, is hostile and asks Charles to leave. However, before his departure, Charles spies in Salem's camp a fair-haired boy, the image of his brother as a child. The child's mother, Mabrouka, reveals nothing, other than the fact that her husband is dead, but she secretly slips to Charles a bundle of papers, the diary of the missing Captain David Holland. As Charles reads the diaries, the film enters into flashback, and we learn David's story. After being left for dead after a tank battle, David is found by Mabrouka and nursed back to health. David falls in love with Mabrouka, and, when he receives misinformation that Cairo has fallen to the Germans, he decides to stay with the Bedouin and marry the beautiful Arab woman who saved his life. However, on learning that the German advance has been halted at Alamein, he prepares to return to combat, leaving Mabrouka his will, in which he bequeathes his title and estate to their unborn child. Charles returns to the Bedouin camp to discover the rest of the story. Salem tells him that David was killed in a guerrilla attack they jointly led against an enemy convoy. Charles offers to forfeit his right to his brother's estate so that David's son, Daoud, can claim his inheritance. However, the film ends with the boy choosing to stay among the black tents of the Bedouin.

The film was based on a short story by Robin Maugham, nephew of the more illustrious Somerset, a veteran of the North African campaign, and a prolific novelist, obsessed with the themes of sexual ambiguity, guilt and fear.[25] The task of converting Maugham's short story into a film was entrusted to Brian Desmond Hurst, a director who had worked in a variety of genres, but who was most famous for his wartime romantic melodrama *Dangerous Moonlight*. Neither Maugham nor Hurst matched the stipulations of realism and restraint that characterized the masculine universe of the classic war film, and reviewers seemed disoriented by the film's willingness to combine battle and romance. *Today's Cinema* summarized the film as one in which, 'though action is prominent, romantic interest is stressed'.[26] *Kinematograph Weekly* described the film as 'bizarre', 'Ethel M. Dell clothed in a *Boy's Own Paper* jacket', but conceded that 'its slick feminine angle' might pay off at the box office.[27] The film's publicity department did little to discourage ambiguity. Having suggested that ex-servicemen and 'newsworthy personalities of the Long Range Desert Group' should be invited to the film's opening night, it then outlined a series of initiatives that placed the film within the discourses, not of the service film, but of orientalized romantic fantasy, for example installing signs in Arabic script, fountains and palm trees to create 'an Arabian atmosphere in your foyer'.[28] The fact that the film was made in colour undoubtedly contributed to its alignment with the feminized spheres of the so-called 'women's film', and its distance from the mainstream British war film, which was usually made in black and white. While Hurst's use of both Technicolor and Vista Vision were undoubtedly intended to emphasize exotic spectacle and to highlight the use of location filming, it is important to remember that colour was often associated in this era with the melodramatic and the feminine, for example in the conveyance of overwrought emotions and unapologetic sensuality through the vivid chromatics of Powell and Pressburger's *Black Narcissus* or the 'women's weepies' of Douglas Sirk.[29]

The selection of colour for *The Black Tent* also suggested an affinity with the spectacular and rousing imperial epics produced by Alexander Korda, and directed by his brother Zoltan, films such as *The Drum* (1938) and *The Four Feathers* (1939). Coincidentally, the year before *The Black Tent* was released, Korda had remade *The Four Feathers* (with a cast headed by Anthony Steel, who would go on to play David Holland in *The Black Tent*) incorporating the Technicolor battle sequences from the original version, under the new title of *Storm over the Nile*. While *The Black Tent* lacked the imperial cavalcade of *Storm over the Nile*, it did incorporate the orientalist imaginary that accompanied, and contributed to, the consolidation of empire, and had been a critical feature in its cinematic representation during the 1930s.[30] Publicity for *The Black Tent* promised that 'western eyes are given a glimpse of the strange and fascinating traditions of the Arab world in the authentic filming of a desert wedding'.[31] Several reviewers highlighted the 'fascinating charm' of the film's exotic locations and costumes, particularly in the wedding sequence, featuring what the *Monthly Film Bulletin* characterized as an 'authentic stomach dance'.[32]

Many of those involved in the making of *The Black Tent* had extensive imperial hinterlands. Anthony Steel was the son of an Indian army officer.[33] The film's producer, William MacQuitty, had been a member of the foreign service of the Chartered Bank of China, India and Australia between the wars, supplementing his career in finance with membership of the Amritsar Club and service in the Punjab Light Horse.[34] As an Ulster Protestant who converted to Catholicism, Brian Desmond Hurst inevitably had an idiosyncratic approach to both Britain and its empire, but, as a film-maker, he remained captivated by imperialism's association with both adventure and spectacle.[35] Having served in the Western Desert, Robin Maugham worked as an intelligence officer in the Middle East in the latter part of the war, returning to the region as a travel writer in the late 1940s. However, his claims of personal affection and political sympathy for the Arabs did not preclude Maugham's screenplay for *The Black Tent* from incorporating a number of stereotypes of the Arab world, including the passive Muslim woman (Mabrouka), the proud Bedouin sheik (Salem) and Ali, the guide who constantly pesters Charles Holland with offers to 'find nice girls' and 'arrange scenes of great delight for you'.[36]

However, for all its stereotypes and preposterous plot, *The Black Tent* testifies to a historical truth that is absent from the classic war films such as *Sea of Sand*. In its idiosyncratic way, it repudiates the myth of the 'empty desert', acknowledging the interaction between the Desert War and the indigenous peoples of North Africa. The recognition of this engagement is clear from the very first meeting between Charles Holland and Sheik Salem, in which the former initiates their conversation with the query 'Did the war make much of a difference to your people?' Salem's reply reverses the usual demoting of the local populations to the shadows of the all-consuming conflict between European arms and armies. 'Oh yes', Salem firmly responds. 'It was a different war for us. We saw much of both sides.' At various points in the movie, Salem offers hospitality to both British and German soldiers, which not merely accords with Western stereotypes of Bedouin *noblesse oblige*, but also has the more radical implication that all Europeans are little more than short-term visitors, a passing phase in the broader non-European history of the North African desert. Significantly, when German officers arrive at a ruined Roman city (a scene filmed at the actual ruins of Leptis Magna) searching for David, they take time to pose for photographs, transient tourists rather than the tribunes of a permanent imperial dominion, with the ruins behind them serving as a mute witness to earlier attempts by Europe to subjugate Africa that had crumbled into dust. The battle of Alamein, the pivotal event in the Desert War (and the one that had most significance for Britons in the popular memory of the war as a whole), takes place off-screen, with David only learning of the great British victory from a Bedouin who is passing through Salem's encampment.

If much of the film's narrative contains the relationship between Britain's war effort in North Africa and the indigenous peoples of the region within a romantic trope, the flashback sequence of *The Black Tent* concludes with David leading a Bedouin unit in an attack on a German convoy. The contribution of the various populations of Libya to the British war effort was not spectacular, but nor was it insignificant. The British recruited a Libyan Arab Force from Libyan exiles in Egypt, while soldiers from Cyrenaica's Sanusi population played a critical role in the reconnaissance ahead of David Stirling's audacious raid on Benghazi harbour.[37] Bedouin acted as guides, accompanied LRDG detachments and assisted escaped POWs and men separated from their units. An officer seconded to the Civil Affairs Branch of GHQ Middle East testified to the way the inhabitants of Libya 'helped us greatly, at considerable risks to themselves, by feeding, hiding and leading back to our lines hundreds of British personnel'.[38] Many prominent authorities strove to draw attention to the Libyans' contribution to British military success. E. E. Evans-Pritchard, a social anthropologist who served as a political officer in the British military administration in Libya after the Germans and Italians were driven out in late 1942, campaigned tirelessly to have Britain give full recognition to Libyan assistance to the Allies during the war, while Anthony Eden paid tribute to the Libyan Arab Force in the House of Commons in January 1942.[39] However, by the time *The Black Tent* was released, such wartime associations had largely been erased from British national memory, impossible to sustain in a postwar era that had seen Britain's power and influence in the Arab world rapidly and dramatically eclipsed. *The Black Tent*, we should not forget, was released in the same year as the Suez crisis, the most chastening manifestation yet of the passing of British pre-eminence in the Middle East. The makers of *The Black Tent* therefore deserve some credit for offering rare acknowledgment of the presence of non-whites in what had become reconstituted as merely an overseas staging of a white man's war.

The Black Tent also tackled an issue that had long disturbed the dominant discourses of race and empire – the challenge of interracial sex and miscegenation. However, it did this within the parameters of established, and often dissembling, literary (and cinematic) conventions. As one reviewer rather clumsily characterized it, 'The love of a European for a beauty of different pigmentation has been a sure-fire romantic hit since Lieutenant Pinkerton wooed Butterfly ... But instead of Japanese geisha houses, the story is set in the Western Desert, more familiar, if only by reputation, to British audiences.'[40] Working within the traditions of the over-heated romantic melodramas authored by Robert Hichens or Edith Hull, the exotic settings of *The Black Tent* allowed the possibility of escape from the conventions of sexual inhibition.[41] David Holland justifies falling in love with Mabrouka in terms of a desert environment that strips away the stifling mores of modern Western life, allowing the attainment of a genuine 'openness of mind and heart'. However, the destabilizing sexual allure of the orient is somewhat muted here. Mabrouka possesses the lustrous hair, dark sultry eyes, opulent jewels and costume of the oriental woman of mystery, but she lacks the libidinous charge of the belly-dancer spy Amina in *Foxhole in Cairo*. Mabrouka is a demure, and essentially passive, character, waiting submissively on her wedding night, and more likely (despite being clothed in this scene in a diaphanous low-cut nightgown whose inspiration owed more to Fredericks of Hollywood than the orient – fantasized or otherwise) to be found playing a sedate game of chequers with David than in the throes of frenzied passion. The disruptive potential of this romantic and sexual relationship across race lines is further diminished by the fact that, as in a number of other British cinematic miscegenation dramas from this period (for example, *Outcast of the Islands* or *The Wind Cannot Read*), what is portrayed here is an interracial romance between a white man and a non-white woman, which thereby, by means of gender, preserves the hierarchy between colonizer and colonized.[42] In so doing, it preserved an element of distance from the anxieties surrounding interracial sex that were becoming prevalent in metropolitan Britain in the mid-1950s, grounded as they were in an almost pathological obsession with the relationships between black men and white women.[43]

It would require a serious stretch of the imagination to see David and Mabrouka's romance in *The Black Tent* as offering the same degree of challenge to the cohesive model of British national identity posed by new forms of sexual exchange emerging in the metropole. However, the ending of *The Black Tent* did share an important feature with many of the debates over interracial marriage taking place in Britain, which was concern over the future prospects of the children of such relationships. Press commentary predicted misfortunes for mixed-race children, who would ultimately find it impossible to fully relate to either white or black culture, in an age in which it was still widely assumed that races would remain essentially discrete and homogenous.[44] *The Black Tent* shared such pessimistic assumptions about the impossibility or undesirability of hybridity. Salem makes clear to both Charles and Daoud that, if the boy goes to England, his Bedouin heritage will be lost entirely, while Charles simply assumes that the son of an English gentleman will need to be raised in 'civilized surroundings'. Daoud's decision to remain among the Bedouin not merely allows Charles to keep his landed estates, but also preserves the mono-racial integrity of the metropole, abandoning the mixed-race child on the outer margins of empire, at a degree of distance and disassociation that would render it impossible for him to disrupt the ethnic absolutism of the 'island nation'.

Interracial sex was only one aspect of a more general uncertainty surrounding the coordinates of sexual categories which characterized Britain in the 1950s. Equally significant was the growing visibility of male homosexuality, and here too *The Black Tent* was willing (albeit covertly) to bring the memory of wartime into alignment with what has usually been presented as a distinctly postwar moment of cultural rearrangement.[45] The film can certainly be viewed as an exercise in queer cultural production, Hurst and Maugham being gay men (the former flamboyantly so, the latter more discreetly).[46] Both men had personally explored same-sex desire within a military context. Hurst fully shared a penchant among upper middle-class gay men in the middle decades of the twentieth century for the muscular bodies and working-class origins of the scarlet-uniformed guardsman, while Maugham's first homosexual relationship had been with his army driver during the Desert War.[47] However, if *The Black Tent* contained a queer 'hidden transcript', it was to be found in its romantic and orientalist registers, rather than its war film elements. Maugham and Hurst appeared disinterested in the potential sexual implications of the lionization of male bonding that had been such a prominent feature of the classic war film. Instead, *The Black Tent's* queer code lies in David's willingness to defy social convention and national–racial exclusivity by marrying Mabrouka. This use of ostensibly heterosexual plots to explore aspects of queer sensibility is certainly a characteristic of Maugham's work.[48] In 1947 Maugham returned to the Western Desert to visit the rocky oasis of Siwa. Maugham's published travelogue played down Siwa's notorious association (reaching back to Alexander the Great) with overt homosexual pleasure, but in one lengthy passage he detailed the highly eroticized dance of the naked male *zaggala*, salaciously dwelling on their apparent lack of sexual shame (Maugham confronted neither the orientalist essentialism that underpinned such forms of objectification, nor the growing pathologization of pederasty by Arab nationalists in this period).[49] Significantly, when Maugham's first-hand knowledge of Arab popular entertainment is incorporated into the *The Black Tent* it takes the form, not of the frenzied all-male bacchanalia he had witnessed at Siwa, but of a brief, and decidedly tame, female belly dance.

Charles Holland – tense, troubled and unmarried – might superficially appear to embody an alienation grounded in Hurst and Maugham's sense of themselves as gay men in an age in which the growing possibility of liberalization of sexual attitudes was still accompanied by ostracization and even outright persecution. However, it is possible that the sense of discomfort represented here was social, rather than sexual, in origin. If the classic war films of the 1950s valorized the restrained professionalism of upper middle-class officers, this not merely had the corollary of erasing the more populist sentiments found in films produced during the war itself, it also left little space for the articulation of aristocratic sensibilities, despite the fact that, as recent research has revealed, the 1950s were something of a decade of upper-class revivalism, as landowners explored the rewards of country-house tourism, reinvented themselves as professional stewards of the countryside, and retained a powerful presence in postwar London culture.[50] In this context, *The Black Tent* can be seen as a cinematic text that registers the continued significance of patrician culture. Indeed, in the opening scene, Charles Holland is to be found in the gardens of his stately home, in this case what appears to be an uncredited appearance of Compton Wynyates, the picturesque redbrick Tudor manor house of the

Sixth Marquess of Northampton. The Desert War provided a compelling site for the articulation of an aristocratic conservative fantasy, the critical components of which were provided by the legacy of the cavalry charge in the culture of the (often only recently mechanized) tank regiments, the rarefied social scene of wartime Cairo and the dashing individualism of irregular warfare.

However, *The Black Tent*'s melancholic message, as Daoud chooses to repudiate the broad acres and title bequeathed to him by his father, appeared to be that aristocratic culture now had little future in the Britain of the estate tax, scholarship boy and technocratic meritocracy. The virtues of respect for tradition and authority, chivalry and clan loyalty associated with the patrician order, no longer to be valued at home, were now much more likely to be found among the caravans of the Bedouin. Moreover, the harsh struggle for survival in the extremes of the desert revealed a self-sufficiency and self-reliance that Britain had now abandoned in favour of the comforting, but ultimately enervating, embrace of a welfare state that offered security from cradle to grave.[51] Maugham was no simple social reactionary. His novels regularly dwelt on how snobbery and class distinction could deform the human personality, and he identified himself as a socialist, not least to torment his patrician father who had served as Lord Chancellor under Neville Chamberlain. However, Maugham's bohemianism and individualism left him uncomfortable with a Britain that he felt had promoted a levelling mediocrity, and *The Black Tent* suggests that he was one of many who found (in the characterization of novelist Geoffrey Household) that the Britain they returned to at the end of hostilities was, to all intents and purposes, 'a foreign country'.[52]

Sexuality, racial difference and the eclipse of empire: *Foxhole in Cairo* (1960)

Foxhole in Cairo relates how the British outwitted Rommel's agents prior to the battle of Alamein and turned the tide of the war in the Allies' favour. Rommel dispatches the playboy and spy John Eppler, who grew up in Egypt with a German mother and an Arab step-father, to Cairo to gather critical information about British strategic plans. Eppler contacts his former lover, the belly dancer Amina, and moves into her houseboat on the Nile. At Eppler's suggestion, Amina lures Major Wilson, who is both prone to heavy drinking and infatuated by the Egyptian dancer, to her houseboat, where she drugs him, allowing Eppler to lift plans from the major's briefcase and relay them by radio to Rommel's headquarters. Eppler, however, is being tracked by the wily Captain Robertson, Britain's naval counter-espionage chief, aided by Radek and Yvette, agents of the Jewish Underground. In the final scene, set on Amina's houseboat, Wilson is shot by Amina, before the latter is stabbed by Yvette, and Eppler is apprehended. It is then revealed that Robertson has used Wilson to pass on false information to the Germans. The film's plot was loosely based on a true story.[53] Eppler was a real person, Robertson is a glamourized (and bearded) version of Britain's Chief Field Security Officer in Cairo, Major A. W. Sansom, and the model for the voluptuous Amina was the star of the Kit Kat Club, Hekmat Fahmy. However critics were unimpressed by the film's repeated claims to authenticity. *Kine Weekly* felt that even the inclusion of official wartime footage failed to compensate for the film's 'atmosphere of theatrical artificiality'.[54]

However, what the critics derided as hokum might be more usefully interpreted as further testimony to the destabilizing impact of both sexuality and imperial demise, not merely on the war film genre, but on the broader British memory of the Second World War. The belly dancer as spy was hardly a novelty, the linkage of female eroticism, oriental dance and wartime betrayal becoming a staple of the popular imagination after the trial and execution for espionage of the exotic dancer and courtesan Mata Hari during the Great War.[55] However, in the specific context of the 1950s, the presence of the orientalized spy-seductress in narratives of the Second World War jeopardized the prerogatives of masculine profession-alism and national superiority which cinematic reconstructions of Britain's wartime achievement were meant to celebrate and promote. In her first appearance, Amina leaves Major Wilson (played, a little too excitedly, by Robert Urquhart) spellbound: 'As a pair of hands part the curtain of beads, the beat of the band becomes more emphatic and a spotlight cuts through the night-club haze to pick up the scantily-covered body of the exotic Egyptian dancer snaking across the floor.'[56] The undulations and shimmies of Amina's curvaceous body are of course in a longer cinematic tradition of male orientalist objectification, her 'harem costume' and suggestive kinetics a crude pastiche of the complex subtleties of oriental dance (although one that, ironically, had been re-circulated back to the Middle East through the night club scene of 1930s and 1940s Cairo).[57] However, they serve here to bring the corporeal and the feminine into the masculine arena of war and politics, where their impact proves impossible to control or contain. Wilson's sexual infatuation literally draws him into the female spaces of Amina's dressing room or houseboat, where his uniform (and the masculine authority it represents) looks incongruous and inconsequential, an insuf-ficient counterweight to the raw sexual power of Amina's half-naked body. Wilson's desire engenders indiscretion and dereliction of duty, risking the very future of the British empire.

It might be argued that Amina's character is simply a marketing expedient, providing a little sexual seasoning to the undoubtedly threadbare war film genre at a time when cinema audiences were increasingly young and male, and film-makers were trying to offer topics and materials that were deemed inappropriate by their competitors in the world of television.

However, the destabilizing presence of orientalized female sexuality on male war narratives was not confined to this cinematic rendering of the Eppler case. Leonard Mosley's supposedly factual reconstruction consistently abandoned its tone of matter-of-fact reportage whenever it discussed Hekmat Fahmy, the real-life model for Amina, in favour of a breathless prose more suited to romantic fiction. Fahmy, Mosley insisted, 'put all her thoughts, her feelings, her ideas and her ambitions into every movement of her dance', and when, 'with shining eyes', she goes to tell Eppler that she has obtained access to British military dispatches, she is 'wearing only a thin dressing gown, and she was wet with sweat and very excited'.[58] Five years after the film was released, Sansom (the model for Robertson) told his side of the story. Those expecting a professional soldier's indignant dismissal of *Foxhole in Cairo* as closer to pulp fiction than reality were to be disappointed. No less than Mosley, Sansom was equally prone to over-heated prose when describing the female protagonists of the Eppler case. Squeezed next to Fahmy in a taxi, Sansom 'felt her soft body close to mine', while his account of his interrogation of Edith, the 'young and pretty' model for Yvette in the film, satisfied the conventions of literary and screen melodrama. Asked if she was willing to sleep with Nazis in order to help the Zionist cause, Sansom records Edith as dramatically proclaiming 'Should I withhold my body while my people are without a home?'[59] In this context, it seems highly appropriate that the code used to carry Eppler's messages to Rommel was based on passages in Daphne Du Maurier's classic work of female romantic fiction, *Rebecca* (which Sansom had actually read for pleasure, earlier in the war), symbolizing the impossibility of quarantining the domains of the feminine and the sexual from a public sphere that nominally acted as the exclusive location for the shaping of military fortunes and national destinies.[60]

Amina's betrayal does not merely expose the potential frailty of British masculine authority. It also reveals that this precariousness was no less evident in regard to race and empire than it was in terms of gender. Amina represents the danger of the colonized turning on the colonizer, with all the ferocious enthusiasm of one who, for too long, had chafed under the constraints of imperial rule. She offered a feminized and sexualized incarnation of the tide of Egyptian nationalist resentment that had become increasingly acute during the 1940s, finally boiling over in the dramatic torching of the social centres of the British colony in Cairo in January 1952.[61] Amina, her eyes blazing, passionately declares to Eppler that 'You know what I feel about the English. They think they own us. My dream is to see the English driven out of Egypt, Germany winning the war and our people free.' The Eppler story had been relayed in another book published in the 1950s, the memoirs of a nationalistic young Egyptian army officer who had turned up at Eppler's houseboat to repair the radio used to send messages to Rommel. The young signals officer's rendering of events fused a virulent hatred of the British with a puritanical contempt for Eppler's playboy lifestyle, spending money on 'girls and easy living', his 'soft and voluptuous surroundings full of bottles of perfume and whisky', the spy himself to be found 'dead drunk with two Jewesses'.[62] The young Egyptian in question was Anwar Sadat, by the mid-1950s a Minister of State in the cabinet and close associate of Nasser, whom he was eventually to succeed as President of Egypt. Sadat's testimony featured in *The Cat and the Mice*, but not in *Foxhole in Cairo*, possibly because Britain was seeking to restore cordial diplomatic relations with Egypt by the time the film was made.[63] However, the visceral nationalist rhetoric of Amina – she agrees to sleep with Wilson in order that 'Egypt will be liberated' – reveals that British memory of the Desert War was not always able, or even willing, to obscure the longer-term geopolitical context in which the conflict should rightfully be placed, namely the eclipse of Britain's Middle Eastern empire and the rise of Arab nationalism.

The end of Britain's Middle Eastern empire was also accompanied by the emergence of the state of Israel, and this new post-imperial geopolitical reality was also to be registered in *Foxhole in Cairo*. Robertson's ability to locate Eppler owes much to his relationship with Radek, the leader of Cairo's secret Jewish underground, and his team of intelligence-gathering female 'lovelies', notably Yvette, a Palestinian Jew masquerading as a Franco-Lebanese cabaret dancer. The film implies a degree of instrumentalism to Jewish support for the British war effort. Radek offers a negative, rather than positive, justification for helping the British defeat the Germans, telling Yvette that, if Britain loses Egypt, 'there will be no freedom for Israel'. When Yvette questions whether Britain will 'give Israel its freedom after the war', Radek's less than unequivocal reply is 'Maybe. If it suits them.' Nor is the film entirely immune from stereotypes of Jews as rootless and mercenary. When Robertson asks Radek for information about Eppler, Radek asks what he will get in return, since 'both parties must have a benefit in a business deal'. The film suggests a marriage of convenience between Britons and the Jewish populations of their imperial possessions, rather than a set of shared values. Yvette (played by Fenella Fielding, whose family were Anglo-Romanian Jews) embodies the ambivalent discourses surrounding Jews and orientalism, her dark sloe eyes, gravelly voice, bejewelled elegance, and tantalizing décolletage all reinforcing a sense of the cosmopolitan exotic, but without the extensive (sexualized) racial alterity accorded to Amina.[64]

Yvette remains an undeveloped character, despite the potential attractions of exploring the relationship between notions of the Jew as incongruous and uncategorizable, and issues of loyalty and betrayal at the dawn of the post-imperial age. The fact that Zionism in the film is associated with an old man (Radek) and a largely decorous woman (Yvette) rather than with the hyper-masculine and heroic 'muscular Jew' who featured in Hollywood portrayals of Israel (in films such as *Exodus*, released the same year as *Foxhole in Cairo*) may suggest that the British were unwilling to offer extended public testimony to the martial fibre of Israelis, lest it cause audiences to recall Britain's decidedly unprepossessing abandonment of its Palestine mandate in 1948.[65] However, the new patterns of power (and Britain's diminished authority) in the Middle East were, albeit unintentionally, cruelly exposed in an interesting piece of choreography in the film's final scene. Robertson arrives late at Eppler's hideout to find two fights already underway, one between Amina (an Egyptian Arab) and Yvette (a Palestinian Jew) and another between Keppler (a part-Egyptian) and Radek (a Cairene Jew), while the body of the hapless British officer Wilson lies lifeless on a bed. Against the backcloth of one of Britain's greatest triumphs in the Second World War (Robertson announces that the battle of Alamein is now underway), *Foxhole in Cairo* closes with what amounts to a premonition of the peripheral, virtually irrelevant, status that awaited Britain in the post-imperial Middle East.

Conclusion

If both *The Black Tent* and *Foxhole in Cairo* are unlikely to receive serious critical re-evaluation, they are not entirely inconsequential. They reveal that it was simply not possible to erase thoughts of race and empire when constructing the national myths of Britain and the Second World War. Paul Gilroy, with whom this chapter began, offers a necessary polemic against an unhealthy obsession with the war years that has permitted a failure to come to terms with either the violence on which empire was predicated, or the trauma that accompanied its demise. However, given its centrality to both official and popular memory, and to the creation of what amounts to a national myth, in postwar Britain, it is clearly neither realistic nor appropriate to pay less attention to Britain and the Second World War. Nor, as this chapter has suggested, does remembering war have to imply forgetting empire. Rather than the zero-sum logic on which Gilroy's analysis rests, what might be more valuable would be to deploy the methodology of what Michael Rothberg calls 'multidirectional memory', applied so impressively in his study of the entangling of literary and cinematic memories of both the Holocaust and decolonization in postwar France. Rothberg demonstrates that the remembrance of one history does not automatically erase others from view, and that the public sphere should be approached as a field of contestation where memories interact in surprisingly productive ways.[66] Historians do not need to pay less attention to the Second World War: they just need to be a little more mindful of how they pay attention, and what they choose to pay attention to.

Notes

1 Gilroy, P. (2004), *Postcolonial Melancholia*. London: Routledge, 87–95; Gilroy, P., (2011), 'Great games: film, history and working-through Britain's colonial legacy', in L. Grieveson and C. MacCabe (eds), *Film and the End of Empire*. London: BFI, 27.

2 To take just one representative text, Bierman, J. and Smith, C. (2004), *War Without Hate: The Desert Campaign of 1940–1943*. New York: Penguin.

3 Bayly, C. and Harper, T. (2005), *Forgotten Armies: Britain's Asian Empire and the War with Japan*. London: Penguin.

4 As is unapologetically evident in Lampson, M. (1972), *The Killearn Diaries, 1934–1946*, T. Evans (ed.). London: Sidgwick and Jackson.

5 Fort, A. (2009), *Archibald Wavell: The Life and Times of an Imperial Servant*. London: Jonathan Cape.

6 Among a number of studies that reassert the primacy of Italy in British policy in the region, Morewood, E. (2004), *The British Defence of Egypt: Conflict and Crisis in the Eastern Mediterranean*. London: Routledge.

7 Bharucha, P. C. (1956), *Official History of the Indian Forces in the Second World War: The North African Campaign*. Bombay: Orient Longman.

8 Moorehead, A. (1944), *African Trilogy*. London: Hamish Hamilton; Moorehead, A. (1960), *The White Nile*. London: Hamish Hamilton; Moorehead, A. (1962), *The Blue Nile*. London: Hamish Hamilton.

9 Bagnold, R. A. (1945), 'Early days of the Long Range Desert Group'. *Geographical Journal*, 105(1), 30–42.

10 Cowles, V. (1958), *The Phantom Major: The Story of David Stirling and the SAS Regiment*. London: Collins, 199.

11 Cooper, A. (1995), *Cairo in the War, 1939-1945*. London: Penguin, 113–19.

12 Medhurst, A. (1984), '1950s war films', in G. Hurd (ed.), *National Fictions: World War Two in British Films and Television*. London: BFI, 35–8. For representative studies of class, Rattigan, N. (1994), 'The last gasp of the middle class: British war films of the 1950s', in W. W. Dixon (ed.), *Re-viewing British Cinema, 1900–1992*. New York: SUNY Press, 143–53; and, for gender, Geraghty, C. (2000), *British Cinema in the Fifties: Gender, Genre and the 'New Look'*. London: Routledge, 174–95. See also Summerfield, P. (2009), 'Film and the popular memory of the Second World War in Britain, 1950–1959' in P. Levine and S. Grayzel (eds.), *Gender, Labour and Empire: essays on Modern Britain*. Houndsmills: Palgrave, 157–75.

13 For example, Plain, G. (2006), *John Mills and British Cinema*. Edinburgh: Edinburgh University Press, 158–69.

14 Review in the *Daily Mirror*, 24 October 1958.

15 British Film Institute, London (hereafter BFI), Large Pressbook: *Ice Cold In Alex* (1958).

16 BFI Screen Online 'UK Cinema Audiences, 1933–2003', http://www.screenonline.org.uk/film/facts/fact1.html/.

17 For a provocative analysis of 'the richly sedimented popular cultural representations' that might emerge from such a process, Eley, G. (2001), 'Finding the people's war: film, British collective memory, and World War II'. *American Historical Review*, 106(2), 818–38.

18 Maugham, S. (1973), *The Black Tent, and Other Stories*. London: W.H. Allen, 1–50.

19 Mosley, L. (1958), *The Cat and the Mice*. New York: Harper and Brothers.

20 This arresting phrase is borrowed from Eley (2001), 819.

21 Summerfield, P. (2009), 'Public memory or public amnesia? British women of the Second World War in popular films of the 1950s and 1960s'. *Journal of British Studies*, 48(4), 935–57.

22 Notably, Harper, S. (1997), 'Popular film, popular memory: The case of the Second World War', in M. Evans and K. Lunn (eds), *War and Memory in the Twentieth Century*. Oxford: Berg, 172–3.

23 See, for example, the reviews in: *Monthly Film Bulletin*, 25 (July 1958), 84; *Sight and Sound*, 27 (Summer 1958), 249; and *Film Quarterly*, 12 (Fall 1958), 42–3.

24 This terminology is borrowed from Kristin Ross's powerful critique of methodological and material 'confinement' in the writing of post-war French history: Ross, K. (2002), *May '68 and its Afterlives*. Chicago: University of Chicago Press, 10. For a rare acknowledgment that colonial wars and decolonization provide an important context for understanding British nostalgia for the Second World War, and 'the speed with which the war assumed a major place in ideas of national identity', see Webster, W. (2001), '"There'll always be an England": representations of colonial wars and immigration, 1948–1968'. *Journal of British Studies*, 40(3), 557–84.

25 Connon, B. (1997), *Somerset Maugham and the Maugham Dynasty*. London: Sinclair-Stevenson.

26 *Today's Cinema*, 86, no. 7479 (13 March 1956), 8.

27 *Kinematograph Weekly* (5 April 1956).

28 BFI Pressbook: *The Black Tent* (1956).

29 Halovich, M. B. (1990), 'All that heaven allows: color, narrative space and melodrama', in P. Lehman (ed.), *Close Viewings: An Anthology of New Film Criticism*. Tallahassee: Florida State University Press, 52–72.

30 Some critics were positively scathing about this re-tread of the classic empire film, damning it as 'fossilized' and declaring that its 'unblanching jingoism' and 'confident Edwardian imperialism' were embarrassingly anachronistic: *Monthly Film Bulletin*, 22, no. 263 (December 1955), 177; *Kinematograph Weekly*, no. 2524 (10 November 1955), 17–18. However, it is worth noting the film's royal premiere, in the presence of the Duke of Edinburgh, and the gushing review 'this splendidly heroic story' received in *Today's Cinema* 85, no. 7392 (9 November 1955), 14.

31 BFI Pressbook: *The Black Tent*.

32 Monthly Film Bulletin, 23, no. 268 (May 1956), 60.

33 BFI Microjacket, Press Release from Elstree Studios, 'The Play's the Thing ... says Anthony Steel' n.d. [1951]

34 MacQuitty, W. (1991), *A Life to Remember*. London: Quartet Books, 32–51.

35 BFI, typescript of unpublished autobiography of Brian Desmond Hurst, n.d. Hurst, who served in Sinai and Palestine during the First World War, possessed a knowledge of Arabic and had been a personal acquaintance of T. E. Lawrence in the early 1930s. Indeed Hurst was, at one point, first choice to direct Alexander Korda's long-desired (but never completed) biopic of Lawrence: Robbins, C. (2005), *The Empress of Ireland: A Chronicle of an Unusual Friendship*. New York: Thunder's Mouth Press, 32–3, 274–7, 277–82. Hurst also directed the Kenyan Mau Mau drama *Simba* (1955). See Webster, W. (2005), *Englishness and Empire, 1939-1965*. Oxford: Oxford University Press, 119–48.

36 Maugham, R. (1973), *Escape from the Shadows: An Autobiography*. New York: McGraw-Hill, 121–6, 141–66; Maugham, R. (1947), *Nomad*. London: Chapman and Hall; Maugham, R. (1947), *Approach to Palestine*. London: Falcon Press; Maugham, R. (1948), *North African Notebook*. London: Chapman and Hall. Maugham also briefly resided in Tanganyika, the inspiration for his (1955) novel *Behind the Mirror*. London: Longmans.

37 Cowles (1958), 115.

38 National Archive, Kew FO 371/50788/U 1031, J. N. D. Anderson, 'Sayed Idris El Senussi', 21 December 1944.

39 Evans-Pritchard, E. E. (1945), 'Cyrenaica'. *Geographical Journal*, 105(5/6), 227–9; Evans-Pritchard (1949), 226–9.

40 *Today's Cinema*, 86, no. 7479 (13 March 1956), 8.

41 Hichens, R. S. (1904), *The Garden of Allah*. London: Methuen; Hull, E. M. (1919), *The Sheik*. London: Eveleigh Nash and Grayson.

42 *Outcast of the Islands* (dir. Carol Reed, 1951); *The Wind Cannot Read* (dir. Ralph Thomas, 1958).

43 Collins, M. (2001), 'Pride and prejudice: West Indian men in mid-twentieth century Britain'. *Journal of British Studies*, 40, 405–10.

44 Buettner, E. (2009), '"Would you let your daughter marry a Negro?" Race and sex in 1950s Britain', in S. Grayzel and P. Levine (eds), *Gender, Labour, War and Empire: Essays on Modern Britain*. Basingstoke: Palgrave Macmillan, 228–9.

45 To take just two seminal works in an extensive field of scholarship: Waters, C. (1999), 'Disorders of the mind, disorders of the body social: Peter Wildeblood and the making of the modern homosexual', in B. Conekin, F. Mort and C. Waters (eds), *Moments of Modernity: Reconstructing Britain, 1945-1964*. London: Rivers Oram, 134–51; Mort, F. (1999), 'Mapping sexual London: The Wolfenden Committee on homosexual offences and prostitution'. *New Formations*, 37, 92–113.

46 Connon (1997), 216–7, 210–1, 236–9; Robbins (2005), 286–8. See also Bourne (2006), 35–46.

47 Robbins (2005), 26–7; Maugham (1973), 116.

48 Most notably in his novel *The Servant*. See Maugham (1973), 169–71.

49 Maugham, R. (1950), *Journey to Siwa*. London: Chapman and Hall, 114–19. For a critique of Western queer essentializing of Arab sexuality, see Massad, J. (2007), *Desiring Arabs*. Chicago: University of Chicago Press.

50 See, for example, Mandler, P. (1997), *The Rise and Fall of the Stately Home*. New Haven, CT: Yale University Press, 311–88; Mort, F. (2010), *Capital Affairs: London and the Making of the Permissive Society*. New Haven, CT: Yale University Press, 56–90.

51 A view articulated in Maugham (1947), 243.

52 The tension between Maugham's progressive-bohemian and patrician-conservative preferences was testified to by his lover Peter Burton: Burton, P. (1985), *Parallel Lives*. London: GMP Publishers, 71. Household, G. (1958), *Against the Wind*. London: Michael Joseph, 212.

53 The authoritative reconstruction of the Eppler case is Kelly, S. (2002), *The Lost Oasis: The Desert War and the Hunt for Zerzura*. Boulder, CO: Westview, 192–232.

54 *Kine Weekly* no. 2763 (15 September 1960), 18; in a similar vein, *Monthly Film Bulletin*, 27, no. 322 (November 1960), 155.

55 Wheelwright, J. (1992), *The Fatal Lover: Mata Hari and the Myth of Women in Espionage*. London: Collins and Brown; Proctor, T. M. (2003), *Female Intelligence: Women and Espionage in the First World War*. New York: New York University Press, 123–44. For a nuanced account of gender and espionage in the Second World War, which rightly emphasizes the variety of performative styles employed by female agents, encompassing the quotidian as much as the glamorous, Pattinson, J. (2007), *Behind Enemy Lines: Gender, Passing and the Special Operations Executive in the Second World War*. Manchester: Manchester University Press.

56 BFI Pressbook: *Foxhole in Cairo* (1960).

57 Karayanni, S. S. (2004), *Dancing, Fear and Desire: Race, Sexuality and Imperial Politics in Middle Eastern Dance*. Waterloo: Wilfred Laurier University Press; Shay. A. and Sellers-Young, B. (2005), *Belly Dance: Orientalism, Transnationalism and Harem Fantasy*. Costa Mesa, CA: Mazda Publishers, 1–27.

58 Mosley (1958), 72, 105.

59 Sansom, A. W. (1965), *I Spied Spies*. London: George Harrap, 128–9.

60 For *Rebecca*, see Mosley, *Cat and the Mice*, 127–8; Sansom, *I Spied Spies*, 117–18. For a highly valuable example of how the histories of intimate life and sexuality may have implications for the study of diplomatic, military and geopolitical power relations: Roberts, M. L. (2010), 'The price of discretion: Prostitution, venereal disease, and the American military in France, 1944–1946'. *American Historical Review*, 115(4), 1002–30.

61 Cooper (1995), 325–36.

62 Sadat, Anwar (1957), *Revolt on the Nile*. New York: John Day, 51–7.

63 Mosley (1958), 109–11.

64 For notions of the Jew being comprehended both within, and without, the

tropes of orientalism: Bar-Yousef, E. (2005), *The Holy Land in English Culture, 1799–1917*. Oxford: Oxford University Press.

65   For the 1950s and 1960s Hollywood 'Jewish superman', Bartov, O. (2005), *The 'Jew' in Cinema*. Bloomington: Indiana University Press, 187–204.

66   Rothberg (2009), *Multidirectional Memory: Remembering the Holocaust in the Age of Decolonization*. Stanford: Stanford University Press.

Key texts

Bierman, J. and Smith, C. (2004), *War Without Hate: The Desert Campaign of 1940-1943*. New York: Penguin.

Bourne, S. (2006), 'Behind the masks: Anthony Asquith and Brian Desmond Hurst', in R. Griffiths (ed.), *British Queer Cinema*. London: Routledge.

Evans-Pritchard, E. E. (1949), *The Sanusi of Cyrenaica*. Oxford: Oxford University Press.

Gilroy, P. (2004), *Postcolonial Melancholia*. London: Routledge.

Kelly, S. (2002), *The Lost Oasis: The Desert War and the Hunt for Zerzura*. Boulder, CO: Westview.

Maugham, R. (1973), *The Black Tent, and Other Stories*. London: W. H. Allen.

Mosley, L. (1958), *The Cat and the Mice*. New York: Harper and Brothers.

Rothberg, M. (2009), *Multidirectional Memory: Remembering the Holocaust in the Age of Decolonization*. Stanford: Stanford University Press.

Sansom, A. W. (1965), *I Spied Spies*. London: George Harrap.

Sadat, A. (1957), *Revolt on the Nile*. New York: John Day.

Summerfield, P. (2009), 'Film and the popular memory of the Second World War in Britain, 1950-1959', in P. Levine and S. Grayzel (eds), *Gender, Labour, War and Empire: Essays on Modern Britain*. Houndmills: Palgrave.

CHAPTER SEVEN

'A story that will thrill you and make you proud'

The cultural memory of Britain's secret war in Occupied France

Juliette Pattinson

Charlotte Gray revealed: The truth behind the British heroine who died forgotten and the scars of her secret war which drove her to become a hermit.

DAILY MAIL HEADLINE, 18 SEPTEMBER 2010

In September 2010, the story of an elderly and somewhat reclusive woman who had died in her home in Torquay featured prominently in the press. With seemingly no relatives or finances to pay for her funeral, Eileen Nearne was to be buried at the state's expense. Council workers clearing her flat found medals and documents revealing her identity as a World War Two agent of the Special Operations Executive (SOE), a clandestine British organization formed in July 1940 to encourage occupied populations to resist and to undertake sabotage and subversion in order to 'Set Europe Ablaze'. The press revelled in this 'forgotten heroine', whose wartime story of resistance, arrest, torture and incarceration in a concentration camp was 'revealed'. She was depicted as a 'real life Eleanor Rigby',[1] a 'real-life Charlotte Gray'.[2] That characters from a popular song, and a best-selling novel and later film, were invoked to describe Nearne underscores the connection between popular culture and historical memory. Although Nearne had been the subject of an article in 1947,[3] had appeared in a 1997 television documentary wearing a wig and using the pseudonym 'Rose'[4] and had featured in several books published during the last 65 years about British agents, hers is not a household name. The unveiling of a blue plaque, and her story featuring in the BBC television programme *Heirhunters* (2012), will undoubtedly have raised her profile.

Despite Nearne's previous obscurity, British agents collectively have a secure place within the cultural memory of the Second World War. The clandestine war did not remain secret for long. Newspaper articles, memoirs, biographies, films, memorials, museum exhibitions, novels and television documentaries, many of which included the involvement of agents in their construction, have all contributed to shaping the public's memory of the SOE. Post-war British culture was replete with tales 'that will thrill you and make you proud',[5] chronicling the exploits of the SOE operatives. For example, the memoir *Ill Met by Moonlight* (1950) about the SOE activities of Billy Moss and Paddy Leigh Fermor on Crete was, according to Somerset Maugham, one of the three best books of 1950[6] and was turned into a film by Michael Powell and Emeric Pressburger, starring Dirk Bogarde, which was the seventh most popular film at the 1957 box office.[7] However, to many British people, especially those fed on a staple of *'Allo 'Allo* (1982–92) and *Wish Me Luck* (1988–9), resistance during the Second World War was predominantly a French phenomenon. More books, television documentaries and films have been produced in English about Resistance movements in France than any other nation's partisan war effort. There are a number of possible explanations for this focus on France. The history of the First World War and France's proximity to Britain has meant that more British people have visited France than other countries with a resistance heritage. Moreover, post-war British school-children through the decades have taken French as a compulsory subject and have been introduced to French history. France had also been the key ally before it had been occupied in June 1940, and the D-Day landings on French soil, in which thousands of British servicemen were involved, had precipitated the overthrow of Germany. Furthermore, in contrast to Holland for example, in which the focus of English-language publica-tions is on the devastating enemy penetration of Resistance networks,[8] there were some tangible French Resistance successes which arguably contributed to shortening the war. There is also an awareness that a British organization was working with local resisters and thus, in reconstructing its own memory of the war, Britain has found a particular place for the French Resistance; indeed, in becoming part of the story of Britain's war, the French Resistance is to an extent Anglicized. However, the most compelling explanation for the focus on France is that, in addition to recruiting men, it also, unusually, deployed women. Of the 480 agents enlisted by the SOE's F[rench] Section, 39 were women, among them Eileen Nearne. Despite this small number, or perhaps because of it, the female agent has captured the public imagination. The novelty of this, in a period in which conventional gender norms prohibited women, at least culturally, from bearing arms, has struck a chord with the public and, as this chapter demonstrates, it is the involvement of women which is central to the cultural memory of the secret war. While my previous publications have used oral history to analyse how the secret war has been privately remembered, this chapter considers a range of media, what Henry Rousso calls 'carriers' and 'vectors' of memory which transmit interpretations of a country's past to audiences,[9] to examine how the secret war has been publicly commemorated, how this has altered over the decades, and how public memories of British clandestine warfare are constructed in terms of gender, nation, class and race.

'Now it can be told': the not-so-secret war in print and film in the 1940s and 1950s

Popular culture was saturated in the 1950s with tales of the Second World War that were based upon fact. War stories were published to great success, targeting an almost exclusively male readership. Kenneth Worpole categorizes these publications into four separate genres: escape, heroism, resistance and war crimes.[10] Many of these accounts of sacrifice and fortitude, including *The Wooden Horse*, *The Dam Busters* and *The Bridge Over the River Kwai*, were adapted for the big screen to feed the insatiable appetite of cinema-goers.[11] Up to 80 films about the Second World War, 30 of which were highly successful, were released in the 1950s.[12] Unlike films produced during the war that sought to show that Britain was stoically enduring hardships and crucially *not losing* the struggle, 1950s films could celebrate how Britain actually *won* it.[13] Moreover, in drawing heavily on a nostalgic memory of the war in which Britain was still powerful, these films acted as a counterpoint to the post-war reality of a declining, austerity-ridden Britain. This was an era, notes Penny Summerfield, in which 'popular culture repeatedly worked over the history of the Second World War in the context of anxiety about Britain's prestige'.[14] As it began to lose its status as an imperial power, beginning with the partition of India in 1947, and in a period of national decline, austerity and an increasingly heated Cold War, Britain looked to its past for tales of glory to provide a foundation for the restoration of national pride. But the tales were all about men;[15] women were relegated to the sidelines, permitted only a 'shadowy presence'[16] as wives and daughters, which contrasted sharply with wartime films such as *The Gentle Sex* (1943) and *Millions Like Us* (1943), in which women were depicted as playing a crucial role. Moreover, these public accounts, both narrative and filmic, of the war only began to emerge in the 1950s; between 1945 and 1949 there was a distinct absence.

This was not the case, however, with accounts about the secret war, as there was a recognition that 'Now it can be told'. This was the title of a feature-length public information film that was released in 1947, but was actually shot in 1944 in the liberated villages of southern France. This 'truly British' film, with its 'discreet trumpet-blowing' and 'lack of braggadocio',[17] starred real-life agents Harry Rée and Eileen Nearne's sister Jacqueline, as well as a number of Frenchmen who had been active in the Resistance and who were 'paid' with tins of corned beef, chocolate and cigarettes.[18] It was a composite story of real events, and acknowledged from the outset the involvement of women in active roles. It was, however, heavily criticised in reviews for the delay in its release; unfortunately, before it could be told, Hollywood had taken several opportunities of telling the story in popular films such as *O.S.S.* (1946), *Cloak and Dagger* (1946) and *13 Rue Madeleine* (1947) about the American equivalent of the SOE, the Office of Strategic Services (OSS). *Punch*'s film critic wrote:

> The climactic scene here, when a Hudson full of rescued RAF men is stuck in a field and a whole village turns out in the middle of the night to shift it, it's as exciting as anything in Hitchcock and much stronger in emotional impact. An excellent film; why couldn't we have seen it months ago, when it was made, and before Hollywood had cheapened its theme?[19]

When it did finally premiere, in February 1947, some operational agents were presented to the audience, including Harry Rée who starred in the film, and Odette Sansom whose award of the George Cross six months earlier (for displaying 'courage and endurance' during her two-year captivity[20]) was well publicized in the press. At this early stage, agents were already beginning to be feted.

Indeed, the SOE featured heavily in the press during the mid-to-late 1940s and early 1950s. The first article appeared in the *Sunday Express* on 11 March 1945 while the war was still being waged (but after the SOE operations in France had concluded following the country's Liberation.) Entitled 'WAAF girls parachuted into France', it named two of the 39 female agents and noted 'The interesting thing about these girls is that they are not hearty and horsey young women with masculine chins. They are pretty young girls who would look demure and sweet in crinoline.'[21] Thus, from the outset, the memory of the SOE was being shaped in particular gendered ways. It was women, not men, who were the focus, and while knowledge of the deployment of young women in highly dangerous work had the potential to be hugely contentious, the focus on feminine appearance pre-empted such controversies. Later articles reassured the public that female agents had returned to conventional womanly roles after their wartime adventures, becoming 'just an ordinary housewife',[22] picturing them in their wedding dress[23] or with their children,[24] and including references to more traditional duties ('[Now the war's over] I am going to stay at home and do some knitting'; 'I can't stay long [to collect my medal]. I have got to get home and put the two children to bed.'[25]) In the first of eight articles entitled 'They Went by Parachute', published in 1946 and 1947 for the monthly magazine *Chamber's Journal*, F Section head Maurice Buckmaster chronicled the experiences of Pearl Witherington with the Maquis, a Corsican word meaning scrubland which was used to refer collectively to small, almost exclusively male, groups of Resistance fighters: 'She was a maquisade; she led 2600 Frenchmen to a notable victory in the woods near Romorantin, and by her efforts prevented an entire German division from coming into the Normandy battle at a critical moment.' He then assured the readers: 'She tells me that she is very glad to have a rest and to turn from war to domesticity.' Furthermore, a 1950 radio script, also called 'Now it can be told', stated: 'Today the greater number are happy wives and mothers, and the others have settled into different everyday jobs.'[26] Such reassurance that traversing gender boundaries in wartime had not resulted in any destabilization of conventional gender norms was crucial, given the revelations in articles from March 1946 onwards that 13 of the women infiltrated into France did not return.[27]

Events such as the war trials of concentration camp staff, the awarding of the George Cross to three female agents (two posthumously) in August and December 1946 and April 1949, the unveiling of a plaque in London in 1948 inscribed with the names of 13 female SOE agents who were killed during the war, and the murder of agent Christine Granville in June 1952, generated much newspaper coverage, fuelling public interest in the SOE's female agents. Contemporary events, such as the unveiling of a memorial, provided an opportunity to revisit the past, orchestrating cultural memory around the wartime activities of female agents. Snippets of gossip about weddings, new jobs and dinner parties being hosted were published, suggesting these were considered to be of public interest, and there were also double-page multi-part series. A weekly seven-instalment serial published in the *Sunday Express* in May and June 1949 revealed to readers the stories of the three George Cross holders, Odette Sansom, Violette Szabo and Noor Inayat Khan, while the *Daily Herald* published nine articles entitled 'Commando Girls' in April and May 1950. Many of these articles invoked the conventions of biography, serving as a memorial and honouring their sacrifice. They are significant because, as Rousso notes, journalism plays a key role in shaping memory through the high circulation figures of newspapers, which far outstrip the sales of books.[28]

A self-representation published in the tabloids was written by Yvonne Baseden, with a three-part serialisation in the *Sunday Express* in 1952. The workings of the 'cultural circuit', which conceptualizes the perpetual cyclical relationship between public accounts and personal narratives,[29] can be seen in operation here: the influence of earlier narrative and filmic portrayals of captivity had undoubtedly shaped Baseden's written account, both implicitly (in a section about her interrogation, she quotes a Gestapo officer telling her 'we have ways to make people talk', a line similar to that which had been used in the 1950 film *Odette* – 'I told you we have ways and means to make a woman talk') and explicitly ('It was like all the prisons you have seen on the films. The cells were in storied tiers with strong wire nets between the floors to prevent suicides.'[30]) Successive representations of the SOE therefore can be seen to have been folded into one another.

Like Baseden, other agents were fully immersed in shaping the cultural memory of the secret war. The first memoir to be published by an SOE agent was *The Dungeon Democracy*, Christopher Burney's searing account, not of his clandestine operations but of his incarceration in Buchenwald concentration camp.[31] Although very few British nationals had been deported to Nazi camps, resulting in this book being highly atypical, it was not released in paperback nor publicized in the 1950s when over 15 new books about the SOE were published. The first account of operational activities in France was *Maquis*,[32] written by George Millar, a pre-war journalist, in his month's demobilization leave following his return from France. It was a publishing success, with 70,000 hardback copies sold in its first print run.[33] As Rousso notes, sales figures help gauge a book's influence.[34] Other books enjoyed similar success: Anne-Marie Walters's account of her wartime experiences, *Moondrop to Gascony*, published in 1946 (and in paperback in 1951), was awarded the John Llewellyn Rhys prize for literature, awarded to the best new book written by authors under 35, another indicator of impact. Furthermore, both Millar's and Walters's autobiographies are still in print today, thereby introducing later generations to the SOE. In addition to these three memoirs published immediately after the war, there were a significant number written in the 1950s: seven personal accounts were published by male SOE personnel, including two books by Maurice Buckmaster; 10 agents, four of whom were women, featured as the subject of biographies; and the experiences of several women agents were recounted in three female-authored books. That male veterans were more likely than their female colleagues to write their memoirs reflects a more widespread pattern in published autobiographies: whereas men represent themselves, women are represented by others. As Wendy Webster asserts, the 1950s was 'an interesting period in the gendered history of national biography, producing as it did a discourse of the "public woman".'[35] The female agents who had trespassed on male terrain during the war presented ideal material for biographers and appealed to publishers eager to attract a female audience while retaining their male readership. The most successful were Jerrard Tickell's highly fictionalized account of Odette Sansom,[36] which had four reprints within a year, is still in print and has to date sold over 500,000 copies,[37] and R. J. Minney's equally hagiographic book about Violette Szabo.[38] The front covers are worthy of study in themselves. The

1956 edition of *Odette* depicts a prisoner, wearing a torn blouse, boldly holding the gaze of her captor who is wrongly depicted as dressed in a (pre-war) black uniform. The black uniform was commonly used by publishers and film-makers as shorthand to invoke the stereotype of the nasty Nazi, rather than the metallic grey uniforms that the Gestapo had by this time donned. The 1971 edition includes a more sexualized image of a meek prisoner seated in a dark gloomy cell, her arms wrapped around her vulnerable body and her back turned in an attempt to protect herself from the gaze of a rather sinister Gestapo interrogator who, legs apart as if strutting back and forth, is stroking his whip in readiness.

Editions of *Carve Her Name With Pride* often feature on the cover a gun-toting woman firing a Sten gun at advancing faceless Wehrmacht soldiers in a rural setting. Those printed after the 1956 film bear more than a passing resemblance to the actress Virginia McKenna, who played Szabo in the film. Some editions include a 'shout-line' quoting Odette Sansom (who by then was Odette Churchill): 'She was the bravest of us all'. Yet Sansom never met Szabo, who was recruited after Sansom had been arrested. Representations of the secret war were thus layered on top of each other.

The success of these biographies attracted the attention of film directors, and consequently they reached an even larger audience. It is these two 'celluloid monuments',[39] both crucial vectors of memory, which are central to the cultural memory of the SOE and of the female agent in particular. Herbert Wilcox cast his wife Anna Neagle in the title role of *Odette* (1950), as he had done in many of his biopic films (about Queen Victoria, Florence Nightingale, Edith Cavell and Amy Johnson), thus underlining the status of Sansom, a Frenchwoman who acquired British citizenship following her marriage to a British man, as a decidedly *British* heroine. Sansom was heavily involved in the construction of her filmic image, acting as technical advisor and touring the locations of her wartime story with Neagle and Wilcox. Claims to historical authenticity were further reiterated by the inclusion of Maurice Buckmaster appearing as himself and providing an introductory monologue ('I know … that this story is a true one'). Evidence of the importance of this film to the cultural memory of the SOE, and to the war more broadly, is that the film came fourth in the list of box office hits of 1950.[40] Significantly, it also did well across Europe, thereby shaping the wider memory of Britain's war effort.[41] The film may well have been instrumental in raising the profile of British agents in France and in the decision in 1952 to rename a street in Montargis in central France Rue Claudie Rolfe, the alias of Lilian Rolfe, another female agent. The film programme from *Odette*'s premiere quoted Sansom:

> It is with a sense of deep humility that I allow my personal story to be told. I am a very ordinary woman to whom a chance was given to see human beings at their best and at their worst. I knew kindness as well

as cruelty, understanding as well as brutality. My comrades, who did far more than I and suffered far more profoundly, are not here to speak. It is to their memory that this film has been made and I would like it to be a window through which may be seen those very gallant women with whom I had the honour to serve.[42]

Despite continually reiterating that she was just an 'ordinary woman',[43] Sansom nevertheless recognized the wider significance of her personal story: 'I have been turned into a kind of Joan of Arc.'[44] Being immortalized in print and film gave Sansom iconic status and turned her in to a household name. Indeed, the interview tapes archived at the Imperial War Museum (which have subsequently been digitized) were simply labelled 'Odette'.[45]

Another agent, one who did not survive the war, also occupies a pivotal position in Britain's memory of the clandestine war. *Carve Her Name With Pride*, R. J. Minney's biography of Violette Szabo, was made into a film of the same name by Lewis Gilbert and Daniel Angel (1958). The parallels with *Odette* were striking, but possibly not unsurprising, given that Sansom was a technical advisor on this film also.[46] There was one key difference, however. Whereas Sansom's wartime affair and post-war marriage to her organiser Peter Churchill were largely written out of *Odette* ('They toned it down rather than turn it into a Hollywood story. And they had the material to do so'[47]) and, moreover, *Now It Can Be Told* was criticised for lacking romance ('Mlle Jacqueline Nearne and Captain Harry Ree make a handsome couple ... Yet they recklessly disobey the first commandment in the Goldwyn Decalogue, and neither kiss nor show the faintest sign of wishing to kiss'[48]), the scriptwriters of *Carve Her Name With Pride* invented a romantic sub-plot involving Szabo, who had been widowed, and her commanding officer 'Tony' – a sign perhaps that a late 1950s audience, many of whom were women, would not accept a film without a romantic sub-plot. Indeed, one review noted that it was 'at once a great war and woman's film'.[49]

These films, which played a key role in shaping audiences' perception of the war, were not only seen by large numbers at the point of their cinematic release but have also acquired a 'permanent life after death',[50] with frequent television screenings since the late 1960s, thus introducing the SOE women to later generations. These films supplied the potent visual tropes that inform the representations of the secret war to this day, thereby securing the place of female SOE agents in the cultural memory of Britain's war effort. And as Geoff Eley notes, the 'memoralizing was itself becoming remembered' in that it was not just the female agents who were celebrated but also the 'richly sedimented popular cultural representations'.[51] In 2008, the fiftieth anniversary of the film *Carve Her Name With Pride* was marked by a commemorative event at the British Film Institute. The BBC four-part series *The White Rabbit* (1967), starring Kenneth More, which is based on a 1952 biography of the SOE agent Edward Yeo-Thomas and is the only filmic representation about a male agent in France, has in contrast been almost completely forgotten.

The late 1940s and the 1950s were undoubtedly the peak of cultural representations of the SOE. Together, these articles, biographies and films, which were shaped by the timing of their release into the public domain, constructed a (nostalgic) version of the national past: a past in which an executed female agent was 'seen by various prisoners in the [concentration] camp and recognised as English by her bravery'.[52] Tales about agents' exploits were part of a wider phenomenon of publishing and film production in which the memory of the war was being reconstructed. Following six years of austerity under a Labour government, the victory of the Conservative Party in the 1951 election elicited a very different political mood. As Kenneth Worpole notes, the war, which had been envisaged as ushering in a New Jerusalem in 1945, was now being recast in popular literature as a war to preserve the established order.[53] Moreover, wartime emphasis on the 'people's war', in which all classes pulled together for the war effort, was erased in films of the 1950s which, as John Ramsden and Neil Rattigan both show, focus on the lone heroism of upper-class officers who seemingly won the war singlehandedly or were aided by other ranks cast as a comic foil.[54] Representations of the SOE, however, do not neatly fit with this interpretation. First, women are placed centre-stage. As a consequence of this cultural centrality, men have been overshadowed and the secret war is almost exclusively depicted as female. Some upper-class men did write their memoirs, such as Oxford-educated Peter Churchill who wrote three accounts (in the third person), but it is the exploits of his later wife Odette Sansom and other female agents, usually mediated by male authors fixated on describing the appearance of these 'girls',[55] that have captured the public imagination. By virtue of their gender, (and the concomitant disruption of social mores precipitated by the recruitment of women in clandestine work), female agents have generated much interest in both popular literature and film. And when an SOE agent was to be the subject of the television programme *This is Your Life* in 1955, it was a female agent, Yvonne Baseden, who was selected by headquarters staff. Baseden had been 22 when she parachuted into France to work as a wireless operator, was in radio contact with Britain from a ditch in a field while her colleagues received the first daylight drop of arms in June 1944, was arrested later that day, interrogated, survived nine months of incarceration in Ravensbrück concentration camp and subsequently married and became a mother. She was thus an ideal representative of the SOE: she was young, attractive and modest, and had assumed a more conventional role following her extraordinary wartime experiences. That Odette Sansom was not chosen was perhaps unsurprising: a married mother of three, she had had an affair with her organizer Peter Churchill whom she subsequently married, and there were questions raised in France in 1950 (and reignited in Britain in 1958 by some who wanted to strip her of her George Cross) as to the effectiveness of what she and Churchill had accomplished. The dominant memory of the war as a conflict fought solely by (upper-class) men, as seen in other cultural representations which succeed in erasing women entirely, was therefore challenged by the public's awareness of young women's involvement in the secret war. The focus on women was perhaps an astute device to deflect attention and ensure that the real secrets of the clandestine war remained secret, an important consideration as the Cold War began to heat up. That these women were shown returning to more traditional roles after the war underscores the extenuating circumstances of the war in which even some women were called upon to do their bit in order that the *status quo* could be preserved.

A second way in which representations of the SOE differ from memories of the war projected in popular literature and film is that traces of the 'people's war' discourse can *still* be found circulating in the late 1940s and 1950s, with references to the varied class backgrounds of the female agents. F Section enlisted several working-class women, most of whom were French nationals or had Anglo-French parentage. The section was more elitist when it came to recruiting men, however, who generally came from middle- and upper middle-class backgrounds, partly because recruitment was largely based on the 'Old Boy Network' and because few men from ordinary backgrounds had the requisite linguistic proficiency. There were a few men who had undertaken manual jobs prior to their recruitment, whom we might presume came from ordinary backgrounds, including an aircraft fitter, a miner, several mechanics, a taxi driver, a carpenter and a jockey. These men do not appear in histories of the SOE. Some of the women from ordinary backgrounds, however, did feature in post-war accounts: a 1948 article about Peggy Knight, for example, is replete with evidence of her 'ordinary' background: 'A little proudly she pointed to the second-hand armchairs she and her husband had re-covered … It might have been any post-war working-class mother talking.'[56] And despite casting Virginia McKenna in the role, Violette Szabo's working-class Cockney background was referenced in *Carve Her Name With Pride* (1958). While the participation of working-class men was erased in post-war stories about the conflict in an effort to restore established class distinctions, the re-establishment of conventional gender norms with the emphasis upon women's domestic role allowed space for a discussion about class.

Nevertheless, while there was recognition of women's participation in the secret war, some of whom were working-class, there was no space for an articulation of race. Noor Inayat Khan, the daughter of an Indian Sufi mystic and his American wife, was always referred to as Nora in early accounts, the Anglicization of her name serving to obscure her Indian identity. The photographs of her chosen to accompany articles were always of her dressed in Western garb in which she passed as white, rather than in traditional Indian clothing. This deracialization of her Asianness can be seen explicitly in the *Sunday Graphic* which assured its readers (erroneously) that she was 'of British stock despite her name'.[57] As Shompa Lahiri notes, 'the post-war British press valorisation of Khan's wartime passing involved an appropriation of Khan's maternal whiteness and disregarding of her paternal brownness.'[58] This saw expression in the deleting of the early chapters of Jean Overton Fuller's biography which chronicled Noor's Indian heritage and the casting of a white actress as Khan in a 1955 televised play.[59] The shared national past constructed in cultural memory thereby erased race, as well as nationality, collapsing identity differences into a common Britishness.

Continuing to be told: literary and visual depictions of the secret war from the 1960s to the 1980s

The cultural memory of the secret war was thus kept alive in the 1940s and 1950s by continual references in the press, the publication of auto/ biographies of the SOE's personnel, and filmic treatments of wartime stories. Over the next 30 years, the SOE had less of a presence in popular culture, as did the Second World War, but it continued to retain a profile with intermittently published first-hand accounts (four by male agents and one by a woman) as well as biographies (two about male agents and three about women). The historical and cultural moment in which they were produced remained as significant as for the representations circulating in the 1950s. The abundance of the SOE testimonies that were published in the 1950s were undoubtedly part of the promotion of both Britain's and France's wartime story, but strikingly they tail off following the re-election of de Gaulle in 1958. Given the rather complex relationship that de Gaulle had with SOE personnel (telling several British agents that they had 24 hours to get out of France in the summer of 1944), the pattern of the SOE publications appears to be in inverse relation to de Gaulle being in power. Moreover, the few accounts that were produced in the 1960s, a period which witnessed the liberalization of sexual mores, the decriminalization of homosexuality and the (re)emergence of a women's movement, bore the distinctive hallmark of that time. Denis Rake's autobiography, for example, published one year after the 1967 Sexual Offences Act, wrote candidly about his relationships with men, including a brief sexual affair with a German soldier,[60] while the *Daily Telegraph* magazine published a photoshoot on the 25th anniversary of D-Day in which Lise de Baissac, then aged 64 and dressed in a calf-length tweed skirt and buttoned-up cardigan, was photographed holding a dagger.

The most widely acclaimed historian of the secret war, and thus a key carrier or vector of memory, is M. R. D. Foot. In 1958, Prime Minister Harold Macmillan sanctioned the research and publication of an official history of the SOE. France was selected as the subject in order to quell the criticisms of three female authors who had campaigned for more information about the executed female agents[61] and to capitalize on the public interest in the wartime activities of the agents generated by the wealth of representations discussed above. Foot was appointed and given access to secret files that were only publicly released in the late 1990s, but he did not interview the many still surviving agents. The book, *SOE in France*,[62] was held up for almost four years by the censors but was finally published in 1966. It served as a counterpoint to the many fictionalized accounts that were in circulation: 'Many authors have been attracted to SOE's work by its undoubtedly dramatic character, a character heightened where work in France is concerned by the presence of nubile young women, some of whom suffered appalling fates ... Many are good thrillers, but bad history.'[63]

The SOE also featured as the subject of fictional representations. The 1960s and 1970s saw an explosion in 'Boy's Own'-style comics and magazines which tapped into this ongoing interest in the Second World War, a phenomenon that Mike Paris has called the 'pleasure culture of war'.[64] Several, including *Commando*, a fortnightly (and later weekly) comic established in 1961,[65] and *Purnell's History of the Second World War*, a weekly magazine from 1966 containing scholarly articles,[66] featured issues about the Resistance. The SOE also attracted the attention of playwrights. David Hare's play *Plenty* (1978), and subsequent film (1985) starring Meryl Streep,[67] was an attempt by a left-wing author writing in a period of disillusionment on the eve of Thatcherism to critique the 'mythic promise' of 1945's legacy.[68] Hare, inspired by reading Angus Calder's seminal text *The People's War* (1969), wrote *Plenty* as an allegory of the devastation wrought by the war. With its chronological disruption, flitting between 1943 and 1962, the play moves across time serving to connote social change.[69] Thus references to the Queen's Coronation (1953) and the Suez Crisis (1956) symbolize the triumphant return of traditionalism and, with its emphasis on hierarchy, an emphatic quashing of the promise of egalitarianism. The main character's personal life is played out against these public events. 'My starting point for the play', Hare asserted, 'was reading a statistic which showed that 75% of the women flown behind the lines for the Special Operations Executive were subsequently divorced during the peace.'[70] While that statistic is not accurate, it prompted Hare to examine 'the cost of a life lived in dissent'[71] by constructing Susan Traherne as highly troubled: she has sexual intercourse with male strangers ('I do like to make a point of sleeping with men I don't know. I do find once you get to know them you usually don't want to sleep with them any more ...'), she has an emotionless affair for 18 months purely to get pregnant, she is infertile, she is unstable, firing a gun above her lover's head, a lesbian relationship is hinted at ('[Alice,] you excite me'), she is restless ('Those of us who went through this kind of war, I think we do have something in common. It's a kind of impatience, we're rather intolerant, we don't suffer fools. And so we get rather restless back in England, the people who stayed behind seem childish and a little silly.'), she settles for marriage to a rather staid man ('I married him because he reminded me of my father. At that point of course I didn't realize just what a shit my father was.'), she destroys her husband's diplomatic career by becoming 'hysterical' and threatening to shoot herself if he is not promoted, her marriage collapses and she is depicted as descending into a cycle of madness in which her husband threatens to commit her to an institution.[72] The film, the screenplay of which Hare wrote, removes the chronological disruption but adds a scene where Traherne is shown in the throes of madness under the influence of drugs. The overriding message is that a woman who has traversed conventional gender boundaries by undertaking active service will struggle to lead a normal civilian life.

There were also a number of television dramatizations: *Moonstrike*, one-off thrillers broadcast in 1963 but now largely lost; *Secret Army*, which ran from 1977 to 1979; *Wish Me Luck*, three series of which were broadcast from 1988 to 1989, with some episodes achieving audience viewing figures of around 18 million per week, and on which agent Yvonne Cormeau was a technical advisor; and *'Allo 'Allo*, which began as a spoof of *Secret Army* and ran for nine series spanning a decade from 1982. These programmes focused upon women undertaking resistance: in *Secret Army*, a Belgian escape line was headed by a woman with the assistance of two other women; *Wish Me Luck* depicted the recruitment, training and mission of two fictional female SOE agents in France; and anorak- and beret-wearing Michelle ('I shall say this only *wance*') had a daring plan to rescue the downed Allied airmen in most episodes of *'Allo 'Allo*. Not only were these programmes popular in their time, but they continue to remain so: repeats are regularly broadcast on both terrestrial and satellite channels, DVDs can be purchased and there are websites dedicated to each. These fictional representations probably did and continue to do more to shape British cultural memory about European resistance than television documentaries and films based on actual events.

Exhibiting the 'Secret War': the Imperial War Museum

The public's perceptions of the secret war in the 1960s, 1970s and 1980s was shaped largely by these fictional television representations, as opposed to the narrative and filmic representations of the 1940s and 1950s which had a true story at their centre. In the early 1980s, proposals were first mooted for a Special Forces exhibition that would challenge these preconceptions and re-centre focus on real individuals. It was to be held at Duxford Airfield near Cambridge in the summer of 1986. But with the re-opening in 1989 of the Imperial War Museum, the national museum of twentieth-century conflict that had been founded in 1917, it was decided that this would house the display. The SOE's operations were covered in the Second World War historical displays, but plans for a new permanent gallery in the south-eastern wing devoted to Special Forces were included in Stage II of the Redevelopment Programme. Over the years of planning, the title was changed to 'Secret War', the focus on solely the Second World War was broadened out to include the entire twentieth century, and decisions were taken to focus solely on British clandestine operations as opposed to chronicling international espionage.[73] Research was undertaken on significant incidents and personalities and it was decided that artefacts rather than text were a more effective way of showcasing the secret war. Over 700 items were selected to be displayed; some were already in the Museum's collections, others were donated by members of the Special Forces Club and had not been publicly viewed before. The exhibition, costing just under a million pounds, opened to the public on 5 July 1995 and a private viewing for 200 guests including the agent Tony Brooks took place that evening with John Paul Getty, one of the private investors who had pledged financial support, officiating at the launch.

The exhibition plays on all of the senses to disorient the visitor and then acclimatize them to the enclosed, claustrophobic environment of the secret war: floors, ceilings and walls slope; areas narrow then open out; some areas are brightly lit, others are very dark; large shadows are cast by visitors on the ceiling; noise from various television screens blares out; the sound of teleprinters, recorded voices, radio static and Morse code can be heard; specially-composed music plays in the background; and the temperature changes. This was intended 'to create a series of environmental narratives that allow the fascinating museum objects to be seen within different atmospheric contexts.'[74] The exhibition's sensory experience was in itself a form of memory.

The entrance to the exhibition on the first-floor gallery is understated – there is no hint as to what lies within except for the sound of the Bond theme music played repeatedly, drawing visitors in to the dark passageway. In a cabinet marked 'It is easy to mistake spy fiction for reality ...', ephemera are displayed, including a *Carve Her Name With Pride* film poster, a television monitor playing clips from various James Bond films, first editions of classic spy literature including John Buchan's *Greenmantle* (1916), Len Deighton's *Spy Story* (1974) and John Le Carre's *Tinker, Tailor, Soldier, Spy* (1974). A more recent addition to this 'Fiction Wall' is a poster from the Bond film *Casino Royale* (2006) starring Daniel Craig. An article written by the exhibition curator noted:

> The core of the exhibition was to lie in the contrast between fact and fiction. It was agreed that visitors would harbour a host of preconceived ideas about the world of espionage. The intention was to help them

identify these stereotypes, properly label them as fiction and then present the equally exciting but true stories of Britain's secret war.

The first area is a 'briefing room' where visitors watch a three-minute film in which an authoritative voice asserts: 'What you are about to see in the exhibition has for years been part of the country's most closely hoarded secret … This is the reality of Britain's secret story against its enemies wherever and whoever they might be.' Visitors then proceed into the light and a space with a sloping floor, and walk around five sections: MI5, MI6, Secret Communications, SOE and Secret Soldiers. Visitors move from the winding section on Secret Communications, which is designed to have a 'clinical feel' to it with its white brightness, into the twilight world of the SOE section with its long, straight passageway reminiscent of a landing strip, a night-time landscape as seen from an aeroplane at low altitude, dark blue lighting, grey and tan (wartime) colours and metallic panels arching up to give the impression of the interior of an aeroplane. The muffled roar of an engine can be heard, as can the cackle of radioed instructions, such as 'Approaching drop zone – Standby'. The air is cooler in this part of the exhibition. The panels provide scant information on the SOE's origins, staff and training, weapons, sabotage, communications, agents' equipment and transportation. The display cabinets, which are deliberately old-fashioned, house items such as the bullet-torn (now repaired) dress of agent Yvonne Cormeau, her briefcase, scarves given to Vera Atkins (a high-ranking member of the F Section staff), medals, coded messages, forged documents, suicide pills and a 'striptease suit' worn by agents when parachuting into enemy-occupied territory. Unsurprisingly, F Section and its female agents are disproportionately represented. The exhibition has been subsequently updated and modernized: visitors can peer through binoculars onto a French landscape, the voiceover in the recruitment and training section of the film *Now It Can Be Told*, which is on a continuous loop, has been dubbed so the accents are not so dated, and there are computers with touch screens so that visitors can 'open' an office filing cabinet and select an agent's personal file. Strikingly, all files are labelled just with the surname, so until 'Szabo' or 'Khan' are opened it is unclear that they are women. The file for Odette Sansom, however, like her interview tape, is simply labelled 'Odette'. The exhibition is undergoing further upgrading for the museum's reopening in July 2013, which will also feature a new family exhibition entitled '*Horrible Histories: Spies*'.

A museum is a crucial way in which the public learns about the past; as Lucy Noakes asserts, it is an authoritative 'site of cultural transmission and public education'.[75] But it is only one version of the past that is presented, as she illustrates with reference to the highly sanitized script that the Imperial War Museum's 'Blitz Experience' adopted. The 'Secret War' exhibition, which foregrounds the SOE's F Section and its female agents, confers historic legitimacy upon the SOE and reaches an even broader audience than the memoirs, films and scholarly accounts.

Thus the secret war, which was so pervasive in the cultural memory of the 1940s and 1950s, retained public visibility throughout the next 30 years. But it was in the last decade of the millennium, as remaining veterans approached the end of their lives and as the 50th anniversaries of the formation of the SOE and of the end of the war were celebrated, that the memory of the SOE was reanimated once more. Yet again, male agents were much more likely than their female counterparts to write their own accounts, with five men publishing their autobiographies since 1990. And women continued to be the focus of biographical accounts with 10 of the 16 books published since 1990 being about the female agents. Female agents have also inspired a number of fictional novels; the most successful, Sebastian Faulks's *Charlotte Gray* (1999), was made into a film of the same name (2003), and a spin-off television documentary called *Behind Enemy Lines: The Real Charlotte Grays* was broadcast in 2002. There have been 10 documentaries utilizing personal testimony, and a film, the director of which was inspired by reading an obituary of Lise de Baissac, was released in 2008 in France (*Les femmes de l'ombre*) and Britain (*Female Agents*).[76] Despite being a fictional and historically inaccurate film, it used similar techniques to establish authority as *Odette* and *Carve Her Name With Pride* had done 50 years previously, with the opening credits featuring a selection of black and white photographs of female combatants from various conflicts. There have been several memorials, including at the site of the first parachutist landing at Valençay (unveiled in 1991), and plaques have been erected at Beaulieu Abbey where the final phase of training was undertaken, at RAF Tempsford and Tangmere from where agents departed for the Continent and at a number of concentration camps where agents were killed. A key element of many of the SOE memorials is the names that are inscribed, bestowing recognition and honour. Memorials, in particular site-specific ones such as these, are a focal point in the construction and iteration of the memory of the secret war. In myriad ways, then, the cultural memory of the SOE was invoked, offering the potential for nostalgia about a shared national past.

Conclusion

This chapter has shown the ways in which some aspects of the secret war achieved cultural hegemony. The SOE operated in various Nazi-occupied countries, as well as the Far East, but the exploits of (male) agents in Italy, Belgium and Burma for example have been almost entirely erased from British cultural memory. Possibly the only exception is the Norwegian resistance, which featured in the popular film *The Heroes of Telemark*

(1965) and more recently *Max Manus* (2008). In contrast, the activities of F Section have received much attention. The drip-feed of articles in newspapers with high circulation figures, best-selling auto/biographies and films which enjoyed box-office success, all of which were produced during a period of nostalgia for the war years and in which agents were often themselves heavily involved in shaping the public's image of the clandestine operative, were key components in the formation of the cultural memory of the secret war in France. In later decades, television documentaries, museum displays and memorials kept the SOE's French operations in the public eye. They produced a remarkably homogenous memory. Read together, this outpouring of cultural representations cumulatively reinforces how the British remembered the war. They serve a very particular purpose in shaping cultural memory: tales of individual sacrifice and heroism were part of a broader cultural discourse about the 'people's war' in which, strikingly, women played a full part.

Indeed, the secret agent that circulated in literary, filmic and visual culture was emphatically female. This focus upon women has presented a highly exceptional feminized rendering of the war. This has resulted in the public being much more familiar with some of the female operatives than with any of their male counterparts. Szabo and Sansom are household names, perhaps partly because 'Violette' and 'Odette' are rather memorable names, whereas few have heard of male veterans such as George Starr and Francis Suttill who played important roles in the SOE. Hence, much of the literature contrasts with other historical fields in which an emphasis is placed on male figures and their activities. The fascination with Violette Szabo, for example, has seen expression through the holding of séances and past life regressions and with some people adorning their bodies with tattoos of her face.[77] An Xbox game released in 2009 called *Velvet Assassin*, 'inspired by the fascinating story and unbreakable spirit of British secret agent Violette Szabo', will introduce the SOE's female agents to a new audience.[78] The gendering of the cultural memory of the secret war is also exemplified by Karen Newman's SOE memorial that was unveiled on Albert Embankment in October 2009. Despite being a memorial to the whole of the SOE in all theatres of war, it bears the bust of Violette Szabo, and an inscription ends with 'in the pages of history their names are Carved with Pride', wording directly associated with Szabo. Thus, while these women represent a numerical minority, collectively (and a few individually) they have occupied a disproportionately large place in the post-war cultural imagination. A compelling explanation for why the female agents have struck such a chord in popular literature and film is that wars are generally seen as being fought by men. The cultural myth that women, the 'gentle sex', are inherently peace-loving, coupled with the belief that 'women give life, not take it',[79] has inhibited women's full participation in combat situations. Yet when women are actively involved in ways that challenge societal codes about femininity, a voyeuristic fascination ensues. This has been seen in the last 10 years with women's involvement, and in particular female casualties, in Afghanistan and Iraq which have generated much coverage. Seventy years ago, female combatants were much less common and, thus, this interest in war women is heightened. These women, often shown in black and white photographs as generally young and highly attractive, appear braver than their male counterparts in risking possibly harsher treatment and execution if caught, and their deaths seem more touchingly tragic because of gendered assumptions about women's nature. Whatever the explanation, these vectors of memory have conveyed, and consequently shaped, a particular national memory of the secret war, and this shows no signs of abating.

Notes

1   *Sun*, 13 September 2010.

2   *Daily Mail*, 18 September 2010.

3   Buckmaster, M. (1947), 'Paris in Spring', *Chamber's Journal*.

4   *Timewatch: Secret Memories* (BBC2, 1997).

5   Headline of series beginning in the *Daily Herald*, 24 April 1950.

6   *London Mystery Magazine*, June–July 1951, 9.

7   *Motion Picture Herald*, poll cited in *The Times*, 8 January 1958.

8   Foot, M. R. D. (2001), *SOE in the Low Countries*. London: St Ermin's; Murphy, C. J. (2006), *Security and Special Operations: SOE and MI5 During the Second World War*. Basingstoke: Palgrave Macmillan.

9   Rousso, H. (1991), *The Vichy Syndrome: History and Memory in France 1944*. Cambridge, MA: Harvard University Press.

10 Worpole, K. (1983), *Dockers and Detectives: Popular Reading: Popular Writing*. London: Verson, 52.

11 Ramsden, J. (1998), 'Refocusing "the peoples war": British war films of the 1950s', *Historical Journal of Film, Radio and Television*, 33(1), 35–63.

12 Pronay, N. (1998), 'The British post-bellum cinema: A survey of the films relating to World War II made in Britain between 1945 and 1960'. *Historical Journal of Film, Radio and Television*, 8(1), 39–54. Here p. 39.

13 Rattigan, N. (1994), 'The last gasp of the middle class: the British war films of the 1950s', in W. W. Dixon (ed.) *Reviewing British Cinema 1900–1992: Essays and Interviews*. Albany: State University of New York, 143–53. Here p. 148.

14 Summerfield, P. (2010), 'Dunkirk and the popular memory of Britain at War, 1940–58'. *Journal of Contemporary History*, 45(4), 788–811. Here p. 809.

15 Harper, S. (1997), 'Popular film, popular memory: The case of the Second World War', in M. Evans and K. Lunn (eds), *War and Memory in the Twentieth Century*. Oxford: Berg, 163–76. Here p. 173.

16 Summerfield, P., (2009), 'Public memory or public amnesia?: British women of the Second World War in popular films of the 1950s and 1960s', *Journal of British Studies*, 48(4), 935–57.

17 *Kinematograph Weekly*, 13 February 1947.

18 'Important Notes', memo, Item 31, *School for Danger* collection, British Film Institute.

19 *Punch*, 5 March 1947.

20 *London Gazette*, 20 August 1946.

21 *Sunday Express*, 11 March 1945.

22 *Daily Herald*, 25 April 1950.

23 *Daily Herald*, 26 April 1950.

24 *Daily Graphic*, 21 August 1946; *Daily Herald*, 24 April 1950.

25 *Daily Graphic*, 21 August 1946.

26 'Now it can be told' (radio script, 4 April 1950).

27 *News of the World*, 17 March 1946; *News Chronicle*, 30 March 1946.

28 Rousso (1991), 277.

29 Thomson, A. (1994), *Anzac Memories: Living with the Legend*. Oxford: Oxford University Press.

30 *Sunday Express*, 23 March 1952.

31 Burney, C. (1945), *The Dungeon Democracy*. London: Heinemann.

32 Millar, G. (1945), *Maquis*. London: Heinemann.

33 Seaman, M. (1999), 'Good thrillers, but bad history: A review of published works on the Special Operations Executive's work in France during the Second World War' in K. G. Robertson (ed.) *War, Resistance and Intelligence: Essays in Honour of M.R.D Foot*. Barnsley: Leo Cooper, 119–34. Here p. 120.

34 Rousso (1991), 278.

35 Webster, W. (2001), 'Representing nation: women, obituaries and national biography', in A.-M. Gallagher, C. Lubelska and L. Ryan (eds), *Re-presenting the Past: Women and History*. London: Longman, 124–41. Here p. 125.

36 Tickell, J. (1949), *Odette: The Story of a British Agent*. London: Chapman and Hall.

37 Starns, P. (2009), *Odette: World War Two's Darling Spy*. Stroud: The History Press, 125.

38 Minney, R. J. (1956), *Carve Her Name with Pride: The Story of Violette Szabo*. London: George Newnes.

39 *Times Educational Supplement*, 27 February 1958.

40 *Motion Picture Herald*, 6 January 1950.

41 *Mercury*, 29 December 1950.

42 Film programme of *Odette*.

43 *Daily Sketch*, 21 August 1946; *Daily Mail*, 5 October 1950.

44 *Sunday Dispatch*, 30 November 1958.

45   Imperial War Museum, interview with Odette Sansom, 9478 (1986).

46   Penny Summerfield notes the parallels within the torture scenes of the two films. Summerfield (2009), 946.

47   Imperial War Museum, interview with Odette Sansom.

48   *New Statesman and Nation*, 15 February 1947.

49   *Kinematograph Weekly*, 1 April 1958.

50   Ramsden (1998), 38.

51   Eley, G. (2001), 'Finding the people's war: film, British collective memories and World War II'. *The American Historical Review*, 106(3), 818–38. Here p. 819.

52   Newspaper unknown, 22 May 1948. Clipping held at FANY (First Aid Nursing Yeomanry) Headquarters, London. All female agents were seconded to the FANYs.

53   Worpole (1983), 72.

54   Rattigan (1994), 150; Ramsden (1998), 56.

55   Osborne, D. (2006), '"I do not know about politics or governments.... I am a housewife": The female secret agent and the male war machine in Occupied France (1942–5)'. *Women: A Cultural Review*, 17(1), 42–64. Here pp. 61–2.

56   Clipping held at FANY Headquarters.

57   *Sunday Graphic*, 22 June 1952.

58   Lahiri, S. (2007), 'Clandestine mobilities and shifting embodiments: Noor-un-nisa Inayat Khan and the Special Operations Executive, 1940–44'. *Gender and History*, 19(2), 305–23. See also Lahiri, S. (2010) *Indian Mobilities in the West, 1900–1947: Gender, Performance, Embodiment*. Basingstoke: Palgrave.

59   Overton Fuller, J. (1952) *Madeleine: The Story of Noor Inayat Khan*. London: Victor Gollancz; Ross, D. 'Madeleine' (BBC, 14 June 1955) starring Rosalie Crutchley.

60   Rake, D. (1968), *Rake's Progress*. London: Leslie Frewin.

61   Ward, I. (1955), *F.A.N.Y. Invicta*. London: Hutchinson; Nicholas, E. (1958), *Death Be Not Proud*. London: Cresset Press; Overton Fuller, J. (1958), *Double Webs: Light on the Secret Agents' War in France*. London: Putnam.

62   Foot, M. R. D. (1966) *SOE in France: An Account of the Work of the British Special Operations Executive in France 1940–1944*. London: HMSO.

63   Ibid., 454.

64   Paris, M. (2000), *Warrior Nation: Images of War in British Popular Culture*. London: Reaktion Books.

65   Montague, R. A., 'Secret War', No. 1344; Handley, F., 'Battleground Brittany', No. 4212; Grehan, G., 'The Fighting Gendarme', No. 4535.

66   See, for example, Barry, R. H. (1968), 'Helping the Resistance, build-up for D-Day', in *Purnell's History of the Second World War*, 5(3).

67   *Plenty* (dir. Fred Schepisi, 1985).

68 See Eley (2001), 829–34.

69 Homden, C. (1995), *The Plays of David Hare*. Cambridge: Cambridge University Press.

70 Programme of 1999 performance of *Plenty* at the Albery Theatre starring Cate Blanchett.

71 Ibid.

72 Hare, D. (1978), *Plenty*. London: Faber and Faber.

73 Imperial War Museum, file R1/SW/01/002.

74 Imperial War Museum, file EXPA 0346.

75 Noakes, L. (1997), 'Making histories: experiencing the Blitz in London's Museums in the 1990s', in M. Evans and K. Lunn (eds), *War and Memory in the Twentieth Century*. Oxford: Berg, 89–104. Here p. 90.

76 *Les femmes de l'ombre/Female Agents* (dir. Jean-Paul Salomé, 2008).

77 Vigurs, K. (2011), 'The women agents of the Special Operations Executive F section – wartime realities and post war representations'. Unpublished PhD thesis, University of Leeds, 178.

78 http://uk.ign.com/games/velvet-assassin/xbox-360-608112/.

79 See Pattinson, J. (2008), '"Turning a pretty girl into a killer": women, violence and clandestine operations during the Second World War', in F. Alexander and K. Throsby (eds), *Gender and Interpersonal Violence: Language, Action and Representation*. Basingstoke: Palgrave, 11–28.

Key texts

Eley, G. (2001), 'Finding the people's war: film, British collective memories and World War II'. *The American Historical Review*. 106(3), 818–38.

Lahiri, S. (2007), 'Clandestine mobilities and shifting embodiments: Noor-un-nisa Inayat Khan and the Special Operations Executive, 1940–44'. *Gender and History*, 19(2), 305–23.

Osborne, D. (2006), '"I do not know about politics or governments … I am a housewife": The female secret agent and the male war machine in Occupied France (1942–5)'. *Women: A Cultural Review*, 17(1), 42–64.

Pattinson, J. (2007), *Behind Enemy Lines: Gender, Passing and the SOE in the Second World War*. Manchester: Manchester University Press.

—(2008) 'Turning a pretty girl into a killer': women, violence and clandestine operations during the Second World War', in F. Alexander and K. Throsby (eds), *Gender and Interpersonal Violence: Language, Action and Representation*. Basingstoke: Palgrave, 11–28.

Pronay, N. (1998), 'The British post-bellum cinema: A survey of the films relating to World War II made in Britain between 1945 and 1960'. *Historical Journal of Film, Radio and Television*, 8(1), 39–54.

Ramsden, J. (1998), 'Refocusing "the people's war": British war films of the 1950s'. *Journal of Contemporary History*, 33(1), 35–63.

Rattigan, N. (1994), 'The last gasp of the middle class: the British war films of the 1950s', in W. W. Dixon (ed.), *Reviewing British Cinema 1900–1992: Essays and Interviews*. Albany: State University of New York Press, 143–53.

Seaman, M. (1999), 'Good thrillers, but bad history: A review of published works on the Special Operations Executive's work in France during the Second World War', in K. G. Robertson, (ed.), *War, Resistance and Intelligence: Essays in Honour of M. R. D Foot*. Barnsley: Leo Cooper, 119–34.

Summerfield, P. (2009), 'Public memory or public amnesia? British women of the Second World War in popular films of the 1950s and 1960s'. *Journal of British Studies*, 48(4), 935–57.

Worpole, K. (1983), *Dockers and Detectives: Popular Reading: Popular Writing*. London: Verso.

CHAPTER EIGHT

The 'missing chapter'

Bomber Command aircrew memoirs in the 1990s and 2000s

Frances Houghton

This is not a gung-ho, press-on-regardless Boys Own Paper account of my experience of flying with RAF Bomber Command; but neither is it an exercise in hand-wringing nor breast-beating and avowals of guilt.[1]

On a sunny day in June 2012, a much anticipated ceremony took place in London's Green Park. As the new RAF Bomber Command Memorial was unveiled by the Queen, the last few surviving aircrew veterans of 1939–45 witnessed the final stages of a 70-year-long battle for official public commemoration of their 55,000 lost comrades. In a popular culture still saturated with referents to the Second World War, the apparent absence of public recognition of Bomber Command's contribution to victory had become an issue of increasing sensitivity among former aircrew. Indeed, since Britain began its cycle of commemorative 50th anniversaries of the Second World War in 1989, mounting levels of disenchantment amongst some Bomber Command veterans, in particular those who had served on the four-engined 'heavy' bombers during the controversial area bombing campaign of the later war years, became evident through a number of newly published memoirs. Together with the odd revised edition of an already existent title, these books formed a new sub-genre of military autobiography that embodied a militant approach towards challenging contemporary public recollections of the bombers' war.

Important studies such as Alistair Thomson's *Anzac Memories* (1994) have cast light upon the dialectic between public memory and the personal rememberings of veterans. His investigation into the working of the ANZAC legend among Australian Great War veterans demonstrates the inherent difficulties of composing private memories that fit with the circulating dominant model of recollection. Thomson found that the personal memories of these veterans had, in many circumstances, been subject to a degree of reshaping as a result of the influence of official and cultural representations of the war.[2] Bomber Command memoirs published since 1990, however, indicate that the relationship between veteran recollection and public memory must also be interpreted as an active, two-way process in which former servicemen seek to establish control over popular memories of 'their' war. These narratives fall into the category of what Henri Rousso has identified as 'vectors' of memory, whereby 'collective' memory of any event is shaped by a series of representations, mediated by groups and individuals, which proffer 'a deliberate reconstruction of an event for a social purpose.'[3] The vectors, or 'carriers', of these representations are defined by Rousso as official, organizational, scholarly, or – as is the case with these war memoirs – cultural.[4] Applying Rousso's model to veteran interaction with public recollections of the Second World War in Britain, this study seeks to explore a ferocious rearguard action fought in literary form by the last remaining aircrew veterans for control of popular memories of 'their' war.

The emotive nature of Bomber Command's place in popular remembrance means that these narratives are particularly well placed to illuminate the shifting and often conflicting affinity between individual and 'collective' memory of the Second World War in Britain. Published military memoirs of Second World War British servicemen have long played a prominent role in what historian Graham Dawson has identified as a flourishing 'pleasure culture of war' in Britain.[5] Bound up in 'Good War' discourses, these narratives enabled post-war generations to experience combat vicariously and enjoyably, secure in the knowledge that honourable victory over the malevolence of fanaticism had been secured. The phrase 'Good War' is frequently used in British and American culture to distinguish the Second World War from other conflicts, implying that the Second World War was the ultimate crusade of righteousness against extreme evil and may therefore be regarded as the epitome of a just war. Because of their consumption as popular entertainment, alongside the inevitable limitations of using personal narratives as historical sources, the inherent value such texts pose to explorations of the Second World War in British cultural memory and popular culture has tended to be overlooked. These books, however, present a rare opportunity to gain an insight into the reverse side of popular memorialization: that is to say, the response of the persons being remembered to the modes in which they perceive they are being memorialized. Whilst inherently a work of private memory, by virtue of its publication the war memoir represents a decision to act in public; to engage in some way with shared social memories of the conflict. As Jay Winter reminds us, remembering is itself a performative act.[6] Literary critic Samuel Hynes builds upon this concept, positing that all war memoirists are 'makers': writing a memoir is an active process where narratives of remembrance are created in which meaning is emergent rather than fixed.[7] Operating within a specific social 'framework', the published military memoir is situated at the intersection of private and public memory.[8] Rousso's model therefore holds significant implications for furthering scholarly understandings of the complex interaction between popular memory of a war and its individual protagonists. Due to their simultaneous proposal and reflection of wider representations of the event, vectors of memory function as two-way conduits.[9] The bomber memoirs under investigation here provide a working demonstration of how, in responding to wider public discourses, published narratives rapidly became a valuable site from which to shape an 'unending battle for how aircrew should be remembered'.[10]

Vectors of memory in conflict

It is evident from several of the texts under consideration that the bomber memoirs of the 1990s and early 2000s were in large part written as a response to the unsatisfactory nature of other vectors of memory in the preceding decades. Official vectors, comprising ceremonies, celebrations or monuments, had remained dismally lacking in comparison to the levels of nationally or locally organized commemoration of other services.[11] These memoirs indicate clearly that former aircrew believed themselves to have been unfairly left out of many such overt symbols of official recognition. A particular focus of resentment in these narratives is the long-running battle to obtain a campaign medal for Bomber Command veterans. At the close of the war, the Command's leader since 1942, Sir Arthur Harris, had requested that a medal be granted to his crews in recognition of their courageous wartime service. Instead, a highly unpopular distinction was made between aircrew who had been operational before D-Day, 6 June 1944, and those who had carried out their tours after this date. In his memoir, *Bread and Butter Bomber Boys* (1995), Arthur White explains that:

> Bomber crews were snubbed by the Government's refusal to award a Bomber Command Campaign Medal in recognition of their efforts and sacrifices. In fact, crews embarking on their tours of operations after

D-Day didn't even qualify for the Aircrew Europe Star but had to be content with the France and Germany Star.[12]

Jim Davis's testimony, *Winged Victory* (1995), conveys a particular sense of bitterness that this distinction had been drawn, noting that:

> The France and Germany Star was given to all the soldiers and other personnel who crossed the Channel after D-Day and, of course, it was also given to those who actually crossed the Channel when the war was nearly over (a matter of a day or so). Every one came under the France and Germany medal. Surely then it would have been fair if all Air Crew who flew on operations against Germany at any time during the war should have been given the Air Crew Europe Star.[13]

With operational flying over Europe continuing to pose considerable risks to bomber crews for many months after D-Day, the division of entitlement to the coveted Aircrew Europe Star remained a contentious issue for Bomber Command. Arthur Harris's own war memoir, *Bomber Offensive* (1947), described this affair as 'the subject of much bitter comment' among aircrew, observing that the France and Germany Star had been bestowed upon 'Every clerk, butcher or baker in the rear of the armies overseas'.[14] From the narratives of White and Davis, it is abundantly clear that the lack of campaign medal for so many of Bomber Command's men continued to sting long after Harris's memoir came into publication.

Davis's emphatic assertion that the refusal to grant all veterans the Aircrew Europe Star represented 'another disgrace' dealt out to Bomber Command implies a regular litany of perceived post-war iniquities passed along to former aircrew.[15] Indeed, it is not solely official vectors of memory that are portrayed in these testimonies as snubbing the bombers' war. Memoirist Arthur White perceived that scholarly sources were equally culpable, indicting the representations crafted by 'so called intellectual arm chair historians'. His opinion of this profession is markedly scathing:

> They were the people fortunate enough to fight World War 2 with the hindsight of ten, twenty or thirty years from the comfort of their 'Poly' or University common rooms and feed their views to 'investigative journalists' of similar ilk who then swamped the media with their indignant outpourings.[16]

Specific cultural carriers of memory are also identified as exerting malign influence over public remembrance of aircrew. Rousso identifies a wide variety of media forms, spanning literature, film, and television, as culturally influential in shaping popular memory, yet in these narratives it is mostly the television documentary which poses an especial concern to the veterans.[17] Although cinematic representations of Bomber Command had largely confined themselves solely to the gallant tale of *The Dam Busters* (1955), the television documentary is cited as a medium of cultural remembrance that was viewed as actively damaging. Jeremy Isaacs's *World at War* series in 1973 portrayed the ordeal of aircrew with some compassion, but it implied that the efforts of the Command had been a waste of time, subscribing to a 'costly failure' interpretation of the campaign.[18] The sympathy for aircrew that had tinged Isaacs's documentary was distinctly lacking in subsequent programmes in which several of the veterans in this study were invited to take part. In his memoir, *Luck and a Lancaster* (1999), pilot Harry Yates relates being asked in 1987 to contribute to a BBC documentary on the Le Havre raid of 1944, in which he had participated. Heavily bombed by the Allies in September of that year, several thousand French civilian lives had been lost in the port. The television programme, Yates was informed, would take former aircrew, such as himself, to Le Havre to meet French survivors and victims of the attack. 'I was suspicious of the BBC's motives, and said so', remembers Yates. 'To me, it seemed all too likely that the RAF crews would be depicted as butchers.'[19] A letter from an assistant producer which outlined the objectives of the programme further reinforced his misgivings. 'The heart of it all', Yates explains, 'was the third aim: "to … personalise a day which saw a particularly high loss of French civilian life."' Whilst acknowledging that televising the recollections of survivors made for 'compulsive viewing', he describes the effect on aircrew veterans as agonizing:

> [F]or ex-aircrew such sorrows are unanswerable. They shift the emphasis away from the greater cause in which deaths occurred and onto the manner of them. They exploit the moral superiority of the victims. The aegis of military duty becomes a contemptible thing. There is such a strong imputation of guilt or complicity, the supposed transgressor can find himself babbling away about following orders before he knows it.[20]

Apprehensive about the depiction of bomber aircrew in other documentaries, and concerned about how the transmission of his testimony might be distorted by the dictates of 'a predetermined critique of the RAF', Yates declined in 1987 to be interviewed, informing his audience that he had 'no desire to be set up like that'.[21] In two revised editions of his 1969 memoir, *The Eighth Passenger*, issued in 1985 and 1993, Miles Tripp also narrates experiencing feelings of pressure to conform to a specific agenda of expectations upon being invited in 1983 to take part in a German documentary which would feature the Dresden raid of 1945. The producer informed Tripp that he would be expected to answer 'the sort of questions' German viewers would ask. These would include queries such as: '"How did you feel knowing that the bombs you dropped on cities would kill civilians?" and "Why did you have to go on destroying our cities when it was obvious to everyone that we had lost the war?"'[22] Tripp firmly replied that if he was 'expected to express remorse' he would not do so: 'Naturally,' he explains further, 'I regretted that many German civilians had died, but equally I regretted that many British civilians had died ... [I]n no way would I criticize the men who had flown with Bomber Command on the Dresden raid.'[23]

Tripp and Yates were not alone in exhibiting a fundamental distrust of television documentaries as a vector of memory. Distaste for the type of television programme that sought to sensationalize the bombers' war by emphasizing discourses of wartime guilt was significantly ratcheted up among former aircrew in the early 1990s. In 1993 a three-part series on the Second World War, *The Valour and the Horror*, produced and shown in Canada the previous year, aired on Channel Four in Britain.[24] The second programme, 'Death by Moonlight: Bomber Command', aroused such a storm of anger among British and Canadian veterans that many made a concerted attempt to take legal action against its director, Brian McKenna. Although the lawsuit proved unsuccessful, it demonstrated the ferociously protective stance many former aircrew were adopting towards cultural mediation of representations of their wartime service. This was also reflected in the different editions of Tripp's narrative. Tripp's experience of contributing to a German television documentary focusing on the bombing offensive was described in an epilogue to the new, revised edition of *The Eighth Passenger* in 1985. The discrepancies between this 1985 edition and a further revised edition published in 1993 highlight that Tripp's defence of the bombers' war increased considerably at the same time as wider levels of veteran dissatisfaction were mounting. Despite his initial stipulation that he would not in any way disparage Bomber Command, the 1985 edition suggests that Tripp enjoyed a fairly affectionate friendship with the German producer of the documentary in which he was participating. In the epilogue to this edition, Tripp narrates how, when he and his former crew went out for dinner in Britain with the filming team one night, their discussion of the programme attracted unwanted interest from a bystander in their hotel lounge. Addressing himself only to the British veterans, this man announced that if the RAF had dropped 'twice as many bombs on Germany', he personally would have been 'very glad'. The response of the aircrew to this outburst is particularly interesting: 'After a moment's stunned silence a babble of voices broke out – and they were our voices, British voices. The Germans said nothing.'[25] Significantly, the 1993 revised edition of the memoir completely omitted this episode. Instead, a vehement defence of Sir Arthur Harris, who had also participated in the programme, was incorporated into Tripp's epilogue.[26] The decision to excise from the 1993 edition this portrayal of Germans being defended by British aircrew might well be interpreted as the reflection of a changing *zeitgeist* in the early 1990s, as old controversies flared anew and attitudes towards hostile contemporary popular memory of the bombers' war began to harden among British former aircrew.

The descriptions in these narratives of predetermined scripts required in some television documentaries thus suggests that, to some extent, former aircrew detected a degree of external demand to conform to a public paradigm of guilty apology for their wartime actions. Frank Musgrove's memoir, *Dresden and the Heavy Bombers* (2005), reinforces the suspicions of Yates and Tripp that veterans of Bomber Command might have been expected by the public to demonstrate remorse for their participation in the bombing offensive. Taking great pains to position his memoir outside the traditional heroic, hyper-masculine type of war memoir which could so easily be absorbed into the 'pleasure culture of war', Musgrove states that it is not 'a gung-ho, press-on-regardless, *Boys Own Paper* account of my experience of flying with RAF Bomber Command'. Yet neither, he declares even more firmly, is it 'an exercise in hand-wringing nor breast-beating and avowals of guilt'.[27] Although due allowance for dramatic effect in this statement must be taken into account, it seems significant that Musgrove's memoir was published in a climate of public apology for historical injustices: a few months before his book appeared, a royal visit to Germany had been marred by newspaper reports that the German media were putting pressure upon the Queen to publicly apologize for the Dresden raid.[28] In thus refusing to mask his wartime service behind traditional stereotypes of heroic masculinity, or to shroud his memoir in a mantle of melodramatic remorse, Musgrove demonstrated a determination not to construct his narrative as a personal apologia simply because he felt he was publicly expected to.

Bomber Command's last battle

By the early 1990s, therefore, former aircrew were notably on the defensive. In contrast to earlier memoirs, veterans increasingly heaped censure upon '[t]hose who have tried to discredit Bomber Command'.[29] Arthur White's reasoning that 'Bomber Command didn't do anything the Luftwaffe hadn't done – they simply did it better' is reflected in Gordon Colquhoun's argument in *How Many for Breakfast?* (1999) that Bomber Command's war was wholly justified: 'We didn't start the bombing you know, ask the people of South London, Coventry and Plymouth.'[30] These narratives are suffused with a considerable sense of anger that the veterans' contribution to the war effort appeared to remain unappreciated by the public. Displaying a solid antipathy for contemporary cultural remembrance of the bombers' war, Broome opines in his *Dead Before Dawn* (2008) that 'Today, the crews of RAF Bomber Command face the sternest criticism from an apparently mindless load of nincompoops.'[31] Bill McCrea also makes this point in *A Chequer-Board of Nights* (2003), using the dedication to his memoir to aim a blunt dig at the critics: 'This book is dedicated to the

55,000 men of Bomber Command who gave their lives so that those who came after had the freedom to question the ethics of their actions.'[32] The powerful authority of survivor testimony is frequently invoked to challenge detractors. Indicating a conviction that only former aircrew may produce an accurate portrayal of the bombers' war for contemporary audiences, Broome remarks that critics (not excluding historians) tend to 'take apart yesterday's necessities with today's modern, often useless, analysis'.[33] Posing a clear statement of intentions, he thus explains that the driving purpose of his narrative is to help his reader to reach a more 'sincere picture' of Bomber Command's wartime efforts than that currently presented.[34]

In thus granting former aircrew a public stage, these narratives also enabled their authors to launch a barrage against specific cultural recollections that they found especially irksome. Prominently featured on this list are the ways in which Air Marshal Sir Arthur Harris and the area bombing campaign carried out under his leadership have been remembered. British popular memory has long reserved a distinctly ambiguous place for the Allied strategic air offensive during the Second World War. As a result of persistent and well-publicized doubts revolving around the military utility and moral legitimacy of the bombing campaign, Bomber Command's wartime role has proved somewhat difficult to fully locate within the 'finest hour' mythology with which British cultural remembrance of the Second World War remains so heavily invested. Post-war controversies centred mostly upon the latter years of the conflict, which saw widespread destruction wrought upon German cities as a result of the 'area bombing' campaign.[35] The devastating conflagration which Allied bombs whipped up in the unfortunate city of Dresden in February 1945 quickly came to represent the terrible epitome of this aerial strategy, a status which was further solidified by Cold War propaganda. Portrayed for seven decades by critics as little more than a slaughter of the innocent, the raid remained hotly disputed in both Britain and Germany well into the new millennium. Indeed, even as the Iraq war loomed in 2003, a new generation of German anti-war protesters mobilized powerful discourses of national victimhood which connected the Allied bombing of Dresden with the proposed British and American air offensive over Baghdad.[36] Ironically, however, wartime raids that could be viewed in a more positive light, due to perceptions of their target status as 'military', have invariably been celebrated in British popular culture. The success of Operation Chastise – the famous Dambusters raid of May 1943 – elevated Wing Commander Guy Gibson VC and his men to such a long-lived status of valour as to lead historian Mark Connelly to remark that British popular remembrance yet remains polarized between the horrors of Dresden and the heroics of the Dams.[37] Connelly thus makes an excellent case for suggesting that this polarization of Bomber Command's wartime experiences within British cultural memory may be viewed as having fostered among ex-aircrew an ever increasing sense that their voices represented a 'missing chapter' in popular recollections of the war.[38]

During the 1990s and 2000s, the concept of this 'missing chapter' began to dominate the published personal narratives of British former aircrew for the first time. Apart from Guy Gibson's posthumously published memoir in 1946, the late 1940s, 1950s and 1960s had seen relatively few Bomber Command memoirs entering the publication lists. During the 1950s, for example, other types of military autobiography narrating the exploits of submariners, commandoes, and prisoners of war positively flourished by comparison.[39] Currently, precise statistics of titles published have yet to be ascertained, but gradually increasing numbers of bomber narratives began to trickle through into the public realm during the 1970s and 1980s. Most of these books consisted of fairly straightforward narration of the author's wartime deeds, providing for a wider audience a flavour of 'what it was like' to serve as a member of Bomber Command during the Second World War.[40] With the dawn of the 1990s, however, the sub-genre of bomber memoirs began to convey distinct messages of dissatisfaction with Bomber Command's place in British popular memory. Alongside a range of personal factors which motivated veterans to take up their pens – including leisure provided by retirement, solitude as a result of a grown family or death of a spouse, or the desire to create a prose snapshot of their youthful identity – external cultural factors also began to exert an important influence upon the construction of these narratives. As a result of decisions taken under the Thatcher government in the 1980s, commemoration of wartime anniversaries rapidly became woven into the fabric of British culture during the 1990s. For Peter Johnson, the coming of these anniversaries spurred him to write *The Withered Garland* (1995). He records that, whilst he had put the war out of mind for years, people increasingly began to ask him 'what happened? what was it like? who did what and why?', which prompted his decision to try to draw some conclusions about his wartime experiences by putting them into narrative form.[41] Frank Broome also cites the vast gulf between 1945 and the early 2000s as an impetus for penning *Dead Before Dawn* (2008), noting that 'It is understandable that after some sixty years, bomber warfare waged upon any nation for any reason must seem almost unbelievable.'[42] As a result of a plethora of 'distorted' representations of Bomber Command, he perceived that 'the appreciation of the RAF bomber effort in World War II now seems extremely tarnished and misleading.'[43]

An increased national interest in the Second World War thus influenced the origin of these texts, yet they were shaped by a bitter backlash to the fascination of new generations. As the 50th anniversary cycle of the war ground into action, the early 1990s saw old controversies surrounding the wartime actions of Bomber Command revive and descend to new depths of ferocity. Much of the debate centred upon plans formulated by the Bomber Command Association to erect a memorial statue of Sir Arthur Harris in 1992 to commemorate the year in which he took over the responsibility of running the bombers' war. Although the sculpture was also intended to commemorate the thousands of RAF aircrew who did not survive the war, with an inscription which read *The Nation owes them all an immense debt*, this was a fact largely lost in the media furore that surrounded the proposal to memorialize the chief architect of Britain's wartime aerial offensive. Harris's most recent biographer has noted that, as soon as the appeal for donations went public in September 1991, the British press seized upon the opportunity to ventilate old arguments about the Command's wartime contribution, while on the German side of affairs, the Mayor of Cologne wrote directly to the patron of Bomber Command, the Queen Mother, imploring her not to take part in the ceremony.[44] Increasingly acrimonious gestures of condemnation marred the statue when it was displayed to the public, with red paint being daubed liberally across it. The Queen Mother was also undoubtedly unpleasantly surprised to be rudely heckled at the unveiling ceremony. In general terms, the British media were probably more sympathetic than many veterans perceived, yet opinion articles such as Geoffrey Wheatcroft's vicious disparagement of Bomber Command's contribution to the British war effort, which claimed that 'it is impossible to defend what was done in our name', could only pour paraffin on smouldering resentment.[45] A marked change thus became discernible in the tone and content of war memoirs being published by former aircrew, who posited that the men of Bomber Command (and most especially their leader) had long been publicly marginalized and were now being actively miscast as villains in contemporary popular discourses.

The defence of Sir Arthur Harris is therefore one of the main themes which characterize this concerted literary endeavour to depict a more 'sincere' cultural representation of the bombers' war. As Johnson remarks, 'The story [of Bomber Command's war] has too often been simplified and portrayed in black and white, mostly black, as having been originated, refined and executed by Sir Arthur Harris and an image on these lines has become all too established in the public mind.' Dismissing this overly simplistic interpretation as 'arrant nonsense', Johnson none the less highlights one of the most difficult challenges the memoirist faced in crafting a response to apparently entrenched popular perceptions of the bombers' war.[46] As Commander-in-Chief of Bomber Command between 1942 and 1945, during which period the 'area' bombing campaign got properly under way for the first time, the increasingly controversial figure of Harris inevitably had to be addressed in order to successfully re-draw cultural images of Bomber Command's wartime role.

In defending Harris, several memoirists bring their guns to bear on an apparent lack of public appreciation of their chief's skillful leadership. An intractable belief that their commander was publicly humiliated immediately after the war informs these texts: he, too, is deemed to have been deliberately left out of official commemoration. The veterans' resentment focuses on the failure of Whitehall to grant Harris a peerage in gratitude for his service to his country. Strong opinions are made clear in several narratives that this decision was intended as a calculated slur. Arthur

White, for instance, expresses a belief that 'Harris himself was snubbed by being the only British Commander to be ignored in the Victory Honours List.'[47] Jim Davis argues that Harris ought to have been 'made a Lord as General Montgomery was', declaring that this omission posed an 'insult' to the RAF.[48] The evident strength of feeling in these memoirs appears, however, to have blinded the authors to the finer details and niceties of the post-war honours system in Britain. As historian Robin Neillands observes, Harris had not in fact been overlooked, having been raised from a Knight Commander of the Bath (KCB) to a Knight Grand Cross of the Order of the Bath (GCB).[49] Yet, whilst the other heads of RAF Commands (including Sholto Douglas of Fighter Command) did not receive peerages either, in the context of public doubts which already existed over the role of Bomber Command, and the battle which had already commenced for control of broader memories of the bombers' war, it seemed to his men that Harris was being openly slighted; a belief which crystallized over subsequent decades. Davis's judgement that this official disdain represented 'a sheer disgrace on the part of Britain ... a stain that our country still bears today' voices a conviction more or less entrenched among those who served with Bomber Command.[50]

As the media tumult swirled around the proposed erection of the Harris statue in 1992, allusions to Harris's culpability in mass murder thus became pushed to the forefront of public debate in Britain and Germany. One memorable German news editorial remarked that, with European unification impending, it was a particularly ill-chosen time to commemorate the achievements of the 'Butcher of Dresden'.[51] Such a blatant equation of the Bomber Command chief with Josef Kramer, the infamous 'Butcher of Belsen', and Klaus Barbie, the 'Butcher of Lyons', had the effect of further fuelling old arguments that had been dredged up and put on parade that the Allied bombing campaign was a war crime paralleled only by the very worst of Nazi atrocity.[52] In this context, it was therefore especially unfortunate that 'Butcher' had also been Harris's service soubriquet. The appellation also had the unhappy effect of suggesting an unmistakable similarity with senior officers from the 1914–18 conflict who remained notorious in British popular memory for sending horrifying numbers of troops through the mincing machine of war on the Western Front.[53] Displaying a conviction that the Bomber Command chief's leadership qualities had thus been woefully misinterpreted, memoirists writing after the watershed of the early 1990s engaged in an indomitable attempt to 'set the record straight' by explaining how their chief's tag had come into being. Determined to rectify public distortions of his former commander's service nickname, Frank Musgrove explains that Harris was ironically dubbed in this manner, 'not because he butchered Germans but because he butchered his crews'.[54] This assertion is clarified by a rationalization that Harris's willingness to sacrifice his crews in the defeat of Nazism earned 'our highest regard: his sheer cussedness, ruthlessness and barbarity made him one "non-operational bastard" whom we could actually respect.'[55] Frank Broome even argued that Harris was fondly referred to as 'Butch' by his 'adoring crews' as a sign of their ultimate regard for his leadership.[56]

The defence of Harris in this literary battle to re-shape popular misconceptions of Bomber Command's wartime role is often closely tied to the question of how much responsibility he bore for the infamous Allied raid on Dresden in February 1945. On 13–14 February, Dresden was the recipient of almost 3,500 tons of Allied explosives which caused a ferocious firestorm.[57] In the weeks following this infamous raid, the British government worked hard to publicly suppress the full extent of its responsibility for the area bombing campaign. The result of this, according to Davis, was that the Command as a whole was 'branded as "Terror Flyers". No politician spoke up, no-one defended the honour of Bomber Command. Top men kept quiet, thinking only of their political futures.'[58] The label 'Terror Flyers' derived from the German term, *Terrorangriffe*, with which Joseph Goebbels, Reich Minister for Propaganda, dubbed the Allied bomber crews. As commander-in-chief of Bomber Command, Harris was the primary victim of this public silence from the highest echelons of government, becoming, as Davis bitterly remarks, popularly 'crucified' as the man responsible for sending the bombers to Dresden.[59]

It cannot be overlooked that Harris himself bore an irrefutable degree of culpability for the raid. Considerable resentment, however, is expressed in these memoirs at the disproportion of levels of blame placed on Harris's shoulders. Johnson, for example, asserts that Harris's overall responsibility for the raid has in fact been 'grossly and unfairly exaggerated'.[60] Similarly incensed by his commander's callous treatment in post-war cultural remembrance, Davis intended to rectify omissions of 'the truth' concerning Harris's connection to the Dresden raid, which he claims had signally failed to appear in any newspaper by the time his narrative was published in 1995.[61] Although many hours of scholarly effort have been devoted to the process of piecing together this 'truth' of how the Dresden raid originated, and who was ultimately responsible for it, these memoirists leave little room for doubt that, in their opinion, Harris has been most unjustly pilloried, and bore a far lesser share of responsibility than has been popularly assumed.[62] The most frequent defence highlighted by their narratives is that the raid had been devised as a response to Soviet requests to assist the advance of the Red Army. Musgrove explains that Stalin himself had 'asked for attacks of this kind to be intensified' at the Allied leaders' Yalta Conference on 4 February 1945, and therefore, as a 'direct consequence', the raid on Dresden was conceived.[63] Davis also asserts that Stalin had 'asked' for this target to be bombed.[64] This insistence that Stalin himself had personally requested the Dresden attack thus posits the city's destruction as the product of politico-military dealings at the very top of the Allied command structure. Although no evidence of such a specific request from Stalin at Yalta was found by the official historians of Bomber

Command, the message in these texts is clear: inflated levels of blame which have 'crucified' Harris for over 70 years in popular British remembrance of the war are misplaced, and should rightfully be apportioned much further up the chain of command.[65]

Also displayed in these memoirs is a profound sense of anger at the manner in which the attack on Dresden was so publicly condemned after the war. A thread of bitterness runs deeply throughout these narratives at the ways in which Dresden seemed to be popularly regarded as an atrocity. The emotionally-charged public image of the raid figures prominently in descriptions of the difficulties former aircrew experienced in reconciling their wartime service with interpretations that appeared at best uninformed – and at worst downright accusatory. As Broome remarks, popular discourses surrounding Dresden elevated the operation to special status as a 'war crime'. This unease dated back to the war itself, yet became increasingly inflated during the 1960s and 1970s as debates on the legitimacy of area bombing (particularly in the context of the United States's sanction of napalm attacks on Vietnam) grew more vocal. Controversial equations were even drawn between Dresden and the Holocaust, with far right historian David Irving's controversial construction of these so-called parallels in the late 1980s and early 1990s, and Jörg Friedrich's inflammatory history of the raid, *Der Brand* (2002; trans. *The Fire*, 2006), adding to the contentiousness of the debate. Inevitably, those who participated in the raid thus became inextricably associated with questionable morality: indeed, Musgrove perceived that he was viewed by post-war civilians 'as someone closely akin to a war criminal'.[66]

A recurrent theme in these memoirs, therefore, is an insistence upon the legitimacy of Dresden as a target. Descriptions of the pre-raid briefings are uncannily similar. Musgrove recollected:

> I had flown bombing missions to Essen, Dortmund, Cologne and Nuremburg: Dresden was just another major industrial city scheduled for attack, with the added urgency that it was now, apparently, impeding the Red Army's advance ... [W]e understood that Dresden was an important communication centre and assembly point for German troops destined for a crucial sector of the eastern front.[67]

Similarly, Broome noted:

> The reason given for the Dresden raid was that it was a Russian support target since the Soviet Army was approximately 70 miles away. In the absence of actual German intelligence at the time, RAF intelligence officers informed the crews that it would be a valuable supply point for the hard-pressed German *Wehrmacht*, as were Breslau and Chemnitz, which had received earlier raids.[68]

Peter Johnson's view of the operation also testifies to the strength of the memoirists' desire to challenge popular misconceptions of the Dresden raid. Elsewhere in his memoir, Johnson depicts himself as a man haunted by his experiences of serving with Bomber Command. However, he too defends the raid on Dresden as entirely legitimate, reiterating the defence put forward by Broome and Musgrove that Dresden in 1945 was the 'hub of the supply systems for the defence of the Reich', and was thus primarily 'a target in support of our great Russian ally'.[69] The articulation of these strategic considerations demonstrates a vehement contention that Dresden was most certainly a legitimate target.

Yet it is clear that these Bomber Command veterans still believed themselves to have been publicly reviled for carrying out the operation, and their narratives illustrate some of the hostility aircrew faced from the public after the war. Musgrove, for instance, reports that upon returning to 'civvy street', as a former member of a bomber crew his prospects when applying for employment were adversely affected: 'Any mention of my being at Dresden,' he recalls, 'and I might as well not have applied. I was branded for life.'[70] Aircrew who had not actually flown on the operation also felt this taint. On the morning of the raid, rear-gunner Frank Broome had reported sick with a sore throat. Yet in the introduction to his memoir his resentment at the widespread condemnation of this raid is clear:

> [S]ixty years later because we flew for Britain and did what the UK government and the British people wanted us to do, some of our good British people (including a Coventry canon) and the odd German from Dresden, think that we committed a war crime. They think we committed a war crime because RAF Bomber Command paid Germany back with interest for the damage done to Britain and occupied Europe.[71]

Broome's memoir makes it evident that simply having served with Bomber Command was sufficient to condemn him in public opinion. The deliberate choice he makes here to align himself with the crews who actually carried out the bombing that night is also reflected in Johnson's narrative. Although he was not operational on the 13 February 1945, as squadron commander it fell within Johnson's remit to draw up the briefing for his crews. Like Broome, he chose to identify himself with the men who conducted the raid:

> Although it happened that I did not fly in the Dresden raid, I was an active member of the team which brought about the destruction of the city and I do not pretend that my responsibility is any the less because I remained on the ground.[72]

The stance Johnson adopts on the issue of Dresden's lawfulness is particularly noteworthy when contrasted to his expression of grave doubts as to the efficiency and therefore legitimacy of the Battle of Berlin during the winter of 1943–4, which he regarded as both morally questionable and a bitter waste of aircrew.[73] Despite harsh criticism of various features of the bombing offensive, he remains loyal to those facets of the Command that have borne the brunt of negative popular memorialization. Asserting a firm belief that the destruction of Dresden represented 'a potent blow in assisting our Russian allies who had borne so much of the burden of the war', he also attempts to soften Harris's public image, noting that 'policies in wartime do not originate with Commanders in Chief'.[74] Johnson's implication that Harris and Bomber Command have been wrongfully imagined as the sole villains of the area bombing strategy is reflected in a curious interplay between the memoirs of Tripp and Musgrove. Originally published in 1969, Tripp's narrative was one of the very first memoirs to recount the experiences of wartime service as aircrew.[75] Like Johnson's book, this text portrays a man who remained haunted by his wartime service. Tripp, however, depicts his participation in the Dresden raid as the chief source of his inner turmoil. Describing the briefing he attended with the other crews before the raid, he reports being informed that the city's population had been swollen by 'a million refugees', later remembering newsreels taken during the early days of the war, which depicted a stream of French refugees being attacked by German divebombers. According to Tripp, the memory was 'instant and vivid and left [him] feeling disturbed'. Some hours later, overlooking the conflagration in Dresden's streets, he 'couldn't forget' the remembered image of the stricken refugees, and narrates dropping his bombs harmlessly into open country instead of on to the flaming city below.[76] In 2005, Frank Musgrove criticised Tripp's tale in his own memoir, expressing a belief that his account of the bombing run had been fabricated. Musgrove had encountered Tripp's story in historian Frederick Taylor's book, *Dresden: Tuesday 13 February 1945* (2004), which contained interviews with several veterans of the raid. Incorporated into a chapter that explored the thoughts and feelings of these men whilst engaged in the operation was Tripp's description of deliberately dropping his bombs away from the target area, repeated *verbatim* from the original edition of his 1969 memoir.[77] Musgrove fails to explain precisely why he does not find this account of events 'credible', but reports a deep suspicion that Tripp's description of the bombing run had been conditioned by increasingly aggressive contemporary public discourses circulating about the Dresden raid in the 1960s:

> After all this time he himself may well believe it; but I am profoundly saddened that he should have to give this version. It is a gloss on events by a man carrying the burden of sixty years of guilt, for a situation that was certainly not of his making. There is no shame in putting his bombs dead centre in the marked target area. The shame is the nation's.[78]

Significantly, Musgrove's wrath is directed, not at Tripp as a memoirist who broke codes of loyalty to Bomber Command, but rather at a hostile and unsympathetic British 'nation' which appeared to have forced a man to edit his own memories of his wartime service, and who, 60 years later still bore a 'burden' of shame for this contribution. Saluting the 'great courage' of the earlier memoirist, Musgrove highlights his own experience of this type of popular pressure, noting that he had been 'tempted over the years to take part in this sort of evasion myself'. Expressing a hope that he had 'not too often succumbed' to any kind of similar inducement, Musgrove poses a direct challenge to the British nation's evident wartime and post-war collusion in eliding knowledge and responsibility of the full implications of the strategic air offensive.[79] Johnson also explicitly throws down this gauntlet, claiming that, 'if the deliberate area bombing of towns when a genuine alternative was available was cruel, inhuman, immoral and stupid, we were all in it together'.[80] The bombers' war is thus shifted into the domain of shared national responsibility.

Conclusion

In conclusion, Bomber Command's last remaining veterans clearly perceived that they had been most unfairly excluded from dominant national recollections of the Second World War. Unhappy with the ways in which they saw their wartime sacrifices being overlooked or misrepresented, and undoubtedly aware that time was running out to rectify this state of affairs, the published war memoir therefore became a valuable weapon in the 'unending battle' for the ways in which aircrew should be remembered. The Rousso model allows us to understand and map the messages conveyed by these publications against shifting public memories of Bomber Command in the 1990s and 2000s. In reflecting and responding to popular representations put forward by official, scholarly and other cultural vectors of memory, these narratives also propose contesting versions which invoke the authority of the survivor to lend weight to their efforts to secure a place for the bombers' battle in a dominant 'Good War' discourse.

Finally, these memoirs also serve a vital commemorative function. In recent years, efforts to memorialize the men of Bomber Command began to stir in Britain, including the unveiling of a commemorative stone tablet in Lincoln Cathedral in 2006, and, of course, the long-awaited dedication of the Green Park monument which took place on 28 June 2012. Yet for all but the very last remnant of aircrew, these endeavours arrived much too late. Written and published long before Green Park was earmarked as a site of public commemoration of the bombers' war, the veteran memoirs of the 1990s and early 2000s thus fill the 'missing chapter', acting as a concerted literary memorial to the tenacity, courage and sacrifice of Bomber Command during the Second World War.

Notes

1   Musgrove, F. (2005), *Dresden and the Heavy Bombers: An RAF Navigator's Perspective*. Barnsley: Pen and Sword Aviation, 1.

2   Thomson, A. (1994), *Anzac Memories: Living With the Legend*. Oxford: Oxford University Press, 7–8.

3   Rousso, H. (1991), *The Vichy Syndrome: History and Memory in France since 1944*. Trans. by A. Goldhammer. Cambridge: MA: Harvard University Press, 219.

4   Ibid., 220.

5   Dawson, G. (1994), *Soldier Heroes: British Adventure, Empire and the Imagining of Masculinities*. London: Routledge, 4.

6   Winter, J. (1999), 'Setting the framework', in J. Winter and E. Sivan (eds), *War and Remembrance in the Twentieth Century*. Cambridge: Cambridge University Press, 6–39. Here p. 9.

7   Hynes, S. (1999), 'Personal narratives and commemoration', in Winter and Sivan (eds), 205–20. Here pp. 205–6.

8   Halbwachs, M. (1992), *On Collective Memory*. Trans. by L. Coser, L. Chicago: University of Chicago Press, 38.

9   Rousso (1991), 221.

10   Yates, H. (1999), *Luck and a Lancaster*. Shrewsbury: Airlife, 144.

11   Rousso (1991), 219–20.

12   White, A. (1995), *Bread and Butter Bomber Boys*. Upton on Severn: Square One Publications, 2.

13   Davis, J. (1995), *Winged Victory: The Story of a Bomber Command Air Gunner*. Ditton: R. J. Leach and Co., 69.

14   Harris, A. (1947), *Bomber Offensive*. London: Collins, 268.

15   Davis (1995), 69.

16   White (1995), 2–3.

17   Rousso (1991), 220.

18   *The World at War* (ITV, 1973).

19   Yates (1999), 144.

20   Ibid., 145.

21   Ibid.

22   Tripp, M. (1985), *The Eighth Passenger* (rev. edn). London: Macmillan, 183.

23   Ibid., 184.

24   *The Valour and the Horror* (CBC Television, 1992).

25   Tripp (1985), 187.

26   Tripp, M. (1993), *The Eighth Passenger* (rev. edn). London: Leo Cooper, 186.

27   Musgrove (2005), 1.

28   Parkinson, D. (2004), 'Germans press the Queen to say sorry for Dresden', *Daily Mail*, 29 October 2004.

29 White (1995), 195.

30 Ibid.; Colquhoun, G. (1997), *How Many for Breakfast?* Seaston: Motoprint, 166.

31 Broome, F. (2008), *Dead Before Dawn: A Heavy Bomber Tail Gunner in World War II.* Barnsley: Pen and Sword Aviation, 4.

32 McCrea, B. (2003), *A Chequer-Board of Nights.* Preston: Compaid Graphics.

33 Broome (2008), 4.

34 Ibid., 7.

35 These controversies have been thoroughly explored in the following: Addison, P. and Crang, J. (eds) (2006); *Firestorm: The Bombing of Dresden 1945.* London: Pimlico; Connelly, M. (2001); *Reaching for the Stars: A New History of Bomber Command in World War II.* London: I.B. Tauris; Nolan, M. (2005), 'Air wars, memory wars'. *Central European History*, 38(1), 7–40; Grayling, A. C. (2006), *Among the Dead Cities: Is the Targeting of Civilians in War Ever Justified?* London: Bloomsbury; Jörg Friedrich, J. (2006), *The Fire.* New York: Columbia University Press.

36 For further information, see Huyssen, A. (2003), 'Air war legacies: from Dresden to Baghdad'. *New German Critique*, 90, 163–76.

37 Connelly (2001), 147.

38 Connelly, M. (2004), *We Can Take It! Britain and the Memory of the Second World War.* Harlow: Pearson Education, 256.

39 Based on the author's ongoing research to collect data from the publishing lists combined in the British National Bibliography 1950–2010.

40 Examples include: Bushby, J. (1972), *Gunner's Moon: A Memoir of the RAF night assault on Germany.* London: Ian Allan; Currie, J. (1977), *Lancaster Target.* London: New English Library; Smith, R. (1987), *Rear Gunner Pathfinders.* London: Goodall Publications.

41 Johnson (1995), *The Withered Garland.* London: New European Publications, 317.

42 Broome (2008), 3.

43 Ibid.

44 Probert, H. (2001), *Bomber Harris: His Life and Times: The Biography of Marshal of the Air Force, Sir Arthur Harris, The Wartime Chief of Bomber Command.* London: Greenhill, 417.

45 Connelly (2001), 138; Wheatcroft, G. (1994), 'Firestorms darken our past: Those who defend "Bomber" Harris's destruction of German cities are wrong'. *Independent*, 7 August.

46 Johnson (1995), 317.

47 White (1995), 2.

48 Davis (1995), 49.

49 Neillands, R. (2001), *The Bomber War: Arthur Harris and the Allied Bomber Offensive, 1939–1945.* London: John Murray, 401.

50 Davis (1995), 47.

51 Ten Dyke, E. (2001), *Dresden: Paradoxes of Memory in History.* London: Routledge, 86.

52 None of these were new arguments: disputes over the just allocation of culpability for wartime atrocity constituted a significant part of the *Historikerstreit* that had been raging between Western historians since the mid-1980s.

53 There are distinct parallels here with the recent efforts of historians to rehabilitate the reputation of General Douglas Haig.

54 Musgrove (2005), 61.

55 Ibid.

56 Broome (2008), 4.

57 Addison and Crang (eds) (2006), xi.

58 Davis (1995), 49.

59 Ibid., 50.

60 Johnson (1995), 343.

61 Davis (1995), 50.

62 Much of this scholarly effort can be seen in the following works that explore the planning of the Dresden raid: Webster, C. and Frankland, N. (1961), *The Strategic Air Offensive Against Germany 1939–1945: Vol. III: Victory*. London: HMSO; Addison and Crang (2006); Taylor, F. (2004), 'Dresden: Tuesday 13 February 1945'. London: Bloomsbury.

63 Musgrove (2005), 69.

64 Davis (1995), 50.

65 Webster and Frankland, (1961), 113.

66 Musgrove (2005), 74.

67 Ibid., 69.

68 Broome (2008), 6.

69 Johnson (1995), 230.

70 Musgrove (2005), 75.

71 Broome (2008), 5.

72 Johnson (1995), 323-2.

73 Ibid., 202.

74 Ibid., 244, 317.

75 Reissued in two separate editions by Macmillan (1985) and Leo Cooper (1993), Tripp's narrative of his wartime experiences remains in its original form (1969), London: Heinemann. The revised editions contain appendices and rewritten epilogues and forewords which incorporate newly released information about Bomber Command.

76 Tripp (1969), 83.

77 Taylor (2004), 281.

78 Musgrove (2005), 108.

79 Ibid.

80 Johnson (1995), 344.

Key texts

Primary texts (memoirs)

Broome, F. (2008), *Dead Before Dawn: A Heavy Bomber Tail Gunner in World War II*. Barnsley: Pen & Sword Aviation.

Colquhoun, G. (1997), *How Many for Breakfast?* Seaton: Motoprint.

Davis, J. (1995), *Winged Victory: The Story of a Bomber Command Air Gunner*. Ditton: R. J. Leach & Co.

Harris, A. (1947), *Bomber Offensive*. London: Collins.

Johnson, P. (1995), *The Withered Garland*. London: New European Publications.

Musgrove, F. (2005), *Dresden and the Heavy Bombers: An RAF Navigator's Perspective*. Barnsley: Pen & Sword Aviation.

Tripp, M. (1969) *The Eighth Passenger*. London: Heinemann.

—(1985), *The Eighth Passenger* (revised edn). London: Macmillan.

—(1993), *The Eighth Passenger* (revised edn). London: Leo Cooper.

White, A. (1995), *Bread and Butter Bomber Boys*. Upton-on-Severn: Square One Publications.

Yates, H. (1999), *Luck and a Lancaster*. Shrewsbury: Airlife.

Secondary texts

Addison, P. and Crang, J. A. (eds) (2006), *Firestorm: The Bombing of Dresden 1945*. London: Pimlico.

Connelly, M. (2001), *Reaching for the Stars: A New History of Bomber Command in World War II*. London: I.B. Tauris.

—(2004), *We Can Take It! Britain and the Memory of the Second World War*. Harlow: Pearson Education.

Dawson, G. (1994), *Soldier Heroes: British Adventure, Empire and the Imagining of Masculinities*. London: Routledge.

Halbwachs, M. (1992), *On Collective Memory* (trans. L. Coser). Chicago: University of Chicago Press.

Hynes, S. (1999), 'Personal narratives and commemoration', in J. Winter and E. Sivan (eds), *War and Remembrance in the Twentieth Century*. Cambridge: Cambridge University Press, 205–20.

Neillands, R. (2001), *The Bomber War: Arthur Harris and the Allied Bomber Offensive, 1939–1945*. London: John Murray.

Rousso, H. (1991), *The Vichy Syndrome: History and Memory in France since 1944* (trans. A Goldhammer). Cambridge, MA: Harvard University Press.

Taylor, F. (2004), *Dresden: Tuesday 13 February 1945*. London: Bloomsbury.

Thomson, A. (1994), *Anzac Memories: Living With the Legend*. Oxford: Oxford University Press.

Winter, J. (1999), 'Setting the framework', in J. Winter and E. Sivan (eds), *War and Remembrance in the Twentieth Century*. Cambridge: Cambridge University Press, 6–39.

CHAPTER NINE

Total war and total anniversary

The material culture of Second World War commemoration in Britain

Janet Watson

It would be difficult to overestimate the importance of the Second World War to British national identity. As the *Guardian* once editorialized, 'As far as the British people are concerned the history of planet earth goes like this. 1) The earth cools. 2) Primitive life forms emerge. 3) Britain wins the Second World War.'[1] This idea, in fact, has had profound influence on British views, as was vividly on display during the extravagant commemorations of the anniversaries of the Second World War. In the midst of 'Total Anniversary' – a term coined by Robert Harris in *The Times*, playing on the idea of 'total war'[2] – another journalist wittily proposed an alternative to the May Day Bank Holiday that would lose its socialist overtones without taking on the jingoism of the sometimes-suggested Trafalgar Day. The new holiday would be 'Who Won the War? Day'. 'Though this proposal might dismay the more internationally minded of our citizens, I believe that it would be thera-peutic,' James Richards wrote in the *Guardian*. 'Whenever the Bundesbank raises interest rates or the Italians beat us at football the question "Who won the bloody war anyway?" rises unbidden from our subconscious.' Richards explained further that 'we should admit that belonging to a nation that fought on alone for a year while the Americans dithered, the Russians sold oil to the Germans and the French set up a collaborationist government means that we can't help feeling the way we do.'[3]

The war has been key to the ways many British people have thought about their nation and themselves as its citizens. Britain, of course, is remembered as having 'stood alone' from the fall of France until the arrival of the Americans. The war seemed to represent a time when everyone got along, when the Empire was secure (and its people somewhere far away), and when Britain clearly mattered in the world.[4] Forty years later, when it was all too obvious to most people that none of those things were true (whether or not they ever had been), looking back at this representation of the war was a way of ignoring the complexities of contemporary Britain. From the miners to the Malvinas and through the 40th anniversaries, Margaret Thatcher was usually adept at the politics of public memorializing. A decade later, when such denial was even more challenging, John Major found navigating the currents of commemoration far trickier, with results that proved to be costly on a number of levels. These anniversaries, then, turn out to be an extraordinary way to look at rapidly changing ideas about Britain and the British, as individuals and groups (including governments) tried to find their place in contemporary global politics and culture. Commemoration became increasingly linked with commodification, with the production of specific visions of the past in the service of ideas about the present. With the vast expansion of anniversary souvenir wares and ephemera, new stories of the war were explicitly being sold to a public that proved very eager to buy, purchasing courage along with coins, tenacity with tea towels, status with stamps, and pride with plates. Visual representations of the war were unavoidable, with commemorative items available at every price point, from special British Telecom (BT) phonecards to fine English china. War stories of all kinds were readily available in the newspapers, bookshops, and on television. In the 1980s, the key commemorative participants were the veterans. In the 1990s, however, the Second World War became increasingly everyone's war, no matter what they had done between 1939 and 1945, or indeed if they had even been alive then. As the glory of the war broadened to include seemingly everyone, however, it became harder and harder to see those who were still excluded; notably, those who fought under imperial flags remained almost invisible.

The 40th and 50th anniversaries of the key events of the Second World War were marked in a wide variety of ways, including newspaper, radio, and television coverage (in both news and 'entertainment' programming); Parliamentary debate and government reports; museum exhibitions; and a plethora of material commemorative objects, which are the special focus here. Historians in recent years have devoted many studies to 'memory' – a field of investigation that has been critical to my own work.[5] However, the more I have engaged with the extensive theoretical literature on memory, and particularly that on 'collective memory', the less certain I am that it is a productive tool of historical analysis, at least for the questions I am investigating here. What intrigues me, and what I find useful and illuminating, are the stories that are told about the past: which stories, when, by whom, for whom, and – especially – to what purpose. Calling these stories 'memories' gives them a kind of aura of scientific validity, of something neurologically incontrovertible rather than culturally constrained. The authority given by lay people to 'memory' is entirely unsupported by neurological under-standings (in which, additionally, 'collective memory' is a contradiction in terms). This project, therefore, though originating in the 'memory boom' in history, takes a somewhat different approach, analysing the wide variety of stories – war stories – that were so powerfully debated between 1979 and 1995, not for what they have to say about the past, but for what they have to say about their particular present (which includes, of course, the powerful effects of claiming 'memory' as a source of often-unquestionable authority).

40th anniversaries: pageantry arrives

A few years ago, I bought a Coalport commemorative plate from eBay, the online marketplace. It dates from 1985, and was made to mark the 40th anniversary of the end of the Second World War. eBay, Google Image and similar sites have changed the ways that we, as historians, can access ephemera; things that might well have never made their ways into conven-tional archives can now be seen and even held and owned by anyone with an internet connection and a little – often a very little – money. I learned a remarkable amount with their help about the ways that commemorative objects, and their increasing commodification, changed in ways that were much more about their own historical moments in British society than they were about the war that was their more obvious subject. Talking – in its broadest sense – about the Second World War changed its focus, and material representations clearly demonstrate those shifts. What had come to be recalled as a war of soldiers and battles became increasingly the war of the people, broadening until 'people' included everyone in the country, no matter what they had done or, indeed, when they had been born. It was another way to maintain an identity of importance built on very specific ideas of accomplishment – ideas that seemed to become broadly inclusive, even as, in some ways, their boundaries were quite subtly being more tightly restricted.

My Coalport plate is a useful example because of the ways that it is both typical and atypical of material culture commemorating the anniversaries of the Second World War, connecting certain well-established traditions to significant changes in representations that were yet to come when it was made. It was typical in a number of ways: it is a fine-china collectible, produced by an English company of long standing (and by this time Coalport was already owned by perhaps the most eminent of those companies, Wedgewood; it retailed for £29.95, which, while certainly not

FIGURE 9.1 *Photograph of a Coalport commemorative plate, celebrating the 40th anniversary of the end of the Second World War (1985). Author's personal collection*

an exorbitant sum, also raised it above the level of casual purchase). The face of the plate presents the traditional triumvirate of military imagery – land, sea and air – in its depictions of the Army, Navy and Air Force in action. At the centre is a respectful reference to the Royal Family, both specifically and institutionally, showing Buckingham Palace, with the Victoria Memorial dominant. Only through that institution are civilians connected to the war; in front of the palace and statue, impressionistic and faceless, are the crowds that famously gathered there on VE Day, 1945. The flags being waved are far more identifiable than the people, with Union Jacks being joined by the banners of other allied nations, including the United States. Perhaps most typical of commemorative ware, the reverse side of the plate quotes Winston Churchill, that most iconic figure of the war for the British.

The Churchill quotation, however, though well known, is still an interesting choice: 'In war, resolution; in defeat, defiance; in victory, magnanimity; in peace, goodwill.' While it invokes characteristics that are often described as being quintessentially British strengths, it is not particularly warlike or glorious, and its reference to post-war international amity is striking in 1985, given the Cold War, the complicated relationship with the European Community, and postcolonial politics at home and abroad.

In other ways, as well, the plate was profoundly atypical. Around the rim there is a list of nations; the United Kingdom and the United States earn the places of honour at the top, but the range is extraordinary in its global nature and in the individual identifications of individual nation-states. There are 29 in total, including former imperial holdings, Commonwealth partners and European allies and resisters, from Australia to China to Gibraltar to Uganda.[6] (It is also striking in its reference to the 'Union of Soviet Socialist Republics', more often either omitted or named only as 'Russia'; in 1985, Cold War politics often precluded any emphasis on the role played by the Soviet Union in the Second World War.) Unusually, despite the VE Day image on the face of the plate, the inscription on the back refers to the 'ending' of the war rather than to VE Day or (much more rarely) VJ Day specifically. That inscription warrants a closer look: 'The names around this plate represent all the Allied nations which worked together to achieve victory in 1945. The design symbolizes the activities of all those men and women, of whatever nationality, race, or calling, who served this noble cause.' This is remarkably inclusive, including women as well as men and defining the relevant 'activities' as clearly being broader than participation in combat. Give the postcolonial tensions seething in Britain and the riots of 1981, the racial inclusiveness is also unusual. This was not, after all, the bucolic and often specifically English image that Margaret Thatcher was promoting when she so regularly invoked British victory in the Second World War as justification for a wide variety of policies, including those that restricted immigrants from many predominantly non-white nations of the former empire.

Margaret Thatcher's relationship with the Second World War was complicated, but it clearly resonated strongly in her vision of the Britain of her premiership. She greatly admired Winston Churchill, and often asserted that he was her chosen model, giving plentiful fodder to political cartoonists and satirists, as well as editorial boards and leader writers.[7] Churchill's shadow was unavoidable when Thatcher declared that intervention in the Falklands was necessary because 'we, of all people, have learned the lesson of history: that to appease an aggressor is to invite aggression elsewhere, and on an ever-increasing scale.'[8] This predilection for applying the past to the present, however, did not make her enthusiastic about engaging more directly with the past itself, or with its participants, who might perhaps limit its possible appropriations for contemporary political purposes. She was, at best, a reluctant commemorator, and more than once had to be dragged into its political theatre. Once there, however, she handled it well.

War commemorations, until around 1984, had been very much about the veterans and their comrades who had not lived to achieve veteran status. Those who had fought relatively close to home visited old battle-grounds if finances permitted, sometimes with wives and families, and sometimes just with comrades. Costs for that kind of travel, of course, were prohibitive for those who had fought further afield, particularly in Asia, as the English members of General Slim's 'Forgotten Army' were known to point out (though they, too, often 'forgot' those who fought who were not British, and especially those who were not white). Commemorative material culture took specific traditional forms, usually narrowly marketed at the veterans themselves and, beyond them, only to a pre-existing narrow collectors' market; the First Day Cover (FDC, the first edition of a stamp which is highly desired by collectors), often a photograph, important postmarks (often from multiple locations), and sometimes with autographs, are perhaps the most typical examples of this kind of item. So philatelists had their place in this market, but that other population of very traditional collectors, numismatists, did not. War anniversaries had not (yet) risen to the level of importance required for commemorative coins. When the Chancellor of the Exchequer was asked about the possibility of a coin to mark the 40th anniversary of D-Day, Ian Stewart responded: 'As special issues of coins are normally reserved for the commemoration of royal events we would not consider issuing a coin to mark this anniversary.'[9]

This restraint, of course, was not because there was no market for commemorative wares, and Stewart's reference to 'royal events' was particularly relevant. The British have loved 'their possessions' for a long time, and other events were marked by material objects for every price range and taste. Ample evidence of that was readily available, and no one had to think far into the past for evidence, even if all years were not quite as dramatically marketed as was 1981, when Royal Wedding memorabilia were omnipresent and images of Charles and Diana were superimposed on everything from tea cups to Rubik's cubes.[10] There was a plentiful market for these kinds of things, just not – or not yet – one that was connected to the Second World War.

Given how well royalty sold – and still clearly does, as the royal wedding of 2011 and the Queen's Jubilee of 2012 both vividly demonstrated – it is perhaps not surprising that the start of the shift centred on a man whose successes in both Hollywood and Washington made him a member of what is often called 'American Royalty' – Ronald Reagan. In 1984, Reagan was up for re-election, and though he was certainly a favourite, making him look more presidential, especially while his potential opponents were still fighting it out between themselves, seemed like a good idea. So, while the Democrats were contesting primaries in a race that was far from decided, President Reagan went on a well-choreographed and well-publicized European tour, planned to impress the audience back home. He started in Ireland, with a focus on his ancestors designed to please Irish Americans. The 40th anniversary of D-Day was an opportunity not to be missed, and he gave one of the most successful speeches of his career above the beaches of Normandy, the famous 'Boys of Pointe du Hoc' speech.[11] Reagan then went to London, where Margaret Thatcher was hosting that year's Economic Summit.

The President's campaign was quick to see the political and electoral opportunities that 6 June 1984 presented, but the Prime Minister and the

Conservatives were more reluctant. While there had been consensus in Britain that the 40th anniversary of D-Day needed to be marked somehow, Hollywood theatrics were not part of the vision. Specific planning did not really get under way until well into the spring of 1984.[12] If politicians in Parliament were talking about D-Day, it was almost always an excuse to talk about something else: the anniversary made for evocative political rhetoric, whether in the service of (to give some examples) relations with the countries of Eastern Europe, the European Community, or the Soviet Union;[13] the need to debate Foreign Affairs;[14] the miners' strike;[15] social security and pensions;[16] the Defence budget;[17] Northern Ireland;[18] or even the status of physiotherapists.[19] D-Day's positive value was both clear and usefully malleable, but none of those political references anticipated the ritualized re-invasion of Normandy that ultimately took place.

British press coverage of the ceremonies in Normandy that June made it quite clear that all the pomp and circumstance was out of place, perhaps even unseemly – very American, and especially very Hollywood.[20] Both the French and British governments seemed more than a little disgruntled by effectively being forced to participate. There was no real history of international political leaders gathering to mark the anniversary of a battle, and this one was particularly delicate given the differences between contemporary alliances in the era of both the Cold War and the European Community and those of 40 years earlier. The ceremony planning indeed led to some sticky moments in relations with West Germany. Though these diplomatic challenges were smoothed over fairly successfully, the whole process certainly did not make Thatcher's government think that further such commemorations were a good idea (and there were clearly many other factors at work in Reagan's landslide re-election that November, though the power of the Pointe du Hoc speech was on display after his death in 2004, when media outlets played the footage repeatedly).

Others in Britain felt differently. Not least among these was the Imperial War Museum, just then launching a major fundraising campaign that it decided could be profitably connected to a VE Festival. Though the American show in Normandy had been mocked and condemned, it had somehow also created the expectation of commemoration: because the 40th anniversary of D-Day had been marked, however problematically, the 40th anniversary of the end of the war seemingly needed to be marked the following year. In the face of these new expectations, early in 1985 the government was forced to state that there would, in fact, be no official events to mark the 40th anniversary of the end of the war, and to make the argument that there was no good to come from reviving the memories of old antagonisms, especially at a time when the former enemies – Germany and Japan – were such important economic partners. Instead of looking back and fostering bygone hatred, it was time to look forward in peace and friendship. Similarly, it would be politically awkward to acknowledge the role of the Soviet Union in the ultimate victory; while it had been possible to exclude them from D-Day ceremonies on the grounds that they had not been there, such tactics were not possible in the case of the end of the war in Europe. These arguments, however, did not resonate with veterans' groups or with much of the public at large. After considerable outcry and extensive press condemnation, the government was forced to reverse its position and plan an event for May 1985.

This was still not, however, political theatre in the ways that the D-Day ceremonies had been the previous year. The main event was a 'Service of Thanksgiving' held at Westminster Abbey. It was officially thanksgiving for peace, but defining peace was complicated, given the levels of violence in the intervening decades; at a minimum it could be considered a thanksgiving for no further world wars in 40 years. The Official Westminster Abbey First Day Cover described how 'H.M. The Queen Leads the Nation in Thanksgiving Service / 40th Anniversary of V.E. Day / Peace and Reconciliation'. It was important that the Queen, rather than the Prime Minister, was officially in charge; the government was interested in keeping contemporary politics as distant from the event as possible (especially given the diplomatic complexities about which heads of state were to be included). This anniversary produced some of the traditional kinds of commemorative objects, like first day covers and china plates. But there were changes, too, including a wider variety of first day covers that moved beyond the depiction of the military to images relating to the country as a whole.

FIGURE 9.2 *Official Westminster Abbey First Day Cover, postmarked London 8 May 1985. Author's personal collection*

The Abbey cover was itself a new idea, with a facsimile signature not of Arthur 'Bomber' Harris or General Slim but of Edward Carpenter, Dean of Westminster at the time. Now the commemoration itself was being marked, broadening the focus from the original military action. Another new kind of cover kept the historical orientation but moved it directly into the realm of the civilian, reproducing the famous photograph from VE Day, with Winston Churchill in the centre of the Royal Family, including not just the King and Queen but also Princess Elizabeth in her uniform and Princess Margaret, on the balcony at Buckingham Palace. They are greeting the masses whose presence is clearly implied but not directly portrayed – the image is of what the people saw, not of the people themselves.

There were also the beginnings of a broader commemorative trade, including less expensive items that targeted a wider (and less military) audience. Many of the goods feel hastily designed, like a mug that is patriotic in its colours and display of the British flag, but does not specifically engage the event in any of its imagery – its 'VE Day 1945–1985' text could be replaced just as appropriately with many others. There was an official souvenir brochure, whose title is printed in a military-style font, and depicts the flag and soldiers (airmen, specifically) against a background of searchlights; its advertisers, including defence contractors and weapons makers, were still clearly assuming a military readership. One thimble also shows how existing souvenirs were rushed to be adapted for the new war anniversary market, and offers a bit of a mixed message for 1985. Winston Churchill was quoted on the back, but the flags on the front are those of Britain, the United States and the Soviet Union (given the status of the Cold War, this perhaps suggests decisions made in haste). Unusually, there is also a poppy in front of the flags. Although poppies had long been a more general symbol for soldiers, diligently kept in the public eye by the Royal British Legion, their specific symbolic roots and primary associations were grounded firmly in the First World War rather than the Second.

These varied images, however – unlike the Coalport plate – all specifically invoked VE Day; the war in Asia was seemingly invisible (though it did get some limited mention in the Official Souvenir, towards the end). The Queen hosted nothing war-related in August, and a question was asked in Parliament about government commemoration of VJ Day. Prime Minister Thatcher herself was on holiday in Australia (ironically, a location where the war in Asia was paramount), but the official government response was that VJ Day had been included in the service in May, which was really about the end of the war, so there was 'nothing specific to celebrate now'.[21] Most commemoratives of that event, however, including the First Day Covers for the ceremony in Westminster Abbey, specifically cited VE Day, so one can understand why this purported inclusiveness might not have been clear to everyone. The Imperial War Museum held a small event to mark VJ Day (though of course much smaller than the multi-day festival it had held in May, and targeted at veterans, not the general public). The few commemoratives specific to VJ Day did not branch out to new audiences but were limited to the more traditional formats, focusing on the military, and allowing artists' renderings of planes in flight and photographs of leaders (usually General Slim) to stand for the broader conflict. If it was problematic to talk about Germany and Japan, it may have been impossible to deal with the loss of Empire and the issues of race in 'British' forces in Asia, given the domestic political vision being put forth by the Conservatives at the time.

50th anniversaries: pageantry comes home

The 50th anniversaries of the war were commodified as they were commemorated, however, in ways that were significantly different in both scope and content from what had come before. Certainly Margaret Thatcher was not the political leader in 1989 that she had been in 1985, but that was a further symptom of social and cultural change rather than its cause. In 1989, it was now possible to mark the 50th anniversary of the Women's Land Army with a First Day Cover; an army, to be sure, but not the kind that had been the subjects of previous FDCs. (Again, Coalport proved to have been a notable exception – to accompany the 1985 plate, it produced four figurines, of Soldier, Sailor, Airman and Land Girl – though the Land Girl was the only one of the four who was not also recognized on the 'All Services' plate.) The transition in how these various anniversaries were commodified between their 40ths and the 50ths cannot be simply explained as a function of numbers; it is not that 50th anniversaries are somehow more special, or resonate more, than other, less 'round', numbers. Looking either backwards or forwards, chronologically speaking, is enough to undermine that theory. There were no great popular commemorations of the 50th anniversaries of the key events of the First World War during the 1960s, on the one hand, and the commodification has only continued to increase for the less 'round' 60ths, 65ths and 70ths of a variety of significant wartime moments that have followed. The current plans to mark the First World War's centennial in 2014 show further how the changes were about the historical moment rather than the round number; commemoration – and its mass marketing – are now expected, assumed. Failing to commemorate has now become an omission, indeed an opportunity for offence.

There was, from the beginning of the 50th anniversaries, an expectation of excess, a ready-made condemnation of the commercial commemorative culture that did not follow at all clearly from British experiences of Second World War commemoration up to that point. This was when the reference to 'total anniversary', as unavoidable as 'total war', appeared in *The Times*, a sentiment clearly shared not only with the *Guardian* and the *Independent*, but also with papers across the tabloid spectrum. And, of course, what made 'total war' *total* was its breadth: no longer about just the armed forces, total war was everyone's war, perhaps especially the civilians' war, and that's what 'total anniversary' was about, too. There was a remarkable change in focus, with the military and veterans no longer at the centre (though certainly also not absent), replaced instead by a predominant focus on civilian 'experience'. Moreover, this was not just the experience of those who had been there, but an experience that could now be everyone's; correspondingly, glory and accomplishment could now also somehow be everyone's. As the number of people who had been alive and aware during the 1939–45 period diminishes over time, the number of people claiming ownership of the 'good war' actually increases.

To make this inversion work, there was a new emphasis on *recreation* over *reproduction*. This new trend was clear from the beginning of the commemorations in 1989. To mark the week of the 50th anniversary of the start of the war, in 1989, the BBC used the news scripts from the 1939 broadcasts, but not the recordings; instead, they were read by a contemporary presenter, Sue Lawley, as if they were happening 'now'. This is not just an issue of the kind of historical re-enactment that has become popular at old battlefields and elsewhere, but a specific rejection of the original in favour of the re-creation. To be sure, there were no original television broadcasts from 1939, but the radio recordings were readily available and were a deeply familiar part of contemporary British culture. Rather than play them again, however, something new was apparently called for. A modern re-visioning of the past was now better than a reproduction of the past, and not just when it came to the news.

Total anniversary was certainly in full swing by 1995 (despite a rather impressive bungling of the D-Day commemorations of 1994 by John Major's government, and particularly by the recently created Department of National Heritage and its proposals for 'spam fritter cook-offs').[22] Memorabilia and souvenirs, at a wide variety of price points, ranged from thimbles and tea towels to plates and mugs to posters and badges and magnets and jewellery and die-cast models and almost anything else. Ideas about what was an appropriate commemorative object had changed in only a few years; while the Chancellor of the Exchequer had dismissed the idea of a commemorative coin for the 40th anniversary of D-Day, the Royal Mint issued a 50p piece to mark the 50th anniversary in 1994.[23] Increasingly, commemoratives had practical as well as collectible value; buyers could not only drink their tea from celebratory mugs but make their telephone calls using one of the series of six special phone cards issued by BT called 'The Time of Our Lives'. These commodities were different from their predecessors, not just in their range of types but in their representations as well; the meaning of commemorating the war was changing in notable ways. While the soldier was by no means absent from this souvenir ware, he was certainly pushed off the place of honour, and when he appeared he was more likely to be depicted in a civilian context than a military one, and particularly likely to be shown coming home. Four of the six BT phone cards, for example, have images of military men reuniting with family members, and all of them show celebratory crowds from 8 May 1945. This might seem to make sense, given that it was the end of the war that was being commemorated, but of course the soldiers did not suddenly all return home on the days that the conflict ceased; portraying them that way made the anniversaries refer much more directly to the post-war period than to the war itself. The war was being marked not as a time of tragedy, violence or death, but as, in BT's words, 'the time of our lives'. The civilian emphasis is also clear on the reverse side of the phone cards, each of which has a pithy little account of the end of the war, and often also a quotation from the day. Number 1 in the series thoroughly domesticates the celebrations: 'And someone in the crowd shouted jubilantly, "I haven't felt so excited since West Ham won the Cup!"'

In 1985, VE Day and VJ Day had been implicitly combined; in 1995 the merge was explicit and official. A government commemorations committee was formed, based in the Ministry of Defence but with membership and responsibilities that spanned many government ministries. Though its articulated purpose was to give both anniversaries the same kind of proper recognition, the emphasis was still overwhelmingly on VE Day; naming VJ Day was, in some ways, an effective way of continuing to subsume it under VE Day while seeming to grant it equal recognition. The key themes of the 40th anniversary commemoration were still present, but were changed in important ways. The Thanksgiving Service at Westminster Abbey in 1985 became in 1995 a Service of Thanksgiving, Reconciliation and Hope at St Paul's Cathedral, with its own first day covers. True, St Paul's holds more people than the Abbey, so there were logistical reasons to hold a larger service there; but it is also true that St Paul's is indelibly associated with the civilian experience of the Blitz, and the new commemorative stamp showing the image of St Paul's with anti-aircraft searchlights lit behind it made that connection explicit. The cover of the new official government programme showed civilian celebrations; the military figures of ten years earlier were gone. Winston Churchill and the Royal Family were mainstays of earlier commemorative wares and continued to play dominant roles; if anything, Churchill became even more omnipresent. The nature of their representations, however, changed in notable ways. Churchill, previously, had been invariably presented as the calm and confident leader; in 1995, he became much more familiar, much more smiley, and was extraordinarily likely to be holding his fingers up in the famous 'V for Victory' sign. He became less of a leader and more of a mascot.[24] Similarly, instead of vintage photographs or discreet silhouettes of the Royal Family, the anniversaries became part of the celebrity royal scene; what seemed to matter, to the tabloids especially, about the VJ Day commemorations was what Diana wore, whether she and Charles were behaving appropriately in public, and that the young princes were there.[25]

Reproducing the past was somehow not good enough any more; it was better to recreate it. The Buckingham Palace balcony scene from VE Day was a regular subject of commemorative wares, thanks to the iconic photograph of the Prime Minister and Royal Family. In 1995, however, a new rendition of the balcony moment told a very different story. Rendered in mosaic, and suitable for framing, the figures on the balcony were also surrounded by patriotic symbolism of the war and the nation, including the figure of Britannia carrying a Union Jack shield, lions, and much smaller shields displaying the flags of Canada, the United States and France. It was not just the context that was different, however. While the photograph showed five figures on the balcony, centred on Winston Churchill, the mosaic reproduction showed only four; Princess Margaret was excluded from this 1995 version of the scene. The shift from five figures to four also served to decentre Churchill; though still important, he now shared centre stage with Queen Elizabeth the Queen Mother. The Queen Mother, in the more than 40 years following the King's death, had become a key figure in the commemoration of the civilian experience of the war, remembered for touring bombed-out buildings and sharing with residents of London, both East and West, the experience of living through the Blitz. This focus on the Queen Mother was further enhanced through the colouring of what had been a black and white image, and the bright blue tiles making up her suit and hat drew the viewer's eye to her rather than her husband the King or her daughter the future Queen, whose brown uniform, rather than emphasizing her participation in the war effort, instead served to make her blend in with the background of the image.

A poster from 1995 also shows this appropriation of the past as a form of validation for its present.[26] An advertisement for a dance, it is clearly meant to seem 50 years old – the event celebrates 'Victory in Europe 1945', the people in the image are wearing 1940s fashions, and nowhere is there any reference to 1995. It was, however, commissioned for a 1995 event and one of the 'period' details is also one of the clearest giveaways: the price is listed as 6½ *guineas* – historical sounding, but also much too much for a 1945 dance ticket (no dance and buffet was that good). These kinds of 'retro' images, re-presenting a nostalgic past for the consumption of a post-war present, proliferated, and also focused heavily on the domestic. In one typical souvenir, women were depicted shopping for groceries both on and off the ration, celebrating victory with its implications that scarcity would end – a particularly ironic portrayal, given how long rationing continued after VE Day. This domesticity was then further compounded, as the image was printed on one of the most domestic items there can be: an apron. Similarly, a popular design that was used on a variety of commemorative items (the same design might well appear on plates, mugs, tea towels and thimbles, for example), again recreated the past for the consumption of its present, offering a new rendering of the scenes of celebration imagined to have occurred on 8 May 1945, complete with British and American flags (and smaller French ones) and the ubiquitous Churchill in the background, fingers of course raised in victory. Numerous variants of this image can be found dating back to 1945 and are remarkable particularly for the men who have climbed the lampposts showing above the amassed crowds; in the re-imaginings, Churchill's image is inserted both larger than life and apparently invisible to the surrounding throngs, who seemingly paid him no heed in their celebrations (quite a descent both literally and figuratively from the balcony of Buckingham Palace). Indeed, there were many souvenirs that *only* represented the 'Home Front', suggesting implicitly that it was those regular people at home, working hard, who had brought about victory in Europe. Even die-cast commemoratives embraced the domestic. Die-cast models have long been the purview of the military aficionado, providing detailed and precise miniature versions of ships, planes, tanks and other vehicles of the armed forces. In a typical set from 1995, though, two of the three models were specifically associated with civilian life: a double-decker bus and a lorry for John Smith's Victory Ale. Even the lone military vehicle, an ambulance, was not a direct part of combat but was instead associated primarily with its aftermath.

The civilian experience – one that could be claimed by so many more people – had overtaken the military for the central position in war commemoration. It went further than that, however. The majority of people in Britain in 1995 could not claim any experience of the Second World War, whether civilian or military, because they were born after 1945. The memorabilia, however, made everyone part of the war experience, gave everyone the right to claim the victory and the status that came with it; status that seemed otherwise challenging to claim in 1995, when Britain was no longer the world power it had been 50 years earlier and also no longer had the geographical scope of the former Empire. Commemoratives underwent some extraordinary changes to make these kinds of appropriations possible. Most people were familiar with military campaign medals, which of course can only be worn by those who fought. Though the official 1995 commemorative badge was available in a style that identified the wearer as a veteran, it was also available to everyone, including a handsome version that clearly seems designed to hang from a jacket like those that were part of military uniforms. An advertisement for another product, prominently displayed on a full page in the official programme, made this new inclusiveness even more explicit. While only veterans could wear regimental and campaign ties, a similar tie was now available, made from either 100 per cent silk or 'easy-care polyester', with the official 50th anniversary commemorative design prominently placed. This, 'the only official VE/VJ Day tie', the advertisement declared, is the tie 'for everyone to ... celebrate and wear ... with pride'.[27] Well, perhaps only men. None the less, it was part of the war that many more people could now claim.

This language of inclusion, however, could also make it that much harder to see who still was being excluded. Shifting attention away from the narrowly military made it, in fact, much easier to talk about VJ Day in August 1995 than it had been in 1945. Fiftieth anniversary official commemorations of the end of the war in Asia focused almost entirely on the horrific experiences of former prisoners of war, including both soldiers and large numbers of civilians – and in Prisoner Of War camps, distinctions between those two groups were in some ways irrelevant, as even the soldiers were not 'soldiering'. The emphasis was not on combat and eventual victory (which would have so clearly also implied loss – Singapore simply could not be transformed into Dunkirk in British eyes, even though the Australians called it just that). Instead, the focus was on suffering, and specifically suffering at the hands of the Japanese, who were presented as fundamentally alien. Only the Japanese were subjected to this kind of uniform and uniformly negative characterization; while the 'Germans' of 1995 were generally distinguished from the 'Nazis' of 1945, virulent racial hatred was regularly directed at all Japanese, often via demands for 'apologies' that could never be satisfied, and complete rejection of anything that might be called an effort towards 'reconciliation'. The focus on Japanese enemies – and clearly they were still enemies, 50 years later, in the eyes at least of the vocal representatives of the numerous survivors' groups of the East Asian campaigns, who repeatedly claimed the authority of their own 'memories', their own 'experience' making them the only legitimate sources about the people and the place – meant that the exclusion of other Asians, fighting and suffering *with* the British, was barely noticeable. The VJ Day commemorations could have been deeply problematic for the image of the nation now being so broadly propagated if the 1995 events had focused on the history of the military during the war years; such a focus could only have drawn attention to the 65 per cent of Slim's 14th Army who were not white, the 16 out of 29 Victoria Crosses awarded in the Far East that went to Indians, Nepalese and Tibetans, and even the nearly 75 per cent of 'British' prisoners of war in Asia who were in fact Indian.[28] Acknowledging those veterans, in turn, would only draw uncomfortable attention to the end of Empire, both in its loss of status for Britain in the wider world, and in the profound changes it wrought in the fabric and structure of British society itself (which was, in fact, far less explicitly discussed in 1995 than it had been in 1985; references to racism were erased by the language of multiculturalism). Commemoration was successful, in contrast, when the focus was shifted from combat to human suffering, shared by soldier and civilian, which fitted neatly into the traditional narrative of the united and stoic British people, rising above their enemies through the superiority of their characters (and eliding – even erasing – other differences among them). Looking at VJ Day this way meant that it was still possible to avoid thinking about how Britain and the world had changed since 1945. Much of the 'Forgotten Army', however, remained forgotten, if anything buried deeper by the illusion of a recognition in 1995 that actually excluded them almost as profoundly as the silences of 1945 had.

While the new emphasis on civilians enabled the explosion of a souvenir marketplace for VE Day, VJ Day's comparable move away from the military made marketing more challenging. How, after all, do you put a starving prisoner of war on a tea towel? Landing craft in Normandy were one thing, but the Burma railway was quite another. As a result, VJ Day commemoratives in 1995 were still most often combined with those for VE Day, as they had been in 1985; all it required was the two additional letters, and then war in Asia was acknowledged without being engaged. The fairly rare commemoratives specific to VJ Day demonstrated the paradox. These tended to be higher-end commemoratives, still targeted more at the traditional military and veteran consumers and their families rather than the broader souvenir market.

Conclusion

On the elegant set of china mugs produced by Ainsley, visibly more refined than the ubiquitous cheap stoneware that filled most souvenir stores' shelves, the diverse 14th Army was only represented by the white (if sunburned) face of its leader, General Slim.[29] Now, in keeping with the times, Slim was artistically re-imaged rather than photographically

FIGURE 9.3 *Photograph of commemorative mug featuring General Slim, celebrating the 50th anniversary of VJ Day (1995). Author's personal collection.*

reproduced. The image is of a man, uniformed yet informally dressed, and explicitly – given the binoculars – at some distance from combat (you could almost imagine him bird-watching). As the aprons and the tie had brought retrospective wartime participation to the masses, here was even a *general* 'for everyone'. 'Everyone', however seemingly broad, still continued to exclude many people, especially those who were not white and were not English; those who might be considered 'everyone else'. Even as the increasing commodification of commemoration reached out to broader and broader potential audiences of buyers, those very souvenirs still showed how many people remained excluded from popular ideas about the war. Material culture demonstrated both the reach and the limits of the appropriation of the war by new generations in Britain.

Notes

1   The newspapers' writer went on to suggest that only other possible events of note were the Beatles' appearance on the Ed Sullivan Show and England's 1966 World Cup victory. *The Guardian*, 7 June 2000. See also Noakes, L. (1997), *War and the British: Gender and National Identity, 1939–1991*. London: I. B. Taurus; Calder, A. (1991), *The Myth of the Blitz*. London: Jonathan Cape; Gilroy, P. (1991), *'There Ain't No Black in the Union Jack': The Cultural Politics of Race and Nation*. Chicago: University of Chicago Press; Paul, K. (1997) *Whitewashing Britain: Race and Citizenship in the Postwar Era*. Ithaca: Cornell University Press.

2   Harris, R. '50 Years On: Is Thatcher Churchill's True Heir?', *The Times*, 3 September 1989.

3   Richards, J. 'The Final Say: Let's Mention the War', *Guardian*, 1 May 1993.

4   This was always, of course, a construction; see Calder, (1991), and especially Rose, S. O. (2003), *Which People's War? National Identity and Citizenship in Wartime Britain 1939–1945*. Oxford: Oxford University Press.

5   See, for example, Nora, P. (1984), *Les Lieux de Memoire*. Paris: Gallimard; Le Goff, J. (1992), *History and Memory*. Engl. trans. New York: Columbia University Press; Mosse, G. (1990), *Fallen Soldiers: Reshaping the Memory of the World Wars*. Oxford: Oxford University Press; Winter, J. and Sivan, E. (eds) (1999), *War and Remembrance in the Twentieth Century*. Cambridge: Cambridge University Press; Watson, J. K. (2004), *Fighting Different Wars: Experience, Memory, and the First World War in Britain*. Cambridge: Cambridge University Press.

6   The complete list of nations, reading clockwise from the top: United Kingdom, Cyprus, Malta, Gibraltar, Canada, Bermuda, West Indies, Singapore, Malaya, Ceylon, India, Rhodesia, Kenya, Uganda, Tanganyika, Australia, New Zealand, South Africa, China, France, Belgium, Netherlands, Norway, Union of Soviet Socialist Republics, Czechoslovakia, Yugoslavia, Greece, Poland, United States of America.

7   See, for example, Thatcher's repeated references to Churchill in Harris, R. (ed) (1997), *Margaret Thatcher: The Collected Speeches*. New York: Harper Collins.

8   Margaret Thatcher, Speech to the Conservative Women's Conference, 26 May 1982. Thatcher Archive: CCOPR 405/82; http://www.margaretthatcher.org/document/104948.

9   Hansard, House of Commons Debate (HC Deb), 9 December 1983, Volume 50, Column 260W.

10   See Cohen, D. (2006), *Household Gods: The British and their Possessions*. New Haven: Yale University Press.

11   For video and text of the speech, see http://www.reaganfoundation.org/tgcdetail.aspx?p=TG0923RRSandh1=0andh2=0andsw=andlm=reaganandargs_a=cmsandargs_b=1andargsb=Nandtx=1742/. This trip was not the occasion of the infamous visit to Bitburg, which occurred the following May, when the President returned to commemorate the end of the war in Europe.

12   'Queen expected to join D-Day veterans on Normandy beaches', *The Times*, 3 November 1983; for Parliament, see HC Deb 09 December 1983 vol. 50 c260W, HC Deb 27 March 1984 vol. 57 c104W, HC Deb 04 April 1084 vol. 57 c588W, HC Deb 06 April 1984 vol. 57 c699W, HC Deb 10 April 1984 vol. 58 cc185–7, HC Deb 25 April 1984 vol. 58 cc506–7W, HC Deb 03 May 1984 vol. 59 cc539–44, etc.

13   HC Deb 05 June 1984 vol. 61 cc151–6; HC Deb 10 July 1984 vol. 63 cc889-980.

14   HC Deb 07 June 1984 vol. 61 cc446–52.

15   HC Deb 07 June 1984 vol. 61 cc456–537.

16   HC Deb 19 July 1984 vol. 64 cc571–609.

17   HC Deb 05 June 1984 vol. 61 cc151–6; HC Deb 10 July 1984 vol. 63 cc889–980.

18   HC Deb 11 June 1984 vol. 61 cc648–734.

19   HC Deb 06 June 1984 vol. 452 cc619–21.

20   Reginald Dale, US Editor, 'American News: Reagan sets off to win European acclaim and impress home voters', *Financial Times*, 1 June 1984; Rich Jaroslovksy, 'Politics '84 – Election Year Extravaganza: Reagan Offers Peaceful Diplomacy Scenes to Counter His Bellicose European Image', *Wall Street Journal*, 6 June 1984; 'D-Day tribute on the beaches', *The Times*, 7 June 1984; Reginald Dale, 'Weekend Brief: Never far away from the old votes back home', *Financial Times*, 9 June 1984; on French President François Mitterand's frustration, see also Reginald Dale, 'Reagan Rubs Raw Nerves in Europe / Controversy over US President's visit to West Germany', *Financial Times*, 19 April 1995. The *Guardian*, in contrast, referred to the 'contrived tedium' of the coverage of Reagan's visit, the D-Day ceremonies, and the summit, calling for more 'hard news' and less of what it termed the 'gigantic balloon of empty tomfoolery', 9 June 1984; even the highly supportive *Financial Times* referred to the coverage of Reagan's participation at the

ceremonies as 'ballyhoo', Ian Davidson, 'Foreign Affairs: One summit really matters', 4 June 1984.

21 'Low-key approach to VJ celebration,' *The Times*, 15 August 1985.

22 See 'Commemoration of the 50th Anniversary of the End of WWII: Post-Exercise Report'. Ministry of Defence, Restricted – Management. Obtained via Freedom of Information request; author's personal copy.

23 There was also a special commemorative £2 coin marking the 50th anniversary of the end of the war in 1995, and another £2 (circulating) coin in 2005 for the 60th. The Royal Mint provides evidence for the overall growth of commemorative culture, especially related to anniversaries, in recent British society, and now issues special coins that relate to a much broader range of events than their previous restriction to royal dates of significance.

24 For the 60th anniversary, St Paul's searchlights were morphed not just into the 'V for Victory' but specifically 'V' for 'VE' – there's a reference to that potential conflation in the 1995 programme cover, but only in small print; it became far more widespread a decade later.

25 See, for example, *Hello!* Magazine, 2 September 1995.

26 Bognor Regis Town Council, 'Grand Victory Dance and Buffet', 8 May 1995.

27 Official Government Commemoration Programme, 1995. 'Easy-care' version of the tie is in the author's possession.

28 *Independent*, 20 August 1995; Kusoom Vadgama, 'Letter: Ah, really sorry and all that', *Guardian*, 15 August 1995. For Victoria Cross statistics, see the list on the Burma Star Association official website: http://www.burmastar.org.uk/vcs.htm/.

29 On one of the two mugs, the reverse side portrays regular soldiers, but they are Americans; the painting portrays the famous scene it describes as 'raising the stars and stripes on Mount Suribachi Iwo Jima'. Slim and the Burma Star are depicted on both. Author's collection.

Key texts

Calder, A. (1991), *The Myth of the Blitz*. London: Jonathan Cape.

Cohen, D. (2006), *Household Gods: The British and their Possessions*. New Haven, CT: Yale University Press.

Gilroy, P. (1991), *'There Ain't No Black in the Union Jack': The Cultural Politics of Race and Nation*. Chicago: University of Chicago Press.

Harris, R. (ed.) (1997), *Margaret Thatcher: The Collected Speeches*. New York: Harper Collins.

Le Goff, J. (1992), *History and Memory*. English trans. New York: Columbia University Press.

Mosse, G. (1990), *Fallen Soldiers: Reshaping the Memory of the World Wars*. Oxford: Oxford University Press.

Noakes, L. (1997), *War and the British: Gender and National Identity, 1939–1991*. London: I. B. Tauris.

Nora, P. (1984), *Les lieux de memoire*. Paris: Gallimard.

Paul, K. (1997), *Whitewashing Britain: Race and Citizenship in the Postwar Era.* Ithaca, NY: Cornell University Press.

Rose, S. (2003), *Which People's War? National Identity and Citizenship in Wartime Britain 1939–1945*. Oxford: Oxford University Press.

Watson, J. (2004), *Fighting Different Wars: Experience, Memory, and the First World War in Britain*. Cambridge: Cambridge University Press.

Winter J. and Sivan, E (eds) (1999), *War and Remembrance in the Twentieth Century*. Cambridge: Cambridge University Press.

CHAPTER TEN

Memory, meaning and multidirectionality

'Remembering' austerity Britain

Rebecca Bramall

'Remembering' austerity?

The historian David Kynaston, author of *Austerity Britain 1945–51*,[1] has in recent years found himself in demand as a talking head, asked to commentate and bring a historical perspective to bear on our current 'age of austerity'. One typical performance was on *Analysis*, a BBC radio programme that explores topical public policy issues. The edition in question examined the return to fashion of an idea of 'thrift', or 'conspicuous austerity', and considered the extent to which British people's spending habits and attitudes to consumption might be shaped by a collective sense of morality, born of past experiences. 'Thrift', the presenter asserted, 'had a hold on the British imagination in the war and post-war years of austerity. Those who lived through that era know the hard reality behind today's revived talk of make do and mend'. Asked to comment on the longevity of the impact of these experiences in generational terms, Kynaston suggested that the 'baby boomers' retained a sense of what their parents had gone through. But there is 'a third generation', he said, born in the last 40 years, who retain 'no sort of memory at all of the austerity years. For them, the notion of getting things repaired, or make do and mend and so on, it's sort of fairyland.'[2]

Since the onset of the global financial crisis there has in the UK been a huge resurgence of interest in the period to which Kynaston refers: to 'austerity

Britain' widely defined, ranging from the beginning of the Second World War through to the post-war settlement and the final years of rationing in the mid-1950s. The focus of this interest has been on the austerity policies implemented during this period to manage the scarcity of food, clothing and other resources that followed from the war effort. The audiences who seem to have the greatest appetite for austerity Britain are, for the most part, far too young to remember the privations of the Home Front and post-war rationing. Opportunities to engage with this period of Britain's past tend, consequently, to happen via cultural texts: through a visit to an exhibition, the use of a 'ration book' recipe book,[3] or the viewing of a television programme, for example. In these texts and contexts particular use has been made of Ministry of Information slogans such as 'dig for victory' and 'make do and mend', and, of course, 'keep calm and carry on', but popular historical knowledge about austerity Britain is also mobilized in many other ways. Images and discourses related to Britain's wartime effort have been taken up by organizations and individuals including the Soil Association, Oxfam, the Royal Mail, Sainsbury's, John Lewis and many other retail and leisure businesses, the Conservative, Green, and Labour political parties, food policy experts, an environmental think tank, contemporary artists and creatives, the theatre producer Cameron Mackintosh, *Wartime Housewife*, *Austerity Housekeeping*[4] and other bloggers, museums and many cultural and educational institutions. Many of these messages have been communicated, publicized or elaborated via the mass media, and in particular via news media, where journalists have used 'austerity Britain' as a frame for the discussion of contemporary events and issues.[5] In addition, both public service and commercial television companies have broadcast a range of programmes which portray the Home Front or austerity Britain, ranging from fictional (or fictionalized) depictions of the period (*Housewife, 49*, *Land Girls, The Night Watch, Doctor Who*), to lifestyle television shows that explicitly reference the period in their title or incorporate historical visual materials such as newsreels or photographs (*Jamie's Ministry of Food, Make Do and Mend, Dig for Victory, Superscrimpers, River Cottage Autumn*), to new genres of television history, such as *Ration Book Britain, Turn Back Time: The High Street, Wartime Farm* and *The Supersizers Go … Wartime*, in which participants 'live through' 'key eras of history', including the Second World War.

When Kynaston argues that the children of baby boomers (born, roughly, between 1965 and 1985) have 'no sort of memory at all of the austerity years', he is not speaking in ignorance of contemporary austerity culture. He just does not see these cultural phenomena as evidence of 'memory' – not even a 'folk memory', as he puts it in an editorial for an austerity-themed issue of the *Independent on Sunday* magazine.[6] In Kynaston's formulation, 'memory' refers to a person's – or, at a stretch, a family's – remembrance of events, people and times they have experienced. It describes a lived relation to the past. In engaging in what they imagine to be practices of 'make do and mend', young people are indulging in 'a little retro-playing'[7] – these practices constitute a visit to 'fairyland', rather than to the exigencies of austerity Britain. Such an understanding of memory accords with the views of many historians and other commentators who have wanted to reserve this concept to describe recollection of lived experiences, but it is a view that has been challenged in recent years.[8] More often than not, scholars in the humanities and social sciences now work with concepts of memory that have been expanded to accommodate different kinds of relation to the past, and in particular those that are conducted through media and cultural texts. 'Cultural memory' is the term most often used, in these discussions, to describe memory that is 'the product of representations and not of direct experience'.[9] In this respect, today's austerity culture can be accommodated within theories of cultural memory. It is a further and distinct tendency in austerity culture that poses more of a significant interpretative challenge.

At the heart of contemporary austerity culture is the idea that there is an analogy to be drawn between today's post-recessionary, deficit-cutting times and Britain in the earlier age of austerity. This historical analogy has been reiterated, secured and made meaningful in a very wide range of texts and contexts. As the cultural activity listed above suggests, the idea that our current 'age of austerity' has a precedent in the wartime and post-war era has proved of value to diverse social actors with distinct and often divergent interests, aims and objectives. Although it is difficult to generalize about this new 'austerity culture', it is evident that much of the talk about austerity relates – either directly, or more obliquely – to the problem of describing, explaining or finding solutions for the current 'crisis'. This predicament is often understood in terms of a conjunction or consonance between economic and environmental imperatives: in one journalist's formulation, a 'new generation' of 'make do and menders' sees 'the economic and the environmental benefits of reducing waste'.[10] Historical comparison and analogy enters into these discussions as means of opening up questions about values, ethics and behaviours, and in particular about the centrality of consumption – or, more accurately, consumerism – in our 21st-century lives. For instance, Kynaston made his remarks about generational experience and memory in a discussion that referenced both the recessionary environment and climate change.[11]

In the context of this allusive and homologous discursive formation, images, scenarios, narratives and other signifying resources associated with austerity Britain tend to be used to address the concerns of the present, rather than to explore, investigate or commemorate the past. The history of austerity Britain is rarely opened up as an object for discussion in these texts and contexts, but is instead used, borrowed, referenced. It is seen as a resource that can be put to work to produce new meanings, in relation to emergent issues. In a television advertisement for supermarket Sainsbury's 140th anniversary, for instance, austerity Britain becomes a moment in the history of the store's achievements and 'firsts', all of which are articulated to present-day concerns: women's equality, fair trade, animal ethics and environmentalism. We see a WVS officer finish her shift at a canteen; she uses the reflection in a Sainsbury's tin to apply her lipstick. '1944: Halved our labels to save resources', the caption reads.[12] It would be difficult to make the claim that this media text is 'about' the past in any straightforward sense; a more persuasive reading would point to the story it tells about the moralities of consumption in 21st-century Britain. The iconography of the 1940s is mobilized to communicate this narrative; its significance is formal, as opposed to substantial.

Kynaston's comment about 'fairyland' captures a prevalent response to this tendency: in austerity culture, the subject and object of history do not match up, he seems to suggest.[13] It is certainly the case that the emphasis in today's austerity culture rarely falls on developing knowledge and understanding of its historical referent, the first age of austerity. If austerity culture is not 'about' the past – if it does not regularly explore, investigate, elucidate or commemorate austerity Britain – what mode of historical consciousness does it activate and manifest? Can interactions with austerity culture be described in terms of a 'cultural memory' of austerity Britain? The issue of meaning in austerity culture poses a significant interpretative challenge in relation to existing theoretical frameworks for the study of cultural memory, a challenge that is addressed in this chapter. With reference to a range of examples, the chapter explores whether a concept of memory can accommodate and lead to insightful analysis of the signifying processes exemplified in austerity culture. This question is positioned in relation to ongoing debates about the role of popular culture and media in shaping historical imaginaries, as well as recent scholarship in the field of memory studies. The chapter contributes to the task of developing theoretically-informed approaches to the analysis of the past in the present, and to debate about the role of the past in shaping our new age of austerity.

Austerity Britain: histories and politics

While this chapter engages with a theoretical and methodological question, the question springs from the imperative to examine the cultural memory of 'austerity' in contemporary Britain. In order to understand what motivates and is at stake in such an analysis it is essential to characterize, in brief, certain debates about the history of austerity Britain, the meanings and political significance that have attached to this period of history, and its place in the national imaginary. To begin, the term 'austerity Britain' demands clarification, a not altogether straightforward task. The concept of 'austerity' was widely used during the Second World War years and the post-war period, and for many ordinary people 'austerity' was synonymous with 'rationing'. Reflecting in 1947 on news of changes to the rationing regime, one diarist for the Mass Observation Archive recorded that:

It was surprising ... to hear that the sweet ration was to be reduced. And this at a time when the sugar supply is so ample that some think it might be taken off the ration altogether. When will austerity cease?[14]

Rationing began in 1939 and continued after the war was over. It did not completely come to an end until 1954, and so there is a compelling logic to Ina Zweiniger-Bargielowska's long periodization of 'austerity Britain' in her study examining rationing 'throughout the entire episode'.[15] Yet it has been a more established practice (and one observed by Kynaston, for instance), to reserve this description for the post-war years only, and usually to describe the specific period from 1945 to 1951. This more conventional periodization became prevalent from the early 1950s, and was popularized through publications such as *Age of Austerity*, a retrospective collection of essays published in 1963.[16] What is at stake in these differing definitions is the distinction between 'wartime' and 'post-war' austerity,[17] a distinction which rests not only on the different political imperatives that motivated rationing policies during and after the war, but is intended to reflect a shift in people's everyday experience of, and attitude to, these policies. As the diarist's comments above confirm, '[i]ntroduced in wartime to restrict consumption in the cause of the war effort, "austerity" rapidly became irksome when victory had been gained.'[18] Historians have invariably linked this identification of a shift in tolerance towards rationing to the transfer of power from the Conservative to the Labour Party in 1945, and to public responses to the welfare reforms and nationalization programme instituted by the Labour government during this and their subsequent period of office. As Michael Sissons and Philip French put it, depending on one's politics, the concept of 'austerity' can operate 'as a justification of the period or as a criticism'.[19]

'Austerity' can therefore be seen to straddle two very significant periods in contemporary British history, the Second World War and the period of the two post-war Labour governments. On the political and critical left, the issue of how the story of these times has been told, and its ideological import, has been a matter of ongoing reflection. Writing in the wake of the Falklands (or South Atlantic) War, Colin McArthur identifies both periods as 'generative' moments in the national imaginary,[20] key to Thatcher's mobilization of British history at the time. More recently, Geoff Eley's survey of the changing political valences of the 'national-popular mythology' of the Second World War suggests that what might be most critical to the national imaginary is a narrative about the relationship between the 'people's war' and the post-war settlement: a memory, more specifically, of a 'British national feeling' that contained 'powerful inflections to the left'.[21] Debates about this relationship have been carried through into today's situation, with revived talk about the place of '1945' in the Labour Party's political consciousness.[22] What this brief survey suggests is that the 'meaning' of austerity Britain has long been an object of struggle and of significant political interest. It underlines the importance of thinking about meaning in contemporary austerity culture, although, as this chapter will go on to suggest, this task may involve taking into account political movements and emergent issues which lie beyond these debates, such as environmentalism.

Lessons from history

Contemporary austerity culture invokes austerity Britain in a particularly instrumental way, often in order to talk about the present and particularly in relation to ideas about excessive consumption and climate change. In light of austerity Britain's contested history (or its history of contested meaning), it is worth considering some further examples of this tendency in more detail. The assertion that austerity culture attends only minimally to the past might seem rather unlikely, given that museums and other cultural organizations have been significant in activating the analogy between past and present. Why else would such institutions engage with the past, other than to develop public knowledge of it? A specific pair of examples should illustrate the extent to which emphasis and meaning in austerity culture is weighted towards present circumstances. These examples take the form of education packs produced by two cultural organizations to accompany specific projects: an Imperial War Museum (IWM) allotment project with The Royal Parks (2007–8), and the British Library's 'Food Stories' website (2007–present).[23] Of the two, the former draws most directly on signifying resources associated with wartime austerity. Addressing the teacher, the authors of the IWM pack explain that it has been designed

> … to give you all the information you need to create your own Dig for Victory themed garden and to demonstrate a few of the many practical ways you can use your 'outdoor classroom' to deliver the curriculum with a focus on healthy living and sustainability.[24]

A sample exercise involves providing children with various statements about 'food in Britain' (for example, 'too much packaging is bad for the environment'), and asking them to identify those statements that are about the past, those that are about the present and those that are 'always true'. The teachers' notes declare that the exercise aims to develop an 'understanding of continuity and change', and to encourage more advanced students to 'discuss whether an allotment could actually solve the problems and issues listed'.[25] While there is an emphasis on establishing the different reasons why people might want to start an allotment now, as opposed to during the Second World War, the latter scenario is recognized and presented precisely as *precedent* rather than as historical object. Sustainability emerges as the primary theme and objective, while 'the Home Front' is the formal material through which the theme is expressed. In creating the education pack, the IWM appears to be driven by an environmental and health agenda.

'Food Stories' is an interactive educational resource that enables students to learn about changes that have taken place in the consumption and production of food over the last century, through the British Library's collection of oral history recordings. Austerity Britain animates a section of the website titled 'changes in eating habits'. By clicking on an image of a ration book, students can listen to a contributor, John Lowery, talk about 'the food he ate as a child during World War II'. It is notable that the 'Food Stories' project is designed primarily for students of citizenship and geography – rather than history – and the accompanying education pack reflects this orientation. For example, in relation to Lowery's contribution, students are asked: 'How many of the foods mentioned by John have you heard of? What kinds of food do you think they might be? Does it sound like a healthy diet to you?'[26] This orientation offers another insight into the extent to which an instrumental approach to this period of history – using it, in other words, to talk about something else – is now seen as appropriate by social actors in educational and cultural institutions often associated with more traditional approaches to history.

The prevalence of this instrumental approach to history in other contexts will come as less of a surprise. In April 2009, the Energy Saving Trust (a social enterprise which offers advice on reducing domestic energy consumption) issued a publication titled *Wartime Spirit*. It opens:

> During the Second World War living conditions were tough and there were limited resources and supplies. Certain values became widespread to ensure resource use was kept to a minimum – the 'waste not, want not' mentality. Even before the war people had a 'thrifty' mentality and while they were busy trying to save money and resources, little did they know they were also being kinder to the planet! Many wartime values are as relevant to us today as they were in the 1940s.[27]

Accompanied by photographs and illustrations from the IWM's archives, the publication continues in this vein, developing analogies between past and present in relation to every aspect of domestic energy use.[28] As in the education packs described above, the history of 'austerity Britain' past is not opened up for discussion; it is treated as over and done, as appropriate material for the task of sketching a precedent or as a 'lesson from history', as an Imperial War Museum marketing campaign put it.[29]

These examples indicate that austerity Britain continues to operate as a significant site of meaning in contemporary culture. This chapter is concerned with the question of whether or not austerity culture can be analysed as cultural memory (or as *evidence* of cultural memory; the distinction is a significant one, and will be explained). In light of these examples, the question bears repeating: should austerity culture be described in terms of 'memory' when historical resources are being used to address emergent concerns about the environment and consumption, rather than to elucidate the past? How should the meanings communicated in these contemporary texts be analysed in relation to the longer history of austerity Britain's political significance?

Cultural memory and meaning

Theories about what 'memory' is, and the role that media and cultural texts might play in activating and shaping memory, have changed considerably in recent decades. Scholars of memory have moved towards a 'structural'[30] or social-constructivist model of 'cultural memory' which understands 'shared memories of the past' as the 'the product of mediation, textualization and acts of communication'.[31] In media and cultural studies, many scholars have worked to emphasize the centrality of media and popular culture in new theorizations of memory.[32] Such approaches to history and memory have emerged in particular from those working on film, television, literature and other cultural texts.[33] Memory research has found great potential in the insight that '[m]emory is always mediated',[34] perceiving that it opens up new ways of interpreting media texts, and their reception and impact.

From a position sympathetic to these claims, the contemporary fascination with austerity Britain could legitimately be analysed via a concept of cultural memory. The fact that representations of this historical period manifest in media texts rather than in communications between members of a family or broader 'mnemonic community'[35] should not, from this perspective, render them inadmissible as evidence of cultural memory or as serious objects of study. On this account, media and cultural texts can foreground the 'social relevance' of the past in the present, enabling memories of experiences we have not lived through – the experience of Home Front or post-war austerities – to become 'part of our archive of memory'.[36] Yet while this dimension of austerity culture can be accommodated, there is little in the cultural memory literature to help us understand and theorize the articulations to new objects and themes identified, for instance, in the 'Dig for victory' and 'Food stories' education packs, which characterize the use of the past in austerity culture.

Part of the problem, here, is that the question of meaning is often avoided altogether in contemporary research on cultural memory. There is a widespread assumption that a media text that *depicts* the past is definitely 'about' the past; that its meaning is secured precisely by the fact that it depicts a 'meaningful' event in the past. Such approaches to cultural memory allow us to recognize a depiction of wartime austerities – such as the Sainsbury's advertisement – as a form, or articulator, of 'cultural memory', but they can end up placing too much emphasis on the past as guarantor of meaning, and failing to acknowledge the fact that 'different pasts reverberate to different effect in different moments of the present'.[37] Another way of putting this is to suggest that, in lieu of a definition of memory tied to experience, the presence of a historical referent in certain texts seems to guarantee that they will be read in terms of the contribution their representations make to cultural memory of that past. The issue is compounded by the fact that researchers who take this approach select and analyse texts that depict – at a denotative level – the past they want to discuss. Making a related critique, Susannah Radstone has noted that the memory paradigm seems to encourage some scholars to read texts *as* memory.[38] An 'epistemological sleight of hand from representation to memory' eliminates the need to associate representations with 'specific social groups and their understanding of the past', through, for instance, studies of how audiences receive and interpret texts.[39] The concept of cultural memory as it is used in some research eradicates the need, in other words, to consider questions of meaning: the texts that theorists choose to analyse simply *are* cultural memory 'of' the events they depict.[40] It is, then, the question of meaning in austerity culture that cannot be sufficiently interrogated via many contemporary theories of cultural memory. Yet for a concept of memory to be productive in the analysis of austerity culture it is vital that it offers a means of interrogating the polysemy of 'historical' representations.

This line of thought points to a need to reconsider what is meant by the notion of the cultural memory 'of' a particular event, period or aspect of the past. It indicates that the 'aboutness' of cultural memory is more complex than we like to think. Michael Rothberg's recent theoretical contribution to the field of memory studies precisely turns on his recognition of the limitations of trying to define or study the cultural memory 'of' a particular event. As he sets out to demonstrate, memory is 'multidirectional': it is always 'subject to ongoing negotiation, cross-referencing, and borrowing'.[41] Rothberg explores how cultural memory emerges 'in dialogue' with subsequent transformations and struggles.[42] Episodes in the Algerian war, for instance, served as a 'trigger' or articulator for Holocaust memory, while in more recent decades 'the emergence of Holocaust memory on a global scale has contributed to the articulation of other histories'.[43] Signifying resources associated with a particular historical event can be used, in other words, to remember another event or issue, or an emergent issue can be generative of cultural memory.

What might the concept of multidirectional memory contribute to an analysis of contemporary austerity culture? It could help us to think more carefully about the ways in which cultural memory of austerity Britain has been generated in relation to post-war struggles and events, including, but not exclusively, those between the political left and right signalled earlier in this chapter. Other points of reference should include second-wave feminism,[44] decolonization[45] and the Falklands War.[46] In this sense, the cultural memory of austerity Britain has never simply been 'about' its historical referent. Articulations of austerity Britain to current debates about consumerism and climate change are, on this account, simply the most recent instances in a much longer history of cross-referencing and borrowing. Indeed, it might be argued – in line with Zweiniger-Bargielowska's history – that the cultural memory of austerity Britain was imbricated from the very beginning in debates about consumption and state involvement in national and domestic economies. The phenomenon whereby austerity Britain is 'made available' for appropriation is not specific or unique to the present moment, but can be understood as part of the fabric of cultural memory.

The 'multidirectional' model of cultural memory facilitates an analysis of austerity culture in which it is recognized that there may be something more at stake in this cultural formation than cultural memory 'of' the Second World War. It compels us to ask questions about textual meaning, and about the processes through which familiar signifiers – a ration book, Ministry of Information typography, 'utility' crockery or even practices of 'mending' and 'digging' – can be articulated to emergent issues and debates, while acknowledging the 'historicity' of these resources. The other, equally important implication of this model is that we may need to look for the cultural memory of austerity Britain in places other than those texts that signify the period at a denotative level. Charged with researching the cultural memory of austerity Britain in the 1960s, for instance, we might turn to an essay by Susan Cooper on austerity food in which she recalls the 'first pineapples and bananas of our lives'.[47] But we might also want to bring into consideration a text such as Judith Kerr's *The Tiger Who Came To Tea*, first published in 1968. Unlike one of Kerr's other books for children, *When Hitler Stole Pink Rabbit* (1971), this story does not make use of signifying resources associated with the Second World War. The *mise-en-scène* is a contemporary one: the young girl and her mother who are the story's protagonists are dressed in fashionable tunics and the kitchen's melamine-topped units are stocked with bright, 1960s crockery. Yet in some important sense the book is clearly 'about' the post-war, and ultimately post-austerity, moment, with the benign tiger figuring the way in which the experience of war was mediated for those remaining on the Home Front. He eats and drinks everything in Sophie's home, including all of the water in the taps, leaving her mother to worry about what to make for 'Daddy's supper'. Sophie's father's return (from the office/war) marks the restoration of the family unit and a return to normality: he has the 'very good idea' of going out to a café for supper. In an evocation of the end of blackout regulations, an important marker of the post-war moment, the family is pictured walking in the twilight down a street in which 'all the street lamps were lit, and all the cars had their lights on'.[48] *The Tiger Who Came To Tea* is, then, 'about' the affective experience of emerging from war and austerity, while it also describes the shift from this post-war era into the 1960s and this decade's further cultural and social change, particularly in relation to gender relations and the family. In relation to Rothberg's model, we might think about this social change as an articulator or activator of the author's memories of austerity Britain. To draw back from this example to make the substantive methodological point: this process of analysing texts for their multiplicity of meanings compels the person making such a reading both to present it as, precisely, a *reading* of a cultural text, rather than the text as evidence of cultural memory, and to make a convincing case for its extension and interpretation in terms of cultural memory, through contextualizing or reception-focused studies.

Conclusion

This chapter has offered a characterization of contemporary 'austerity culture' and has discussed the value and appropriateness of a concept of memory for an analysis of this formation. Attention has been drawn to the extent to which austerity Britain is being used to describe and debate present-day issues and concerns, in particular those relating to consumerism and climate change, and to the fact that theories of cultural memory do not easily accommodate or facilitate the analysis of these processes of meaning-making. One exception is Rothberg's multidirectional model of memory, which questions assumptions that are often made about the meaning of 'historical' representations. It is important to be alert to the ways in which the resources of the past can operate as the material for metaphor or analogy and as the medium through which emergent issues can be communicated. Conversely, evidence of the 'cultural memory' of a particular event or experience may be found in other places, being expressed through other symbolic resources, than we might expect.

One answer to the questions raised in this chapter might be to suggest that austerity culture could be analysed in terms of representation, rather than memory, using the methods of textual, semiotic and discursive analysis developed for these purposes. Certainly these methods tend to accommodate questions of meaning with much greater sophistication than some approaches in memory studies. Informed by cultural studies and discourse theory, such an analysis of austerity culture might proceed to unravel and elucidate the ways in which the resources of the past have been articulated to new objects and themes. Cultural texts, discourses and practices do not have to be analysed via a concept of memory in order to make evident the presence of the past in the present. However, a concept of memory does have at least three potentially enabling features, which will be set out by way of a conclusion to this chapter. First of all, scholars' use of a concept of memory is often motivated by a desire to describe the ways in which engaging with cultural texts can have politically transformative effects. This dimension of memory studies is commendable, and can be located in a long tradition of left-political scholarly work in which concepts of 'memory' have played an important role.[49] In light of this tradition, 'memory' is a concept worth retrieving and reinvigorating in relation to new theoretical paradigms and emergent political projects. This must involve, however, a more sophisticated approach to questions of meaning and salience than is entertained by the mere matching of events in the past to their perceived correlative in the present: the Second World War, for instance, to the present conflict in Afghanistan. Memory studies has been slow to attend to uses of the past which fall outside of the sphere of identity politics, such as in environmental social movements and discourses. As the example of austerity culture reveals, the resources of the past can be brought to bear in a dynamic and sometimes unpredictable fashion on new objects, themes and desires, and for memory studies to constitute an effective site of politics it is important that it remains open to this potentiality.

It is, however, also imperative to bear in mind the extent to which the possibilities for such new articulations are organized and informed by what has come before – by, precisely, the past. Rothberg is committed, at a theoretical level, to an 'open-ended sense of the possibilities of memory'.[50] His diachronic work on cultural memory, which involves carefully tracing the interplay and cross-referencing of themes, topics and tropes in public discourse about distinct historical events, creates a resource that could be used to qualify this optimism and sense of potentiality. Though it may theoretically be the case that signifying resources associated with austerity Britain can be used to generate meaning in relation to emergent projects or struggles, it is critical to recognize, in Stuart Hall's formulation, the 'givenness of the historical terrain'. Hall describes here the way in which the 'ideological terrain' of a 'particular social formation' has been 'powerfully structured in that way by its previous history'.[51] Making a similar point in a different context, Richard Terdiman has observed that 'the space for interpretation has stretched to the horizon. What is necessary now is to see how it might be bounded.'[52] In relation to the analysis of austerity culture, we might think of this boundedness in terms of the 'given' histories and politics of austerity Britain. Hall's framing may help to describe the extent to which the political possibilities that follow from, say, the Green Party's mobilization of the Home Front as a rallying call to environmental action might be circumscribed by this givenness.[53] Use of a concept of memory will not necessarily bring such a perspective to bear on emergent cultural formations, but it might help to encourage it.

The language of signification and signifying practices can account for the kind of 'memory' required to interpret and generate meaning from, for instance, a ration book in the context of debates about climate change and Britain's food security.[54] But such an approach might generate a rather ahistorical, flattened-out reading of austerity culture. To analyse austerity culture via a concept of representation, rather than memory, might be to attend less carefully to the *historicity* of the resources in question. Why is the present scenario being organized, explained and imagined via resources that denote austerity Britain, as opposed to something else? What role does the historicity of these resources – which we might conceptualize in terms of texture, intensity, or 'difference' – play in producing meanings about the present? What fantasies and desires do these historical resources animate?[55] Together with the other reasons presented, the importance of these questions provides a final reason to consider the advantages of continuing to work with a concept of memory. The children of the baby boomers *do* have a 'sort of memory ... of the austerity years', but as this chapter has shown, we need to consider how this description of historical consciousness, and particularly its implication about meaning, can be reformulated and renewed.

Notes

1   Kynaston, D. (2008), *Austerity Britain 1945–51*. London: Bloomsbury.

2   'Analysis: the threat of thrift', BBC Radio 4, broadcast 5 March 2009. See also Hatherley, O. (2009), 'Lash out and cover up: austerity nostalgia and ironic authoritarianism in recession Britain'. *Radical Philosophy*, 157, 2–7.

3   See for example Fearnley-Whittingstall, J. (2010), *The Ministry of Food: Thrifty Wartime Ways to Feed Your Family Today*. London: Hodder and Stoughton.

4   *Wartime Housewife* (2009–present), blog. http://www.wartimehousewife. com/; *Austerity Housekeeping* (2011–present), blog. http:// austerityhousekeeping.wordpress.com/.

5   See, for example, Elliott, L. (2012), 'London's 1948 Olympics: the real austerity Games'. *Guardian*, 30 March; or Harris, P. (2009), 'Blitz spirit of 2009: As crunch deepens, thrift tips that saw Britain through the War can help again'. *Daily Mail*, 2 April.

6   Kynaston, D. (2008), 'The Austerity issue; don't panic', *Independent on Sunday*, 2 November 2008.

7   Mower, S. 'Prêt-à-rapporter'. *Telegraph Online*, 14 April 2009.

8   See for example Eley, G. (2001), 'Finding the people's war: film, British collective memory and World War II', *American Historical Review*, 106(3), 818–38. Here p. 818.

9   Rigney, A. (2005), 'Plenitude, scarcity and the circulation of cultural memory'. *Journal of European Studies*, 35(1), 11–28. Here p. 15.

10   Lonsdale, S. (2009), 'Make do and mend: restoring the good things in life'. *Telegraph*, 22 January.

11   BBC, *Analysis: the threat, of thrift*, 5 March 2009.

12   'Sainsbury's: Trying Something New For 140 Years' (2009). Television advertisement.

13   Another way to interpret Kynaston's comment would be to align it with what

Raphael Samuel calls 'heritage-baiting': the critique of spectacular, affective, commodified 'heritage' culture, or indeed wider debates about historical consciousness in postmodernity. On the former, see Samuel, R. (1994), *Theatres of Memory*. London: Verso, 259–73; on the latter, see Jameson, F. (1984), 'Postmodernism, or the cultural logic of late capitalism', *New Left Review*, 146, 53–92; Lowenthal, D. (1985), *The Past is a Foreign Country*. Cambridge: Cambridge University Press; Wright, P. (1985), *On Living in an Old Country: The National Past in Contemporary Britain*. London: Verso; Harvey, D. (1989), *The Condition of Postmodernity: An Enquiry into the Origins of Cultural Change*. Oxford and Cambridge, MA: Blackwell; Walsh, K. (1992), *The Representation of the Past: Museums and Heritage in the Post-Modern World*. London: Routledge.

14 Taylor, G. (2005), in S. Garfield, *Our Hidden Lives: The Remarkable Diaries of Post-War Britain*. London: Ebury Press, 463.

15 Zweiniger-Bargielowska, I. (2000), *Austerity in Britain: Rationing, Controls, and Consumption, 1939–1955*. Oxford: Oxford University Press, 1.

16 Sissons, M. and French, P. (1963), 'Introduction', in M. Sissons and P. French (eds), *Age of Austerity*. London: Hodder and Stoughton.

17 McKibbin, R. (1998), *Classes and Cultures: England 1918–1951*. Oxford: Oxford University Press, 41–2.

18 Tomlinson, J. (2000), 'Labour and the economy', in D. Tanner, P. Thane and N. Tiratsoo (eds), *Labour's First Century*. Cambridge: Cambridge University Press, 58.

19 Sissons and French (1963), 9.

20 McArthur, C. (1984), 'National identities', in G. Hurd (ed.), *National Fictions: World War Two in British Films and Television*. London: BFI, 55.

21 Eley (2001), 820.

22 Glasman, M. (2011), 'Labour as a radical tradition', in M. Glasman, J. Rutherford, M. Stears and S. White (eds), *The Labour Tradition and the Politics of Paradox*. http://www.lwbooks.co.uk/ebooks/labour_tradition_politics_paradox.html/.

23 Russell, P. and Lobbenberg, A. (2007), 'Food stories', *British Library*. http://www.bl.uk/learning/resources/foodstories/index.html/.

24 Imperial War Museum (2007), 'Dig for Victory Teachers' Pack', *Imperial War Museum*. http://cwr.iwm.org.uk/upload/package/79/DigForVictory/schools.htm.

25 Imperial War Museum, 'Dig for Victory Teachers' Pack', 3–4.

26 British Library (2007), 'Food stories: teacher's notes'. http://www.bl.uk/learning/citizenship/foodstories/teacher/teachernotes.html/.

27 Energy Saving Trust (2009), *Wartime Spirit*. http://www.energysavingtrust.org.uk/About-us/Media-centre/Library/Green-Barometer/Green-barometer-7-Wartime-spirit. Pamphlet.

28 Hinton, E. and Redclift, M. (2009), 'Austerity and sufficiency: the changing politics of sustainable consumption'. *Environment, Politics and Development Working Paper Series*, 17. http://www.kcl.ac.uk/sspp/departments/geography/research/epd/HIntonRedcliftWP17.pdf/.

29 Imperial War Museum (2009), 'Lessons from history'. Advertisement.

30 Klein, K. L. (2000), 'On the emergence of memory in historical discourse'. *Representations*, 69, 127–50. Here p. 130.

31 Rigney, (2005), 14.

32 See, for example, Lipsitz, G. (1990), *Time Passages: Collective Memory and American Popular Culture*. Minneapolis: University of Minnesota Press; Huyssen, A. (1995), *Twilight Memories: Marking Time in a Culture of Amnesia*. New York: Routledge; Hoskins, A. (2001), 'New memory: mediating history'. *Historical Journal of Film, Radio and Television*, 21(4), 333–46.

33 See, for example, Sturken, M. (1997), *Tangled Memories: The Vietnam War, the Aids Epidemic, and the Politics of Remembering*. Berkeley, CA: University of California Press; Middleton, P. and Woods, T. (2000), *Literatures of Memory: History, Time and Space in Postwar Writing*. Manchester: Manchester University Press; Landy, M. (2001), 'Introduction', in M. Landy (ed.), *The Historical Film: History and Memory in Media*. London: Athlone Press, 1–22; Grainge, P. (2003), 'Introduction: memory and popular film', in P. Grainge (ed.), *Memory and Popular Film*. Manchester: Manchester University Press, 1–20; Landsberg, A. (2003), 'Prosthetic memory: the ethics and politics of memory in an age of mass culture', in P. Grainge (ed.), *Memory and Popular Film*. Manchester: Manchester University Press, 144–61; Cook, P. (2005), *Screening the Past: Memory and Nostalgia in Cinema*. London: Routledge.

34 Radstone, S. (2005), 'Reconceiving binaries: the limits of memory', *History Workshop Journal*, 59, 134–50. Here p. 135.

35 Misztal, B. A. (2003), *Theories of Social Remembering*. Maidenhead: Open University Press, 15.

36 Landsberg (2003), 155.

37 Schwarz, B. (2005), 'Afterword: "strolling spectators" and "practical Londoners" – remembering the imperial past', in J. Littler and R. Naidoo (eds), *The Politics of Heritage: The Legacies of 'Race'*. London: Routledge, 221.

38 Radstone (2005), 136; Radstone, S. (2008), 'Memory studies: for and against', *Memory Studies*, 1(1), 31–9. Here p. 35

39 Kansteiner, W. (2002), 'Finding meaning in memory: a methodological critique of collective memory studies'. *History and Theory*, 41(2), 179–97. Here p.192; see also Confino, A. (1997), 'Collective memory and cultural history: problems of method'. *American Historical Review*, 102(5), 1386–403. Here pp. 1391–2.

40 Zelizer, B. (1995), 'Reading the past against the grain: the shape of memory studies'. *Critical Studies in Mass Communication*, 12(2), 214–39. Here p. 232.

41 Rothberg, M. (2009), *Multidirectional Memory: Remembering the Holocaust in the Age of Decolonization*. Stanford, CA: Stanford University Press, 3.

42 Ibid., 7.

43 Ibid., 17, 7.

44 Minns, R. (1999), *Bombers and Mash: The Domestic Front, 1939–45*. London: Virago.

45   See Francis, Chapter 6 in this volume.

46   McArthur (1984); Eley (2001).

47   Cooper, S. (1963), 'Snoek piquante', in M. Sissons and P. French (eds), *Age of Austerity*. London: Hodder and Stoughton, 54.

48   Kerr, J. (2006), *The Tiger Who Came to Tea*. London: HarperCollins (first published 1968).

49   See, for example, Bauman, Z. (1982), *Memories of Class: The Pre-History and After-Life of Class*. London: Routledge and Kegan Paul; Popular Memory Group (1982), 'Popular memory: theory, politics, method', in R. Johnson, G. McLennan, B. Schwarz and D. Sutton (eds), *Making Histories: Studies in History-Writing and Politics*. London: Hutchinson, 205–52; Ashplant, T. G., Dawson, G. and Roper, M. (2000), 'The politics of war memory and commemoration: contexts, structures and dynamics', in T. G. Ashplant, G. Dawson and M. Roper (eds), *The Politics of War Memory and Commemoration*. London: Routledge, 3–86. On the concept of memory in feminist scholarship, see Hirsch, M. and Smith, V. (2002), 'Feminism and cultural memory: an introduction'. *Signs*, 28(1), 1–19.

50   Rothberg (2009), 312. Rothberg can, however, be seen to foreclose on his own optimism. His book is ultimately 'about' the Holocaust: its subtitle is 'remembering the Holocaust in the age of decolonization'. Thus his reading of discourses of decolonization under the sign of the Holocaust undermines his openness, at a theoretical level, to the productive mobility and polysemy of memory, while providing an illustration of the extent to which the political terrain of memory studies is bounded and given.

51   Hall, S. (1996), 'The problem of ideology: Marxism without guarantees', in D. Morley and K.-H. Chen (eds), *Stuart Hall: Critical Dialogues in Cultural Studies*. Abingdon: Routledge, 24–45. Here p. 42.

52   Terdiman, R. (1993), *Present Past: Modernity and the Memory Crisis*. Ithaca, NY: Cornell University Press, 350.

53   Simms, A. (2011), *The New Home Front*. Green Party pamphlet. For further discussion see Bramall, R. (2011), 'Dig for victory! Anti-consumerism, austerity, and new historical subjectivities'. *Subjectivity*, 4(1), 68–86.

54   See, for example, The Ministry of Trying to Do Something About It (2009), *Ration Me Up: Carbon Ration Book*. London: New Economics Foundation.

55   For further discussion of austerity as an object of desire, see Bramall, R. (2012), 'Popular culture and anti-austerity protest'. *Journal of European Popular Culture*, 3(1), 9–22.

Key texts

Eley, G. (2001), 'Finding the people's war: film, British collective memory and World War II', *American Historical Review.* 106(3), 818–38.

Hurd, G. (1984) (ed.), *National Fictions: World War Two in British Films and Television.* London: BFI.

Klein, K. L. (2000), 'On the emergence of *memory* in historical discourse', *Representations*, 69, 127–50.

Kynaston, D. (2008a), *Austerity Britain 1945–51.* London: Bloomsbury.

—(2008b), 'The Austerity issue: don't panic', *Independent on Sunday*, 2 November.

Radstone, S. (2005), 'Reconceiving binaries: the limits of memory', *History Workshop Journal*, 59, 134–50.

Rothberg, M. (2009), *Multidirectional Memory: Remembering the Holocaust in the Age of Decolonization.* Stanford, CA: Stanford University Press.

Samuel, R. (1994), *Theatres of Memory.* London: Verso.

Sissons, M. and French, P. (eds) (1963), *Age of Austerity.* London: Hodder and Stoughton.

Wright, P. (1985), *On Living in an Old Country: The National Past in Contemporary Britain.* London: Verso.

Zweiniger-Bargielowska, I. (2000), *Austerity in Britain: Rationing, Controls, and Consumption, 1939–1955.* Oxford: Oxford University Press.

INDEX

Page references in bold indicate a key text reference